DIAMONDS IN THE ROUGH

BASEBALL STORIES FROM ALASKA

DIAMONDS IN THE ROUGH

BASEBALL STORIES FROM ALASKA

LEW FREEDMAN

EPICENTER PRESS
ALASKA BOOK ADVENTURES

ACKNOWLEDGMENTS

Thanks to all the Alaska Baseball League officials and players who helped provide information and background for this book.

A special nod of appreciation goes to league founder Red Boucher, Fairbanks Goldpanner general manager Don Dennis, and Anchorage Glacier Pilots coach Jack O'Toole, who have the longest memories of all.

—Lew Freedman

Epicenter Press is a regional press founded in Alaska whose interests include but are not limited to the arts, history, nature, and diverse cultures and lifestyles of the North Pacific and high latitudes. Epicenter seeks both the traditional and innovative in publishing high-quality nonfiction books and contemporary art and photography gift books.

Publisher: Kent Sturgis
Editor: Roger Brigham
Text and cover design: Elizabeth Watson
Proofreader: Sherrill Carlson
Printer: Transcontinental Printing

Library of Congress No. 00 132263

To order extra copies of DIAMONDS IN THE ROUGH, mail $14.95 plus $4.95 to Epicenter Press, Box 82368, Kenmore, WA 98028. Washington residents add $1.30 for state sales tax. You also may order via fax to (425) 481-8253, via phone to (800) 950-6663, or at our website, EpicenterPress.com. Visa, MC accepted.

Booksellers: Retail discounts are available from our trade distributor, Graphic Arts Center Publishing', Box 10306, Portland, OR 97210.

First printing May 2000

10 9 8 7 6 5 4 3 2 1

PRINTED IN CANADA

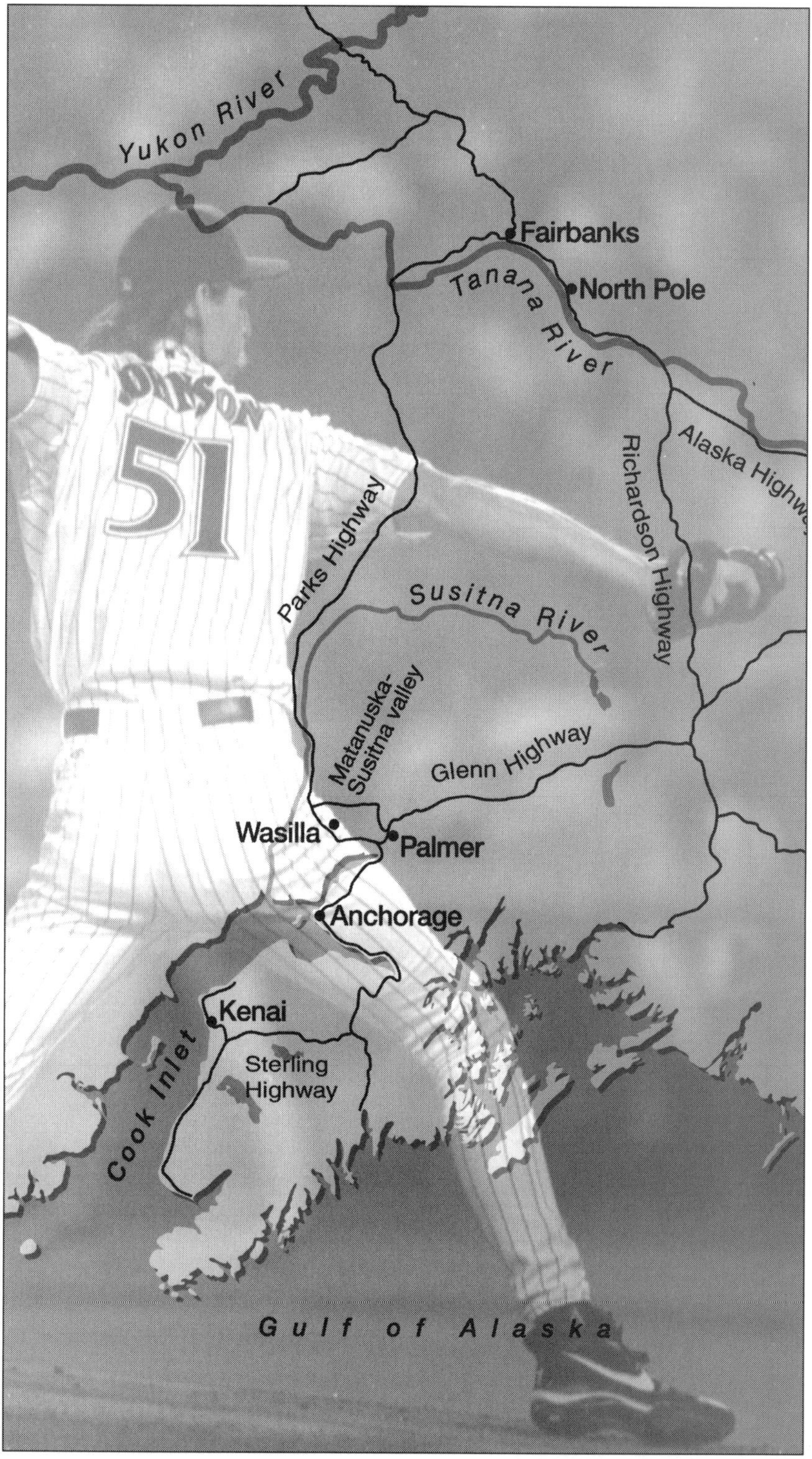

Yukon River
Fairbanks
North Pole
Tanana River
Alaska Highway
Richardson Highway
Parks Highway
Susitna River
Matanuska-Susitna valley
Glenn Highway
Wasilla
Palmer
Anchorage
Kenai
Sterling Highway
Cook Inlet
Gulf of Alaska

CONTENTS

Welcome Satch!
Indians
Think First of First National Bank of Anchora
and Support Anchorage Baseball

1
THE EARLY DAYS

Whaling boats, fur coats and Satchel Paige

SATCHEL PAIGE in Alaska. Sounds a bit like Shoeless Joe comes to Iowa, the evocative fantasy premise of the movie *'Field of Dreams.'*

But if Shoeless Joe Jackson descending from heaven to play baseball on a field constructed under the direction of mystical voices was fanciful, Paige's presence in Anchorage at Mulcahy Stadium in August, 1965, only seemed so.

By 1965, two decades after the construction of the Alaska Highway linking "Seward's Icebox" to the Lower Forty-eight by vehicle, Alaska was starting to grow up. Except that television was tape-delayed, and live, big-name entertainment was woefully short in supply.

Baseball? Well, there was no Alaska Baseball League yet, only the Fairbanks Goldpanners starting to make noise up north. In the absence of either the Major Leagues, or a league of their own, it made perfect sense that a touring Satchel Paige would create a major stir for Alaskans.

Satchel Paige. Perhaps the greatest pitcher of all time.

◄ Alaskans were thrilled in 1965 when Satchell Page, then 59, visited Anchorage to play a four-game exhibition series with local ballplayers.

The name conjured images of a nearly buried American baseball past. A past when black men were sinfully banned from organized baseball and forced to barnstorm, or to compete in the old Negro Leagues. There their talents might be put on grand display, but rarely extolled in mainstream media.

In his prime, in the 1930s and 1940s, the great hurler with catchy rules for better living and a fastball that blurred batters' vision, was understood to be the equal, if not superior, of any other man flinging a ball. Paige was so good that despite the undeniable darkness of his skin, he forced himself into American consciousness and was the recipient of a splashy spread in *Life* magazine. Still, that Paige did not receive the opportunity to flash his skills in the majors until he was in his forties was an injustice common in a country both simpler and cruder, more innocent and more overtly prejudiced, than it is today.

Only the most naive would suggest there was no racism in Alaska, but in certain quarters there was assuredly a sense that the Last Frontier was more tolerant, more of a melting pot. Perhaps it was because of the military influence, or because of the perceived ruggedness it took to put up with the harsh character of the land. But among those welcomed in Anchorage were black singers such as James Brown, Aretha Franklin, Lou Rawls and Billie Holliday. They found a receptive audience at the Mermaid Room and other spots in town.

In the days before satellites brought signals from above and Alaska was wired for cable, the populace was starved for live entertainment. Pat Osborne, a first-hand witness to the Paige pitching phenomenon as a youngster, and later a music promoter, said that in 1960s Anchorage it did not take much to draw big, to fill a 2,000-seat arena with hard bleachers.

"Lassie and Sky King would fill the West High gym," said Osborne.

When Paige landed at Anchorage International Airport, he bumped into former vice president Richard Nixon, changing planes for a fact-finding trip to Southeast Asia. Nixon's career was ascendant. Paige was simply trying to coax a few more strikes out of his rubbery arm. Nixon was looking for the right gate. Paige was looking for the Mulcahy mound.

Paige was perhaps fifty-nine years old (he did his best to hide his age) and scheduled to participate in a four-game exhibition series with local ballplayers. Before the week was out, he pledged to settle in Anchorage as the manager of a new summer baseball club to be called the Alaska Earthquakers.

The name was selected because the Good Friday, 1964, earthquake of seventeen months earlier was fresh on everyone's mind. The shattering shake registered 9.2 on the Richter Scale as the most severe in North American history.

It was not as if anyone believed for more than five seconds that the itinerant Paige would really move to Alaska, but it made people feel good.

No one could make up for the prime, big-stage years Paige was cheated out of, but by the time he reached Anchorage, he was an icon. He was the man

Jack O'Toole, now a Pilots coach, played right field and coached third while Satchel Paige brought the baseball spotlight to Alaska in 1965. LEW FREEDMAN

whose phrase, "Don't look back, something might be gaining on you," had become part of American lexicon.

The four-page program for the exhibitions splashed "Welcome Satch!" across the front. But really, Alaska was always welcoming to baseball.

An early drawing of baseball being played in Alaska was produced by Albert G. Spalding in his 1911 book, *America's National Game.* Spalding, the founder of the sporting goods manufacturing firm of the same name, featured a humorous picture of men wearing hooded, thick fur coats and swinging bats. All while playing the game on a diamond laid out on an ice sheet that was presumably deep water, since a ship can be seen parked in the background.

Accompanying the picture are quotes from an 1894 account of baseball in the north written by General Frederick Funston, soon to be a hero of the war in the Philippines. Funston wrote a story for Harper's Round Table publication about what he viewed and learned in March, 1894.

Following a twenty-day snowshoeing trip across "northeastern Alaska" with Natives, Funston found himself at Herschel Island with numerous whaling vessels. Hemmed in by ice floes, the crews had been stuck in place for months.

"It was on the great national game of Base Ball that officers and men most depended to break the tedium of their long imprisonment and furnish needed exercise," wrote Funston.

Balls and bats were broken out after ships settled into the ice for the season. A league of seven teams was created. Officers banded together, as did seamen. They spent the winter pursuing the "Arctic Whalemen's Pennant" in

the Herschel Island League. One rule stated that games would be played no matter the weather. This proved problematic when the temperature dipped to forty-seven degrees below zero.

"All winter, regardless of blizzards and of bitter cold, the games went on, three or four each week," wrote Funston.

The men played with enthusiasm in nasty cold, howling winds and falling snow. Games were shortened to four innings in December, though, when the darkness of the shortest days of the year marked the calendar.

"All the whalemen were dressed in the Esquimau fur costume, only the face being exposed, and on their hands wore heavy fur mittens," went Funston's story.

The Fort Richardson military team went 18-0, thanks in part to future Major League Hall of Famer Richie Ashburn (kneeling, fifth from left). COURTESY OF CHUCK SMITH

Errors, he suggested, were quite common given the bulky handwear and the slippery footing. Funston felt the goings-on provoked considerable interest from the Native population in the Bering Strait and in Point Barrow.

"Men, women and children became typical Base Ball cranks (fans), and there was never a game without a large attendance of Esquimau," reported Funston. "A fact that impressed me very much at one of the games that I saw was that the crowd of several hundred people watching our national sport at this faraway corner of the earth, only twenty degrees from the pole, and thousands of miles from railroads or steamship lines, was more widely cosmopolitan than could have been found at any other place on the globe. From the ships were Americans, a hundred or more, men from every seafaring nationality of Europe—Chinese, Japanese, and Malays from Tahiti and Hawaii. The colored brother, too, was there, a dozen of him, and several of the players were Negroes. Esquimau of all ages were everywhere, while the red men were represented by the eleven wiry fellows who had snowshowed with me from their home in the valley of the Yukon."

Spalding expressed amazement that baseball found its way to the land of the polar bear and the seals of the arctic ice and proclaimed, "That Base Ball follows the flag is abundantly proven. . . It has been played by our soldiers and sailors wherever they have carried the stars and stripes."

This thesis was supported in many parts of the world. Alaska was no exception as the territory matured from a wide-open region being explored to one more thickly settled.

Anchorage, now Alaska's largest community with 250,000 people, was founded as a tent city on the banks of Ship Creek in 1915. The men came looking for jobs, but they brought baseball with them for pleasure.

On Fifth Avenue in downtown Anchorage today, there is a marker serving as part of a walking tour. It notes the community's early interest in baseball.

"In 1915," the marker reads, "vigorous young men flocked to Ship Creek looking for work on the new railroad. The employment officer would scan their applications, look them up and down, then squint his eyes and ask, 'What position do you play?' "

By the start of World War I, baseball had captured the hearts and minds of Americans. Ty Cobb was in the midst of his run of twelve batting titles with the Detroit Tigers. Babe Ruth was then a Boston Red Sox pitcher. Cy Young, Honus Wagner and Christy Matthewson were some other greats of the era.

Of course new Alaskans wished to play baseball. It was America's hobby. During that first summer of Anchorage's existence, a diamond was carved out to accommodate games played by teams stocked by the fresh arrivals.

"At game time," the marker relates, "the whole town turned out. There was even an all-women's team battling it out with the men. The handicap? All men had to bat left-handed and run the wrong way around the diamond, left leg first."

Soon players sought other competition. In August, 1916 a rivalry sprang up between Anchorage and Seward. In modern Alaska the two communities are connected by 120 miles of highway. The trip was a bit more adventurous some eight decades ago. Players and fans began their journey by sailing along Turnagain Arm. Then they pumped themselves on hand cars along the tracks of the railroad.

The Anchorage team lost the inaugural series to Seward and the local

The first Alaska Baseball League team was the 1960 Fairbanks Goldpanners. Top row, left to right: Mel Gredig, Don Merchant, Gene Hammel, Floyd Watson, Al Bauer. Bottom row: Freddie Harris, Augie Acuna, Red Boucher, Lou Webb, George Meis. Not pictured: Barry Bernstein. COURTESY OF RED BOUCHER

paper hinted that things were not quite on the up-and-up because Seward utilized "an imported battery of professional ballplayers."

Ironically, a half century later, the Alaska Baseball League's foundation would be laid on the backs of imported players, albeit collegians.

When the Seward team traveled to town for a Labor Day rematch in September, the Anchorage club recorded a revenge triumph. A peculiar poem, written to the rhyme of "Casey at the Bat," commented on the sporting extravaganza. It read:

"Don't come unless you're loaded
"Don't come unless you're right
"Don't come unless you're ready
"To Kiss the Game Goodnight."

They say victors write the history. Apparently, they write the poetry, as well.

World War II transformed Alaska. Military bases such as Fort Richardson and Elmendorf Air Force Base in Anchorage and others in and around Fairbanks introduced thousands of men to the territory. After the war, the United States maintained a massive military presence in Alaska.

Inevitably, many stationed in the north had baseball in their blood. The military bases fielded teams in the local city leagues and many were top-notch.

Surely the most talented and distinguished ballplayer during the post-war

As this Fifth Avenue tour marker notes, when workers flocked to the tent city of Anchorage in 1915, they brought a passion for baseball with them. "Vigorous young men flocked to Ship Creek looking for work on the new railroad," the marker says. "The employment officer would scan their applications, look them up and down, then squint his eyes and ask, 'What position do you play?'" LEW FREEDMAN

period was Richie Ashburn, who became a Hall-of-Fame outfielder for the Philadelphia Phillies and then a long-time broadcaster before dying of a heart attack at age seventy in 1997.

Ashburn was inducted into the Army in September, 1945 and served for eighteen months. Most of that time was spent in Alaska. In 1946 he was the star of a terrific Fort Richardson team that the squad's second baseman Chuck Smith remembers fondly.

Smith, the only member of that military team who settled permanently in Alaska, said the group was a veritable all-star team. It was unbeaten while playing all around Alaska. Ashburn, ultimately a career Major League .308 hitter and a two-time batting champion, was a minor leaguer in Utica, New York, when he became a soldier.

"He was a tremendous ballplayer," said Smith, who in addition to a long career in public education, culminating in a stint as superintendent of schools in Fairbanks, was involved with clubs in the Alaska Baseball League. "He could bunt .350. He was lightning on the bases. I had never seen the equal of him. He just did everything a little better than everyone else. The only thing that could have kept him from stardom was injury."

Smith himself was a pretty fair player who had a short minor-league career. His rise was halted by injury.

While Ashburn later became famous as a smooth-fielding centerfielder who covered territory with gazelle-like grace, his Alaska years were marked by one peculiarity. At the time, he was Fort Richardson's everyday catcher. Perhaps it was an early example of the Army testing its be-all-you-can-be campaign.

Satchel Paige, of course, was never an Army type. He was free-spirited, a witty man with a lanky build, blessed with a deceptively powerful right arm. He could talk as good a show as he pitched, and man, could he pitch. When he was younger, he sometimes waved his outfielders in as a display of disdain for batters, then struck them all out. Paige whimsically popularized his legendary rules for long life, including not "angrying up the blood" with fried foods.

As he approached sixty, Paige was surely not as fast or free-wheeling as he used to be, but he remained a consummate showman.

In Anchorage, local players were proud to be Paige's foils or teammates. He pitched three innings at a time for a team each day, then switched sides as each game progressed.

Jack O'Toole, an Anchorage Glacier Pilots coach for more than thirty years, played some right field during the Paige series and coached third base. He remembers not Paige's speed, but his mound cunning. Of course, beside his wicked fastball, Paige had duped batters for two generations with a "hesitation" pitch.

"He could throw all that junk," said O'Toole. "He had a hell of a sinker. We had fun. He was probably wondering what he was doing in Alaska. He was here probably to make a thousand-dollar bill."

Clearly, O'Toole, a fixture on the local baseball scene, was not fooled into believing Paige was going to register to vote in Alaska. Paige, though, did a good job pretending he'd been overwhelmed by Alaska and sounded earnest about becoming the boss of the budding Earthquakers.

"Lately, I've wanted to leave barnstorming baseball to settle down to help the sport," Paige was quoted as saying. "And Anchorage seems to me the place to do it. I loved Anchorage at first sight, and I'm the man who can build this team up. I'm the man who knows baseball players and can get them up here to play. This will make Anchorage in the baseball world."

Paige's promotional agent at the time was Abe Saperstein, the man who invented the Harlem Globetrotters basketball team. Paige said getting out of his contract with Saperstein would likely be no problem.

"There is only a hundred-to-one chance Abe will object to my staying up here," said Paige.

Carrying on the charade, Paige announced a day later that Saperstein had given him the OK to hang out in Anchorage.

No doubt such chatter was to hype the gate. Or else it was Paige playing a card to negotiate a better touring deal for himself from Saperstein, a strategy he had employed many times over the years.

One page in the program featured a photo of Paige in a Cleveland Indians uniform, and the herald, "Satchel Paige, Regarded As The Greatest Pitcher of Them All." The games were scheduled for Thursday, Friday and Saturday, August 26, 27 and 28 at night and the "grand finale" on the afternoon of Sunday the 29th.

Teasing the fans as the exhibitions unfolded, Paige made a fresh announcement.

"I'm going to bear down Sunday," he said. "I may even go the distance if the weather's right."

As it turned out the weather was quite chilly and Paige did no such thing.

Pat Osborne was an eleven-year-old Little Leaguer when Paige came to town. He attended the games in uniform in order to get in free, and he walked to the park by himself from his nearby home. Even then he recognized that Satchel Paige was somebody special.

Osborne obtained Paige autographs on the cover of the program where Paige was shown winding up and again wearing his old Cleveland Indians' uniform, and another autograph on a baseball. Once, Osborne's dad gave him a fright, taking the ball down from a shelf and using it to warm up a cousin. Scuff marks remain clearly visible on the ball from that faux pas, but so does the writing: "Best Wishes, Satchel Paige."

Osborne, now in his forties, has gray hair and white in his mustache and tiny beard, but as a youth he was attracted by the scene. Adults playing ball instead of kids, the big stadium, games under the lights. Later, he learned Paige might well have been the man chosen to break baseball's color barrier instead of Jackie Robinson, and how significant a figure Paige was.

"What made him memorable was his impact on baseball and civil rights," said Osborne. "Those guys weren't just trying to break through to another job, but a race barrier."

Paige, of course, did not stay in Alaska after the exhibitions. Most likely when Paige died in 1982, he had never set foot in Alaska again. Nor did the Anchorage Earthquakers ever get off the ground.

Neither Paige nor the Earthquakers "made" Anchorage in the baseball world. His appearance was stage-setting. But soon enough, high-caliber baseball was being played in Anchorage and all over Alaska.

2

THE FAIRBANKS GOLDPANNERS

Blazing the trail

COURTESY OF RED BOUCHER

RED BOUCHER became the George Washington of the Alaska Baseball League by accident.

In 1960, a year after migrating to Fairbanks following a lengthy career in the Navy, Boucher was operating a sporting goods store called Pan Alaska Sports. He was new in town and settled in Fairbanks instead of Anchorage only because when he exited the Alaska Highway, the Interior community was closer.

Some local sports figures approached him that spring to sponsor a still-on-the-drawing-board team. They needed bats, balls and uniforms to make it a reality.

Boucher was a soft touch for this appeal because he was a lifelong baseball fan whose devotion to the game exceeded his on-field ability. As a youth he was a 5-foot-9½, 148-pound righthanded pitcher. Walter Johnson, the fire-baller of the Washington Senators, was his hero. Of Johnson it was said, "You can't hit what you can't see."

Boucher was not so similarly talented.

"I could spit faster than I could throw," he said.

During his Navy days, Boucher managed a military team in Panama

Since the mid-1960s, one of the team's first financial supporters, Bill Stroecker, has been serving one-year stints as Goldpanners president. On big game nights he often takes his turn in the ticket booth. LEW FREEDMAN

which played exhibitions against a team handled by Tom Lasorda, later a Hall-of-Fame manager for the Los Angeles Dodgers. There were wild times.

"We used to stage fights (between the teams) just to get the crowd in," said Boucher. "Nobody ever won. We just rolled in the dirt."

The Fairbanks organizers were thinking big when they came to Boucher. They said they had ballplayers lined up from Colorado. Boucher drew up a uniform design patterned after the St. Louis Cardinals' 1930s Gas House Gang of Dizzy Dean and Frankie Frisch.

Then the players reneged on coming to Alaska. Then the organizers discovered time conflicts of their own. It seemed Boucher had an investment in a closetful of empty suits. Oh yes, and as the only original planner remaining, he also had a schedule to fulfill. It was May, just forty-five days till opening day.

"It was left in my lap," said Boucher.

No one ever accused Boucher of being a why-me guy who sat back moaning and whining. If Boucher ate the cost of the uniforms, Alaska baseball would have hit a dead-end before really beginning. Instead, he attacked. From his Navy days, Boucher knew people with Major League connections.

He telephoned Bobby Doerr, who for fourteen years played Hall-of-Fame second base for the Boston Red Sox. And he telephoned Al Hollingsworth, a former National League pitcher, then a Red Sox scout. They offered winning advice. Boucher was told that a guy in Tucson, Arizona named Abe Chanin was starting a publication called "Collegiate Baseball." Just maybe he had a line on players willing to take a chance on Alaska on short notice. Boucher called Chanin and he said, "I've got a friend at the University of Arizona."

The friend was Wildcats coach Frank Sancet. Sancet liked the sound of Boucher's pitch. He put six young players on a plane to Fairbanks.

"The players he ended up sending me turned out to be the nucleus of the Panner club," said Boucher.

Boucher scrounged up a few locals and fielded a ten-man team in the local military league. The team was a seat-of-the-pants operation and practiced at a junior high school field. The players had been promised living quarters and jobs, but at first Boucher had neither.

"They had to live at my apartment," he said. "I had them cutting lawns."

And occasionally selling sporting goods in his store. Mr. Spalding would have been proud.

When Steve Agbaba, a legendary Alaska broadcaster, baseball aficionado, and all-around character, saw Boucher scrambling, trying to balance the tasks of forming a team, babysitting out-of-town players, and running a business, he asked, "What the hell are you doing?"

At times, it may not have looked much like Boucher knew. But he never really doubted that his baseball team would be around for the long haul.

Sportswriters and other skeptics periodically teased Boucher about his efforts. His team was variously called "Boucher's Imports," or "Boucher's Panhandlers," because it always seemed to be begging for funds.

There was no abundance of players, either. Once, Boucher put himself up to bat. He got a scratch single. People initially laughed at the squad, but the team finished 11-7.

In 1961, the Goldpanners improved to 12-4. By 1962, it became apparent that the team Boucher assembled far exceeded the previous quality of local play. His club's record was 24-7. By then the team's success was respected, and when the name "Goldpanners" stuck, that pretty much put to rest the Panhandlers tag. Most importantly, Boucher had the confidence and persuasiveness to wangle an invitation to the National Baseball Congress World Series in Wichita, Kansas.

Boucher didn't feel constrained by geographical borders and wanted to spread the gospel of Alaska. After beating an Anchorage team to ensure legitimacy as a state qualifier, Boucher still had to convince the NBC his unknown Alaska bunch was worthy.

Wichita was the proving ground for non-professional teams. An institution in summer baseball, the tournament dates to 1935, and, in fact, Satchel

Paige participated in the first one. The NBC was a showcase for talent from the hinterlands. Pro scouts flocked to Wichita seeking undiscovered gems.

Wichita instantly fell for the Goldpanners, the nickname, the entire Alaska package. The Goldpanners were called the "Alaska" Goldpanners. Boucher insisted. It was his way to promote the state. While the team still officially maintains that prefix, over time everyone else in the league adopted the habit of referring to the team as the "Fairbanks" Goldpanners.

Above all, the Goldpanners became popular in Wichita because they could play. Fairbanks finished second in the tournament. A team begun so humbly in itty-bitty Fairbanks only two years before fell just a game short of winning the national championship.

Dick Lobdell, the long-time Anchorage Glacier Pilots broadcaster and board member, was working for KFAR radio in Fairbanks in 1962. His partner, Bill Whaley, went to Wichita to call the games, but it was 105 degrees there. Whaley couldn't stand the heat, so he wanted out of the kitchen. Lobdell stayed behind in Fairbanks.

"Bill called me up and said, 'I've had it,' " said Lobdell. " 'It's too damned hot. I'm coming home.' "

So the station improvised, using the time-tested, on-air method of re-creating games. Boucher phoned the station with scoring decisions, then Lobdell produced a broadcast.

"We went into the control room and we had all the sound effects," said Lobdell.

The unknown Goldpanners were seeded thirty-second, last in the draw when the double-elimination tournament started, but the club won six games in a row to reach the semifinals.

The shortstop for that Fairbanks team was a young man named Emmitt Wilson. His background differed from the many college players on the roster. And so did his future in the game: he eventually became commissioner of the Alaska Baseball League.

Born in 1937, Wilson grew up in the San Francisco Bay area. He attended San Jose City College, a junior college, but signed a professional contract with the Pittsburgh Pirates organization in 1960. He played in Hobbs, New Mexico, and Kingsport, Tennessee, Class D ball under the old minor league structure.

"I did all right," recalled Wilson. "I could run and throw. I was a Punch and Judy-type hitter. If the ball took more than two bounces, I had a chance of beating it out."

Wilson's pro aspirations were squashed in 1961 when he was drafted into the Army and shipped to Fort Richardson in Anchorage. He represented the post on an all-star team, and as a member of the local Playboy Lounge team

Dan Cowgill played for the 'Panners in the Seventies. Now he's calling the shots as manager. LEW FREEDMAN

played some games in Fairbanks against the Goldpanners. Wilson remembers it once took eleven days to play three games because of incessant rain.

Boucher recruited Wilson for the 1962 NBC squad, and Wilson had to obtain permission from his commanding officer to go.

Wilson now has a full head of white hair, but he is erect and youthful appearing, with a sharp memory. The two things he remembers best from the journey to Kansas is the how Boucher motivated the team and how Fairbanks rallied around the cash-poor club from a distance.

Located on the banks of the Chena River, Fairbanks owes its 1901 origins to gold-rush dreams. Although now a thriving city of 60,000 people within the North Star Borough, the community in the 1960s seemed very much a small town, a town without pretensions that was a little rough around the edges and comfortable with the description.

When Boucher decided to take the Goldpanners to Wichita, he made the fortuitous decision to to seek support from Bill Sneddon, publisher of the *Fairbanks Daily News-Miner.* Sneddon lobbied local businesses and fifteen firms put up $350 apiece.

Players and backers backed out at the get-go, but Red Boucher (center, between son Patrick and coach Jack O'Toole at Mulcahy Stadium) got Alaska's summer baseball program rolling. He was inducted into the National Baseball Congress Hall of Fame in 1999. COURTESY OF JACK O'TOOLE

One key contact made was Bill Stroecker at First National Bank. Stroecker, whose father Ed was one of the community's first prominent ballplayers, was an avid fan. Not only did Stroecker offer money, he stayed involved with the Goldpanners. Nearly forty years later, Stroecker, who advanced to the presidency of his bank, was still a member of the team's board of directors and president of the team.

To whatever degree Boucher was optimistic about the Goldpanners' skills, he was not rich enough to keep his team in Wichita indefinitely.

"We couldn't afford to stay in downtown hotels," said Wilson. "We had no air conditioning."

During the tournament, the players checked out daily, packed suitcases, and brought them to the clubhouse. When they won another game, they checked back in for another night.

"We kept winning and we ran out of money," said Wilson.

Appeals for money were made in Fairbanks.

"I'm told they took a wheelbarrow and ran it through the bars to keep us playing," said Wilson.

A well-wisher's telegram was mailed. It contained a huge list of people who gave small amounts of money to keep the quest for the national title going.

"Red read every name on that list to the team," said Wilson.

In the semifinals, the team trailed, but a player named Jim Dolin hit a wind-blown, three-run homer to put the Goldpanners into the championship game against the Wichita Dreamliners, a powerhouse featuring all former professional players.

Besides the Alaska mystique, another reason the Goldpanners found swift acclaim at Wichita's Lawrence-Dumont Stadium was their station as underdogs. It was the young whippersnappers against the hardened oldtimers.

"No one had ever brought a team of college kids," said Lobdell.

Larry Davis, commissioner of the NBC since 1960, said Boucher and the Goldpanners made an immediate splash.

"Boucher was so popular," he said. "He had some showmanship. He was a crowd pleaser. Plus, he had a lot of talent. Then they always had real decorative uniforms and Goldpanners was a catchy name."

However, the Dreamliners won the championship, 7-6 in the last inning, on what Wilson remembers as a controversial call at home plate.

The always enterprising Boucher immediately extended an invitation to the Dreamliners to travel north the next June to play in the annual Midnight Sun game. The Dreamliners came and that helped jump-start the tradition of bringing well-known Lower Forty-eight clubs to Alaska.

"I give credit to Red," said Lobdell. "Not too many people could have done it that fast. Red was a hustling promoter. It was well known he was not a baseball man per se. He was not an X and O guy. He was a promoter and motivator."

Although the Goldpanners finished second, their surprise effort pleased fans in Fairbanks.

"We came home and they threw us a victory party you wouldn't believe," said Wilson.

Wilson received permission from the Fort Richardson CO to stick around.

"So I stayed a week," said Wilson. "That's where I met my wife."

And that's how he began his career as a Goldpanner.

3

THE COLLEGE STARS

Tom Seaver and others change the face of the sport

THE WAY Red Boucher remembers it, he was minding his own business in Fairbanks one day in early 1964 when the phone rang. Rod Dedeaux, the esteemed coach of the University of Southern California baseball team, was calling.

"Red," he said, "I've got a guy I want you to try out. He's got some experience at Fresno City College and I'm trying to decide whether to give him tuition and books money. Let me know if you think he's worth it."

Then Dedeaux hung up. Boucher accepted Tom Seaver for his summer roster.

Seaver, later nicknamed "Tom Terrific" in a Hall-of-Fame, 300-win pitching career primarily with the New York Mets, was worth it.

During two summers in Alaska—Seaver returned to pitch for the Goldpanners in 1965—Seaver and Boucher developed a friendship. Boucher proudly displays autographed Seaver photographs in his office, in addition to signed letters. When Seaver was inducted into the Hall of Fame in Cooperstown, New York, in 1992, Boucher was an invited guest. Boucher owns—and wears—a T-shirt from that induction day. More than once, Seaver has thanked Boucher for the assistance he received in Alaska.

"I just want to take a moment to express my appreciation, Red, for the opportunity you made available to me and the time you spent helping me as a Goldpanner," Seaver wrote in one letter. He said his time in Alaska represented a "vital step in my progress."

Seaver made his mark early with the Goldpanners, but as of 1999, an astounding total of 161 players who wore the Goldpanner uniform had advanced to the Major Leagues—more than half of the ABL's three hundred such graduates.

The Goldpanners were very much a fledgling outfit in the early years. Nobody in town really knew who Boucher was. But if Boucher made the Goldpanners, the Goldpanners made Boucher. When the Fairbanks team represented the community well, Boucher was noticed.

"All of a sudden I was Mr. Something," said Boucher.

Boucher began his own life with virtually nothing. His father, Henry Aristide Boucher Sr., died at age twenty-seven, when Boucher was only eight, the lingering results of a mustard gas attack during World War I. Boucher's mother, Helen, placed him and his brother in an orphanage because she couldn't take care of them. She suffered from multiple sclerosis.

After twenty years in the Navy, reaching the rank of chief petty officer, Boucher sought a fresh start when he came to Alaska. When his Goldpanner supporters backed out in 1960, Boucher resolved to make "the best damn team I can."

The way, he soon realized, was stocking the club with collegians, an approach since adopted by most of the country's major summer teams. His recruiting may have been take-what-I-can-get at first, but by 1963, partially through his Dedeaux connection and his extraordinarily successful USC program, the Goldpanners were fielding players destined for the pinnacle of the sport.

"I never picked a Goldpanner I didn't look in the eye," said Boucher.

They had to have a winning spark, he said, and he traveled Outside on his own nickel to recruit. The rare player he didn't meet, who was chosen for him, was Seaver. Seaver had the goods anyway.

"Tom Seaver made Tom Seaver," said Boucher. "There's never been a more determined individual who played ball for me."

He was not, however, the first notable Goldpanner.

Three players off the 1963 team – Dave Dowling, Chuck Hartenstein and Mike Paul – became Major Leaguers. Dowling, in fact, had the greatest single Goldpanner pitching season. He finished 11-3 with an 0.85 earned run average.

Years later Dowling said that although he had a friend in Fairbanks before he joined the team, his basic knowledge of Alaska stemmed from Robert Service's renowned poetry and the Johnny Horton song "North to Alaska."

"I was sort of intrigued to see what Service was writing about and Horton was singing about," said Dowling, who came from the University of California at Berkeley.

Although his career was very brief, Dowling, a dentist in Washington state, became the first Goldpanner and Alaska Baseball League player to make the majors when he pitched a game for the Chicago Cubs in 1966.

Showcasing his talents in Wichita at the NBC tournament made his pro career possible, said Dowling, who said one other thing sticks in his mind about Fairbanks in summer—mosquitoes.

He said he would urge any player to try the ABL "and bring insect repellent with them."

The Goldpanner cast was even more impressive by Seaver's first season. Seaver was one of seven Goldpanners on the 1964 club who progressed to the majors. Besides Seaver, Graig Nettles, Curt Motton, Rick Monday, Paul, Gary Sutherland and Jimy Williams saw Major League action. Nettles, of course, was an all-star.

As the reputation and success of the Goldpanners spread, top-notch players routinely went north to play for Boucher. Men who became stars enjoyed formative summers in Alaska. Joining Seaver and Nettles on the 1965 team was pitcher Andy Messersmith. Later came Bob Boone, one of the greatest fielding catchers of all time, and pitcher Bill "Spaceman" Lee, the left-hander with the world-class sense of humor.

Lee, part of the USC pipeline, said he expected to be cold the whole time he was in Fairbanks, but the real eye-opener was the quality of players.

"What you were doing was playing with the best talent in America," said Lee, the former Boston Red Sox hurler who was known for punting wads of bubble gum into the bleachers at Fenway Park. "If you succeeded in Alaska, you'd eventually succeed in the American League and National League."

And then there was multi-talented, but always perplexing, Dave Kingman.

Kingman, who hit 442 Major League home runs, even if he could barely keep his batting average above his weight, was originally a pitcher, but Boucher wanted to use him as an everyday player.

"I told Dedeaux, 'You've got to put that kid in the lineup,'" said Boucher. "'He hits moon shots.'"

Back then, Kingman was just as much pitcher as slugger. Stan Zaborac, general manager of the Mat-Su Miners, remembers watching the kid throw and wondering just what would become of him.

"He was scary wild," said Zaborac. "He'd throw in the nineties. He'd just rare back and throw."

Boucher said Kingman put a lot of pressure on himself.

"He threw smoke," said Boucher. "But once he gave up a big inning and

Outfielder Tim Nettles, whose father Graig and uncle Jim played for the Goldpanners in the 1960s, played for the Panners in 1998. Lew Freedman

came back to the dugout and said, 'Coach Boucher, I let you down.' I said, 'No, Dave, you didn't let me down. Your place is to be an everyday player."

Although some say it has never been done, Boucher swears Kingman hit a home run over the Growden Park left-field wall that came down on the roof of the Fairbanks Curling Club across the street, a memorable blast that might approach 500 feet.

"I can see it landing now," said Boucher.

Although Kingman made it as a home-run hitter with the Oakland Athletics and other teams, in a Major League career spanning 1971 to 1986, his lifetime average was .236.

The collection of Fairbanks' talent was astonishing, though it was raw and the players were several years shy of their primes.

Dick Lobdell, who was a Goldpanner broadcaster in the 1960s before moving to Anchorage, said Seaver "was not an overpowering pitcher when he was in Fairbanks." And Nettles, "was having troubles, believe it or not."

A classic Goldpanner story involves the 1964 team. Nettles was struggling. And so was young Rick Monday. Only one could make the season-ending roster for the NBC tournament. Given Nettles' and Monday's futures, with benefit of hindsight, it's easy to say there must have been someone else to cut.

"At the end of the season, Red cut Rick Monday," said Lobdell. "The next year Monday had a great season at school and became the number one college draft pick."

Well, miler Jim Ryun was cut from a school track team, and Michael

Jordan couldn't make his varsity high school basketball team as a freshman, so these things happen.

Emmitt Wilson, who was then acting as a player-coach, said he was involved in the choice.

"It was my suggestion we keep Nettles," said Wilson. "But Monday, you could see the potential."

Monday starred at Arizona State and become a well-respected Major League outfielder.

The Goldpanners were ahead of the curve fielding teams of collegians, so they had the pick of the crop. Generally, the recruiting was West Coast-based, and Boucher and USC developed a special rapport.

"He was Mr. College Baseball," said Boucher of his lucky link-up with Dedeaux. "Rod helped and encouraged me more than anyone else."

The Goldpanners' depth was phenomenal. Jim Nettles, Graig's younger brother who played in Fairbanks in 1966 and 1967, said he felt fortunate to be invited north after his freshman year at San Diego State.

"I was the last guy picked on the team," said Nettles, who also became a Major Leaguer, enjoying a six-year career with the Minnesota Twins and other clubs. "It was, 'Well, let's take a chance on this guy.' "

Nettles said Boucher was an inspirational field leader.

"I was in awe," said Nettles.

Flying into Fairbanks, said Nettles, the plane carrying several players was delayed in Seattle. The players didn't arrive until a morning later than scheduled. Boucher met them and drove them right to the field.

"You missed a whole night's sleep," said Boucher, "but you can catch up in September."

The players were woozy, but once the workout commenced, everything went smoothly.

"He got us fired up," said Nettles.

Boucher's philosophy was simple. You had to take your obligations seriously. Players were expected to work at jobs in the community from 8 A.M. to 4 P.M., then report to the ballpark at 5 P.M. for baseball.

"The first order was to discipline them and motivate them," said Boucher.

That was Boucher to a T. Lobdell said Boucher wasn't a strategist and Boucher agreed. "I didn't know crap," he said. "Motivate them and get the hell out of the way."

Lobdell remembers once Boucher felt he had to crack down because the team was becoming complacent. Boucher waved twenty-two plane tickets and shouted, "Anyone want to go home?"

No one did. Most were like Jim Nettles, who felt being a Goldpanner was special.

Before starring in the majors, Graig Nettles teamed with the likes of Tom Seaver, Rick Monday and Andy Messersmith to make the Goldpanners a national power in the 1960s. COURTESY OF RED BOUCHER

The 1964 Goldpanners. Future Hall of Famer Tom Seaver is second from the left, middle row.

COURTESY OF RED BOUCHER

"It was an elitist thing," said Nettles, who now operates a baseball training center in Puyallup, Washington. "We were so good. Our whole pitching staff made it to the Major Leagues."

That sounds like the kind of story an oldtimer would tell to impress a younger generation of players, much like the walking-uphill-both-ways-to-school tall tale.

But Nettles is not exaggerating. On the 1966 and 1967 squads, throwers Lee, Tom House, Jim Barr, Rich Hand, Brent Strom, Mike Adamson, Greg Garrett, and Don Rose all did advance. Given how difficult it is to make the majors, how much luck, as well as skill, is necessary, the odds of something like that occurring must be 10,000 to 1.

Fairbanks appreciated what it saw. There was no cable TV, no Major League games beamed into town. If you wanted to watch baseball, you headed out to the stadium.

"Back in those days, there wasn't that much to do," said Lobdell. "Coming out to the ballpark was the thing to do."

The ballpark itself was located a few miles from the airport in a less-developed neighborhood. Originally known as Goldpanner Field, it was built on a dump site—by Boucher and his early ballplayers themselves—with donated lumber.

Before the Goldpanners became an institution it was hard to get any assistance from the local government, so the field was not especially well-cared-for and lacked good grass covering.

"The only reason I ran for public office," said Boucher, "was because they wouldn't give me grass seed."

Needless to say, when Boucher reached the city council, then became mayor, his park was better groomed.

The stadium was eventually called Growden Park. It was named for a popular local man because of a tragedy. Chuck Smith, later president of the Valley Green Giants, coached a local American Legion team. One of his top players was Jimmy Growden. Growden grew up, married, and became the basketball coach at Fairbanks' Lathrop High School. On the day of the Good Friday Earthquake, Growden and his two sons were in Valdez, ground zero. They were swept away by a tidal wave.

"A real loss," said Smith.

Once they started winning big, the Goldpanners averaged between 1,200 and 1,500 fans a night and drew as many as 5,000 for the Midnight Sun game played in connection with the Summer Solstice.

The community embraced the Goldpanners. When Smith was principal at Main Junior High, his invited speakers included Boucher, Seaver, and Dedeaux. After listening to the three of them a budding player should have been able to grasp the nuances of throwing a curveball.

A Goldpanner support squad of sorts was started. This was not to be confused with the Dallas Cowboys cheerleaders. These were teen-aged girls seeking to be part of the action.

Jinx Whitaker, now the operator of a Fairbanks art gallery, said becoming a "Goldpannerette" was a big deal when she was sixteen. Besides distributing programs at the park, her job was "to look cute." The teens wore blue-and-gold shirts and directed fans to their seats, while trying to cozy up to the visiting college boys.

"It was my first experience with humility," said Whitaker, who remembers being more-or-less snubbed by Seaver. "I thought I was the cutest thing going. After all, I was a Goldpannerette."

Cruising Second Avenue downtown with one group of players, the darkly tanned Whitaker was totally confused when asked if she was a Native, as in an Eskimo. Being a Goldpanerette never represented a quantum leap for her social life.

"I never even saw a party," said Whitaker. "I was naïve. Actually, that was the only year I understood baseball."

By the mid-1960s, after their remarkable 1962 NBC debut, and with beefed up scheduling, the Goldpanners were posting dominating records. The marks notched for the rest of the decade—45-12, 34-19, 38-19, 50-13, 45-10, 37-8, and 41-18—were overwhelming.

The Goldpanners were so good they had outgrown their Alaska roots in

In 1967, after being named National League rookie of the year with the New York Mets, Tom Seaver returned to Fairbanks for a public appearance and autograph session. Seaver's stay with the Fairbanks Goldpanners signaled the start of a wave of top college talent to showcase their talents in the Alaskan summers. COURTESY OF RED BOUCHER

one sense. Although in early days the roster included a mix of military players, locals, and collegians, it was now almost all collegians. One player who keenly felt the difference was Wilson.

Wilson, the shortstop on the revered 1962 Goldpanner NBC runnerup team, was discharged from the Army in October of that year. He returned to San Francisco and went to work as a labor foreman for a construction company, a job arranged by his father, Forrest.

He thought he was done with baseball. But Boucher tracked him down the following May and asked if he wanted to come back.

"I missed baseball, so I said, 'Yeah,' " Wilson said. "My dad was real upset with me."

So distraught his son was throwing away a seemingly solid career on a whim that Forrest didn't speak to Emmitt for ten years.

Wilson returned to Alaska in 1963 and stayed. His real job at first, ironically, was working for a construction company, but he was the shortstop again when the team returned to the NBC. This time the Goldpanners played their way to Wichita. They flew to Seattle, then went by bus to Eureka, California, and Grand Junction, Colorado, among other stops.

"The fans were even more supportive," said Wilson. "We stopped at every radio station and Red promoted Alaska and his baseball team."

After the season, Wilson decided he had to find a real career. He went to work for Alaska National Bank as a teller and over the next nine years worked his way up to vice president in charge of consumer credit. In 1971 he became the state's deputy director of commerce under Governor Bill Egan and served as commissioner of commerce in the cabinet for two years.

Wilson played for the Goldpanners from 1962 to 1968, though after the first few years he was squeezed out of the starting lineup. Still, Wilson developed friendships with Seaver, Boone and Graig Nettles. They came over to his house, wrestled with his kid.

On Nettles' first day in town in 1964, Wilson said he took him to a bar, Tommy's Elbow Room, and they hung around drinking until 4 A.M. In the Land of the Midnight Sun, when they emerged, it was bright, not dark. Nettles couldn't get over the sun shining in the middle of the night.

"He was just amazed," said Wilson. "We sat at the corner of 10th and Noble on the curb and he was just marveling at it."

For that matter, although Seaver retains a more-or-less pure image, Wilson remembers a more fun-loving guy.

"Over the years he's been able to develop an apple pie, milquetoast image," said Wilson, "but he was as big a prankster as any of them."

Seaver, said Boucher, was a jokester, but he was more of a go-along guy. If you were looking for the smoking gun on a prank, he said, "Graig Nettles was the instigator."

Still finding himself, Seaver did not put up humongous pitching numbers in Fairbanks. He was a raw specimen, not yet his full 6-foot-1 and 195 pounds. In a mound meeting during Seaver's first game for the Goldpanners, Seaver was told to change directions, either move his pitches more inside, or outside, Wilson can't remember.

"Tom says, 'I would, but I don't know how,' " said Wilson. "He had a very live fastball. He didn't know where it was going."

Zaborac, another old wise man of the ABL, said Seaver had the tools when he saw him.

"He was just impressive," said Zaborac. "The potential was there."

Seaver made all the adjustments necessary to live up to that potential.

By certain standards, Seaver was a late bloomer. He was not drafted out of high school in Fresno, so he stayed home to play for the local college. He was very enthused when Dedeaux made a tentative scholarship offer. USC had only five to give that season and that's why Dedeaux wanted Seaver to prove himself in Alaska.

Seaver flew to Alaska alone. When he got off the plane he wasn't quite sure whom he was looking for or who was looking for him. He was greeted by Heida, Boucher's wife at the time, who was from Iceland. The Goldpanners were in the middle of a game. She brought a uniform and drove Seaver directly to the ballpark. He changed, walked into the dugout and shook hands with Boucher.

Boucher sent Seaver to the bullpen and told him to warm up. Boucher had already made it clear that jet lag was not any kind of excuse, so that first night Seaver found himself called into a 2-2 game in the sixth inning against the Bellingham Bells. He struck out the first batter.

Seaver stayed at the Bouchers' home and enjoyed Alaska. In a biography *Seaver,* written by Gene Shoor, about ten pages is devoted to Seaver's summers in Fairbanks.

"Alaska was something else," said Seaver. "You simply can't realize what a magnificant place it is unless you've been there. And it's a lot different than most people picture it.

"I can remember my first trip there. I expected it to be so cold. I wore a heavy sweater and a topcoat as I got off the plane. But Mrs. Boucher was just wearing a sleeveless dress."

Seaver was flabbergasted by the middle-of-the-night sunlight. Once, he woke up about 3 A.M. and feared he had overslept for his job as a groundskeeper.

At the season-ending NBC tournament in Wichita, Seaver excelled, winning two games and swatting a grand-slam home run.

It was at Wichita the next year that a still unsure-of-himself Seaver received some very solid feedback about his future. He pitched in the losing semifinals game, but was approached the same day by Major League hitters Bob Boyd and Rod Kanehl and told he was going places.

By 1967, Seaver was with the New York Mets. Along with Danny Frisella, a former Goldpanner teammate.

Jack Lang, a New York sportswriter, wrote a story about them. The lead read in part, "From the top of the world to the bottom of the National League . . . '

Frisella talked about the strangeness of playing night games without the lights being turned on and said the only way he could sleep was by placing tinfoil over his windows—a tried-and-true Alaska method of making summer sunlight resemble night.

Seaver spoke of his own troubles sleeping and the surprising mildness of the temperatures. Although he didn't mention it, about a week a year Fairbanks' usual summer readings of sixty-to-seventy-five escalate into the low nineties.

Following his rookie year there is no evidence Alaska was a big topic in Seaver interviews.

"You knew Seaver was going to be OK," said Lowell Purcell, who broadcast Goldpanners games when Seaver played in Fairbanks.

Seaver's career statistics were far better than OK. He played in the majors for twenty years and finished with a record of 311-205.

There have been other great Goldpanner players, but one of the earliest remains the greatest.

4

THE ANCHORAGE GLACIER PILOTS

Building on a natural rivalry

THE CREATION of the Fairbanks Goldpanners and their swift metamorphosis into a national-caliber team pretty much ruined a juicy rivalry with Anchorage. No longer could the average local Joe compete. No longer was the big game of the season a war between teams representing the state's two largest cities.

"By 1965 or 1966, it was 'Oh, crap,' whenever we played them," said Lefty Van Brunt, who was then player-coach for the Anchorage All-Stars. "Around 1964 was about the last time we gave them a game."

Facing the Goldpanners became an ordeal for Anchorage clubs. They got clobbered all the time. Once, Van Brunt recalled, the score of a game was 22-0 after five innings. The once-exciting series was starting to sound more like Notre Dame-Prairie View football.

Steve Langdon, a first baseman on some of the Anchorage teams, said the going got increasingly difficult.

"Of course, we got pounded," said Langdon, whose son Trajan became Alaska's greatest-ever basketball player.

Still, the Anchorage players had some good moments. Langdon said in consecutive games he stroked a home run off Bill Lee, then swatted a double off Brent Strom. Those guys were future major leaguers.

Langdon, now a college professor, also was a victim when Lee retired the Anchorage side on three pitches—all changeups.

Anchorage's baseball beginnings dated to those 1915 holiday games with Seward. In the next half century, World War II and the discovery of oil on the Kenai Peninsula altered the landscape, expanded Alaska's population, and increased interest in the 49th state.

But Alaska still had a lot of catching up to do. Although airline service improved, distance was still a barrier. Television shows were not seen on the same day in Alaska as the rest of the United States. There were no professional sports teams. Facilities were unsophisticated. And the weather was inhospitable for baseball. When big-league clubs departed for spring training in February, Alaska might be under six feet of snow. When opening day rolled around in April, most of Alaska was still thawing.

The seasons of the north did not match the calendar of the rest of the world. In a sense, that was part of Boucher's genius. The Goldpanners' playing season was June and July in Alaska, by mid-August in Wichita. That schedule jibed perfectly with collegians' summer breaks.

If dog mushing, seal hunting, and whaling were the main spring activities in the small villages of Bush Alaska, Anchorage considered itself as mainstream American as apple pie, and, in adaptable form, at least, equally enthralled with baseball.

Baseball broadcaster Dick Lobdell grew up in Anchorage when it was a one-public-high-school town (now there are six), graduating from old Anchorage High School in 1955. There was no high school team and no high school league, so he played catcher, then third base, in summer American Legion ball. At a time when it was especially difficult to get noticed in Alaska, he also played at Fresno State.

The Legion teams for high school-aged players were named for sponsors like the Kiwanis, or Mountain View Auto Supply. Also, the military bases fielded teams. A couple of times a season, there might be a series with a Fairbanks Legion team.

Lobdell, a heavyset man with glasses and graying, Fu Manchu facial hair, is now in his sixties. In the same year he finished high school, Lobdell was a member of the first Alaska team to compete in American Legion regional play. The team, coached by his father, flew to Seattle and took a train to Billings, Montana. For the last segment of the ride they shared the train with the Yakima, Washington, team, the defending national champion.

"I remember it like it was yesterday," said Lobdell. "They looked like they were all twenty-five years old."

Pilots fans get their fill of the sun in the third base stands at Mulcahy. LEW FREEDMAN

Call that natural intimidation because of Yakima's reputation. What was to be feared was the difference in the level of experience the teams brought to the diamond. The Alaska team, as Lobdell remembers, played maybe twenty-five games, while teams from places in warmer climates (just about everywhere) played many more.

That year Billings had an ace pitcher named Dave McNally, later a star for the Baltimore Orioles. Once play began, though, it seemed as if everyone else had a pitcher destined for the Major Leagues. The Alaskans lost 8-0 to Albany, Oregon, and 16-0 to Lewiston, Idaho, and were eliminated from the tournament in two straight games. It seemed as if the distance between Anchorage and Montana was far more than 2,000 miles.

"We found out exactly where we needed to go from there," said Lobdell.

One man devoted to improving the quality of baseball in Anchorage was Van Brunt. Born George, he was called Lefty by everyone because he was the only left-handed kid in his San Francisco neighborhood. Even his mother called him Lefty.

When he was growing up in the 1930s and 1940s, Van Brunt thought his arm might take him somewhere. There wasn't any Little League then, but Van Brunt showed his skills pitching and in the outfield for Mission High and in American Legion. The New York Giants scouted him.

Van Brunt was sixteen when he signed and seventeen when the Giants assigned him to the Class C Pittsburg, California, Diamonds in 1949. Van Brunt, still rail thin and firmly muscled at sixty-eight, then stood five-foot-eleven, but weighed only 150 pounds, and that was if his uniform was drenched in sweat. He won his pitching debut, 5-2, over Visalia and in his next game his pinch-hit double helped win another game.

Van Brunt's manager was Vince DiMaggio, the least known of the three Major League DiMaggio brothers. In what might be termed history's worst pep talk, DiMaggio surveyed Van Brunt's talents and said, "I don't know what they see in you."

The Giants saw enough in Van Brunt to keep him around for another season, briefly placing him in Class B at Waterloo, Iowa, before returning him to Pittsburg.

But that was the end of Van Brunt's pro career. His next uniform belonged to the U.S. Air Force, which deposited him in Alaska. When Van Brunt was discharged in Seward in 1955 he married his wife Pat, who while always indulging him his passion, said she didn't know what she was in for over the next forty-five years.

"I knew he was a baseball fan," she said. "I didn't know he was a baseball nut."

The Van Brunts moved to Anchorage the same year Lobdell finished high school. Lefty was twenty-four and while beginning what became a thirty-four-year career as a longshoreman for Alaska Freight Lines, he played ball for the Elmendorf Rockets in the city league.

As the years passed, Van Brunt's tentacles reached into all corners of local baseball. He played some, coached Little League, then coached American Legion. By 1967 he was president of the Anchorage Adult League. So he truly was at ground zero when the Goldpanners ran roughshod over Anchorage players.

So was Jack O'Toole. O'Toole, now nearly eighty years old, is the grand old man of Alaska baseball. Originally from Detroit, O'Toole was brought to Anchorage by the Army in 1945. In the 1950s and 1960s, city league ball was in its heyday. O'Toole, a bar owner by trade, filled in at second base for a couple of seasons and remembers when games were played at an old field at Sixth and C Streets. It was across the street from the old Ambassador night club, which had a liquor store.

"We conned the guy into a deal where the first guy who hit a home run got a case of beer," said O'Toole.

That affected early-game pitching strategy.

The city's main park moved to 10th and B Streets in the early 1960s, then the present stadium was built with money from a bond issue. Lights were installed in 1965, the year Satchel Paige came to town. The stadium was named for William Mulcahy, a civic booster who had been in the forefront of numerous volunteer projects in the 1940s and 1950s.

O'Toole was a Little League coach and coached two Pony League state champions in the slightly older division, tutoring such players as Wally Hickel Jr., son of the former governor, Steve Langdon, and Jack Slama, a future Alaska Baseball League commissioner.

It was apparent the city was hot for baseball. The Paige exhibitions showed it. So did attendance when the Goldpanners came to town, even though games were likely to be no contest.

Every state has its great, bragging-rights rivalries between high schools, colleges, or cities. At that time in Alaska, if there was more than one high school in a community, it hadn't been there long. The University of Alaska Anchorage and the University of Alaska Fairbanks, later to become intense rivals in intercollegiate sports, weren't yet members of the NCAA.

But sparks of a rivalry between the communities of Fairbanks and Anchorage were igniting. Often they revolved around which would become the state's most important center of commerce. Later, after the Trans-Alaska Pipeline was built and after Anchorage far eclipsed Fairbanks in population, residents of the two cities still sniped at one another. Anchorage citizens called Fairbanks "Squarebanks," ostensibly because it was so dull. Fairbanks citizens called Anchorage "Los Anchorage," supposedly a derogatory comparison to Los Angeles and its smog.

Although all of this was still to come, it galled the Anchorage baseball community that the Goldpanners, whom it must be remembered initially appropriated the name "Alaska," routinely mashed the old town team at will.

"They had better town baseball down there than we did in Fairbanks," said Goldpanner founder Red Boucher. "But when we brought the college kids down it was too much. We kicked hell out of them."

Those most tuned-in to Anchorage baseball—onfield men and businessmen, Van Brunt and O'Toole, Bernie Kosinski and Joe Keenan, Roger Cremo and others—began talking, If Fairbanks can do it, why can't we? The old Thompson's Restaurant in downtown became the main gathering place. The Mermaid Room bar also hosted a session or two.

In 1968, a consortium of businessmen tried to form a team, but at the last minute it didn't have enough money.

"We were one backer short," said Van Brunt.

In Fairbanks, Boucher watched the moves closely. While he had a monopoly on recruiting talent, in the broader picture he knew it would be better if there were another Alaska team. It was prohibitive to foot the entire travel bill for NBC rivals like the Wichita Dreamliners, the Bellingham Bells, the Humboldt Crabs, or the Grand Junction Eagles.

"It was an extension of the NBC tournament," said Boucher, "but it cost us money. I thought, 'We've got to get another team up here.' "

Another team could share costs. So Boucher and his chief assistant, Don Dennis, took proactive roles nurturing Alaska expansion.

"It was staged," said Dennis. "We were intimately involved. . . . "

Simply put, dollars and cents made good sense.

"We were paying one hundred percent of the cost of teams coming to Alaska," said Dennis. "We could see right away that if you bring up two teams simultaneously and then switch, it would be better."

There was also a worry that the Goldpanners might bore fans by sweeping eight-game series. If the Goldpanners won 11-0, fans might decide that particular visiting team wasn't worth bothering with and sit home till the next series.

"I used to pray a new team would come into town and win," said Dennis. "Or at least have a really good ballgame."

To help the Anchorage boosters get going, the Goldpanners scheduled a July, 1968 best-two-out-of-three series against the Anchorage All-Stars at Mulcahy Stadium. The Anchorage organizers planned to pass the hat to raise money.

While the fundraiser was a good idea, there was little doubt of the games' outcome. In fact, the Goldpanners were so confident they would easily win the first two games, they scheduled a return flight to Fairbanks earlier than the starting time of a third game. The Goldpanners made their plane.

The days of skewering Anchorage with a mere shrug of the shoulders were about to end, though.

The Anchorage backers hired California's Chapman College coach Paul Deese as manager. Deese met with the Anchorage organizers for dinner at the Top of the World Restaurant in the Hotel Captain Cook and liked their spiel. Then Joe Keenan took him to Fairbanks to meet Boucher and an agreement was hatched. A new Anchorage team, operating with collegians, would cooperate with the Goldpanners to bring foes to Alaska.

In the summer of 1969, Alaska's second team, the Anchorage Glacier Pilots, made its debut.

Glacier Pilots. Another flavorful nickname. The airplane opened up Alaska, made its remote, tundra areas accessible, leading to better communication, growth, tourism, and not the least, improved mail delivery. Bush pilots were respected and admired figures in Alaska, seen as dashing and romantic swashbucklers who survived dangerous missions. Most of which was true. So calling a team "Glacier Pilots" was both inspired and historically accurate.

However, this team owed its name to one particularly popular glacier pilot, Bob Reeve. Bill Tobin of the now-defunct *Anchorage Times* newspaper, is given credit by the team for pushing for the adoption of the Glacier Pilots name as a way to honor Reeve.

"He was the one who had the notoriety," said O'Toole of Reeve, "The Seattle Pilots got started the same year. Their Pilots were Boeing."

When George "Lefty" Van Brunt was a young pitching prospect from San Francisco, his manager, Vince DiMaggio, told him he didn't know what anyone saw in him. What the baseball fans in Anchorage saw was a dynamic personality who helped launch the Glacier Pilots and still coaches pitching for the team. LEW FREEDMAN

Reeve was as famous as any Alaska flyer. His biography is called "Glacier Pilot" and he and his wife Tilly, who married in 1936, were big supporters of the team. Reeves' exploits were well-documented as he moved from Valdez to Nabesna to Fairbanks to Anchorage, where he settled in 1942. His visibility gave the new team a positive public association.

Reeve died in 1980, but Tilly remained a member of the board until her death in 1993. The season after she died, the team yearbook cover featured photos of Tilly Reeve, Bob Reeve, and an airplane. The yearbook also contained a detailed tribute to Tilly, calling her the team's "fairy godmother" because she frequently made cash donations to pay bills.

"Yes, the Pilots' board of directors had only to let Tilly know they were a little short and that they would repay as soon as they could and Tilly would ask, 'How much do you need?' " the story read.

Meanwhile, Deese assembled a team. For starters, he signed up seven of his own NCAA Division II champion players. Two men heavily involved in the inaugural year were Van Brunt and O'Toole. Although Van Brunt was out of baseball from 1970 to 1984, more than thirty years later they both remain in Pilots uniforms.

The basic goal, of course, was to beat Fairbanks. Or at least play the Goldpanners tough. Don Dennis, who succeeded Boucher as boss of the Goldpanners when the team organizer left baseball that year, said he expected the Pilots to be respectable.

"I saw them as another Grand Junction or Bellingham," said Dennis, "that we'd win three out of four."

The Pilots were better than that right away.

"Deese was the toughest SOB I ever played against," said Boucher. "But I thought it was fantastic."

A peculiar transaction sparked one of the most auspicious rookie campaigns of any team in history. In the middle of the 1969 season a Glacier Pilots pitcher signed a pro contract and departed. That left the Pilots short on mound talent. Fairbanks had eleven pitchers on the roster, too many for efficient use. So, in a gesture of sportsmanship, the Goldpanners offered Deese a pitcher, showing him a list of three guys to choose from.

Deese selected a young man named Steve Dunning, out of Stanford, who had done little in Fairbanks. Soon after his acquisition, Dunning started against the Baseline Collegians, a Boulder, Colorado, team loaded with talent, including future Major League star Burt Hooten.

Dunning was transformed. He mowed down batter after batter. Suddenly he was the second coming of Cy Young. He struck out nineteen men and won.

"His first game!" exclaimed Dennis, still shaking his head over the development three decades later.

Dunning, of course, went on to a Major League career with the Cleveland Indians and other teams.

The Glacier Pilots went on to win the national championship, taking the National Baseball Congress World Series by surprise in their first year of existence. The national title. That was something Fairbanks had not managed in their game efforts throughout the 1960s.

"Dunning is one reason they won the national championship," said Dennis. "They had no chance of doing what they did. It was out of nowhere. I was shocked. No, no, no, I never thought they'd be that good."

How good were the first Pilots? Well, not only did they throw a rapidly maturing Dunning at people, they had Jim Crawford in the rotation. Crawford went on to the Houston Astros and other clubs. And they also featured future Major League star Chris Chambliss toting lumber. Not to be overlooked is Jack Brushert, who later became Pilots general manager for a spell in the early 1980s. Even if he didn't go as far as Chambliss, Brushert recorded an astonishing season, batting .406, still the second highest average in team history, with a still-standing record .860 slugging percentage. He clouted 18 home runs.

Brushert was one of the Chapman players excited by the chance to see Alaska and he'd heard of the Goldpanners.

"Even in Southern California people had talked about going to Fairbanks," said Brushert.

Brushert remembers John Stepp, the Pilots' representative at the airport, taking all the players out for breakfast then housing them at an abandoned hospital for a night before families came to get them.

"One by one we were picked up and whisked away," said Brushert. "It was a long summer. We worked all day and played baseball all night."

Brushert said he had a demanding construction laborer's job where he hauled cement and two-by-fours.

"I woke up in the morning and I couldn't straighten my fingers," said Brushert.

Chambliss had a distinguished Major League playing career and was the hitting coach for the 1998 World Champion New York Yankees team that won a record number of games.

He remains one of O'Toole's favorites.

"You could see there was a lot of talent there," said O'Toole. "He had just one year in the minors, then bang, right up. He will become a manager one day, I think."

Chambliss came out of UCLA and hit .343 for the Pilots during the regular season. At Wichita he upped that to .583, stole seven bases and scored 10 runs. The performance made him the Most Valuable Player.

Much later, Chambliss reminisced about his stay in Anchorage.

Chambliss said he had no idea what to expect when he headed to Alaska. He did wonder if it would be snowy in summer. Now past fifty, bald, with a graying mustache, Chambliss said the baseball portion of the summer paid big dividends for him. Given the long college season, advancing to the College World Series in Omaha, playing for the Pilots and finishing up at the NBC, Chambliss probably played in a 130 games.

"I always talk about that season as a great introduction to professional ball," he said.

To Chambliss, Deese was a seasoned field leader who proved to be a perfect manager for the new team.

"Paul was an excellent baseball man," said Chambliss. "He was just very organized. A real fine tactician on the field."

Chambliss really bloomed at the NBC. The hotel was the old Broadview, where Bonnie and Clyde used to reside, and after the Pilots fell into the losers bracket, Brushert remembers the players making airline reservations every day. They kept winning close games, though.

In the semi-finals in Wichita the Pilots met the Goldpanners. How delicious. Two Alaska teams fighting it out for national supremacy. Anchorage won, 5-3, and Chambliss drove in two runs with the Glacier Pilots' only hit out of the infield.

Then the Glacier Pilots defeated the Liberal Bee Jays of Kansas, 5-1, in the championship game, scoring five runs in the eighth inning, three coming on a home run by Brushert.

"It was a great year," said Brushert. "It was like a dream come true. I remember being very nervous in the game. We got a great pitching effort from Jim Crawford. Liberal was the favored team. Nobody expected us to be in it. Nobody was rooting for us."

Scouts flocked to Chambliss. It was hard to resist the compliments thrown his way and he decided to abandon UCLA. Chambliss was drafted the following January and in less than two years he was in the majors.

"I was in great position to go pro," said Chambliss.

It was an unforgettable debut in the national limelight for Chambliss, and for the Glacier Pilots.

NBC commissioner Larry Davis was as amazed as anyone when the Pilots showed up and took the crown.

"It's tough for a first-year team to come in here and win this," he said.

Little did Davis know that Alaska teams were about to become fixtures in the top echelon of his tournament.

5

THE PENINSULA OILERS

Bingo!

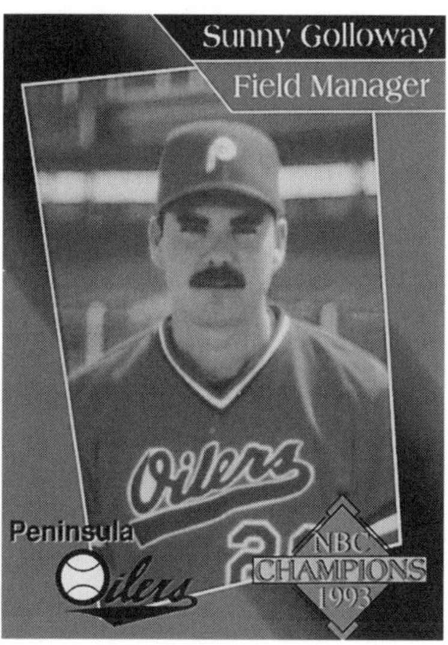

EARLY GAME night. Members of the visiting Alaska Baseball League team filed into the solid old building in Kenai. They walked past groups of citizens seated at rows of brown formica-topped tables, sitting in brown-backed chairs beneath a sign reading "Peninsula Oilers Bingo."

And you thought it was Peninsula Oilers baseball. Well, it's both.

The players headed to their beds in the back room, with its cinder block walls, two bunks per cubicle. Just as they got settled, the cry of "Bingo!" rang through the air. We have a winner. The players, fresh from the ballpark, echod back through the wall, "Bingo!"

You have heard of the old television show, "Bowling for Dollars." This is Bingo for Baseball.

The Peninsula Oilers became the third member of the Alaska league in 1974. By 1982, however, the team was looking at budget shortfalls. How to keep the club alive and thriving?

Bingo.

The idea was a winner. People who don't even care about baseball make contributions to the team simply by participating. By playing their own game

Mike Baxter, the Oilers director of baseball operations, shown here trying to entice the local fans with team yearbooks during the 1998 season, has been with the club since its early days. LEW FREEDMAN

of chance, they give the team financial security without taking major chances.

"We really lucked out when we bought this building," said Mike Baxter, the Oilers manager of baseball operations. "We had to buy it, or lose it. It really fits our needs."

At a time when the club did not have much money in the bank, it took a risk and purchased the building that saved it.

The building contains team offices, the bingo parlor, and housing for visiting teams, a benefit since hotel rooms are difficult to obtain during the height of the tourist season. Once in a while, the functions overlap.

Take rainout nights. The players have nothing to do, so they join the bingo games. Members of the Glacier Pilots or Goldpanners may be wearing their uniform pants because of a last-minute cancellation, and they'll slide right in next to bingo players from the Kenai Peninsula.

"If one of them bingos," said worker Peggy Baxter, wife of Mike and head of the team's gaming division, "the place explodes. If they get to where they need one number, the whole team's around them going, 'C'mon, c'mon.' "

Players also sneak in a little action on game nights if the baseball ends early. One night, members of the Kamloops Sandpipers of British Columbia got back early and happily joined in.

"I was planning on taking their money," said catcher Andy Meng.

Instead, Meng and teammates lost about seventy dollars. Of course, it went to a worthy cause close their heart: Alaska baseball.

The mass-sleeping arrangement is just a doorway away from the bingo parlor. The quarters are more functional than fancy and the digs have been jokingly nicknamed "The Bingo Hilton."

The Hilton chain itself makes no claims to proprietorship. The accommodations are not four-star. But neither are they notably uncomfortable, though some players do say it is best to be near the front of the line for the showers if you feel the need for hot water.

Reaction to the Bingo Hilton varies with one's age. The older the player is, the less enthralled he may be with the surroundings. The younger player is less fazed. It may also depend on how long ago the night was spent since in the old days the cots were reportedly less cushy than the current beds.

"I've spent nights there," said Glacier Pilots broadcaster Dick Lobdell. "For older guys, it's not that great. But for the players, it's like a big dorm."

Another older fellow, Stan Zaborac, the cornerstone of the Mat-Su Miners team, said the Bingo Hilton was always fine for him.

"I stayed at the Bingo Hilton many a time," said Zaborac. "For me there was a comfortable bed. I snored and drove everybody out and got lots of rest."

Really, the situation is fine for college-aged guys on a road trip. However, not every visiting squad knows what to expect. A pitcher named Todd Bay for Kamloops was making his third trip to the Bingo Hilton when asked to describe his feelings about it.

"My first year, I thought, 'I gotta come back just to see the looks on guys' faces,' " said Bay. "The Bingo Hilton is sort of like the Hotel California—you can never leave. I personally would like to go to a bingo hall every place we stay. It honestly brings the team together."

Bingo and baseball bring the Oilers together, financially.

"It works out," said Mike Baxter. "Most of the time the games and the bingo go on at the same time, so we don't get in each other's way."

The Oilers scheduled bingo nights are Monday, Tuesday and Thursday, year-round. Another non-profit outfit conducts bingo on the premises Wednesday and Friday. Bingo is usually over by 10 P.M. If a team is staying in the back, though, said Peggy Baxter, they've got to be advised of house rules.

"You always remind them not to run through the bingo hall in their shorts," she said.

Words to live by. Don't go out in public in your underwear.

Bingo is such a hit for the Oilers, the late Coral Seymour, a former general manager, once estimated that it provided up to seventy percent of the team's operating budget.

Home-team players don't live in the Bingo Hilton. While visiting guys are squeezed into the back room, Oilers are parceled out to families who treat them like sons. Maybe that's just part of the homefield advantage.

Just as the Goldpanners were appropriately named for links to the gold rush and the Glacier Pilots' name was tied to Alaska's important era of aviation development, the Kenai Peninsula Oilers were named because of the area's early identification with the oil industry.

Although most people think of the trans-Alaska Pipeline and the Prudhoe Bay oil fields in the far north when picturing the state's key resource industry, the first major oil find in Alaska occurred at the Peninsula's Swanson River in July, 1957, when a geologist named Bill Bishop hit the mother lode.

The Oilers got their start much the same way as the Glacier Pilots. The two existing Alaska teams were eager for expansion. It just made good financial sense to add a team in the state instead of continuously flying more teams in to play both clubs.

Kenai is more than 500 miles from Fairbanks and about 150 from Anchorage, so it was close enough to improve on out-of-state trips, but far enough away to develop an independent fan base.

The Goldpanners' Don Dennis, Ed Merdes, a Fairbanks businessman, and Paul Deese, the Pilots' manager, traveled to the Kenai area in 1973 and met with business and civic groups to stoke interest. At the time the city itself had only about 3,500 people. Dennis is sure that Seymour, who ultimately became the essential operative in the Oilers' franchise, was in the audience at an initial meeting.

Seymour, a man who had a gruff exterior and a soft side, did everything from handling the groundskeeping and maintenance chores to holding the titles of general manager and president.

"He was a hard guy to get to know," said Mike Baxter, who joined the Oilers in 1978. "He did a lot of things for a lot of people. Little League. Somebody in need. Financial things. Most people didn't even know about it.

"Coral wanted to see things done right. He'd jump in and tell you and that's how he rubbed some people the wrong way. He had an opinion and he

The late Coral Seymour could be a tough and gruff negotiator as general manager for Peninsula, but his sweat and generosity got the Oilers off the ground and kept them pumping. COURTESY OF THE PENINSULA OILERS

was willing to share it with you. Once you got past that and saw what a great guy he was, he was the guy out there painting the fence and fertilizing the field."

Naturally enough, oil industry figures became major backers of the Oilers. Seymour himself made his career working for an oil services support company.

Some early Oiler management officials had to go the extra mile to establish the franchise and make sure it survived. Baxter said they took out loans or mortgaged their homes. Seymour was always in the mix and that included helping out from his own pocket and with his own sweat.

"He sold ads, he pushed the broom, he was the guy with the shovel in his hand," said Baxter.

The Oilers did have a ballpark when they got going in the summer of

1974—the simply labeled Oiler Park. They also had a reputable manager. Just as the Goldpanner management recognized that it was important the Pilots be able to provide serious competition, the Goldpanners and Pilots understood that the new Oilers had to be roughly their equal.

Once again a fledgling Alaska team turned to Chapman College. The Oilers hired Bob Pomeroy, a Deese successor who also had experience coaching the Boulder Collegians, a summer team. It was late to begin recruiting, so Pomeroy relied heavily on Chapman guys.

Pomeroy, now in his sixties and living in Mission Viejo, California, where he sells electronic scoreboards after a second career in athletic administration, said that when the Kenai officials wooed him, they took him fishing on the Kenai River and he caught a fifty-pound king salmon.

"I thought it was a kick," he said.

The pristine green waters of the Kenai River have always been a terrific tourism lure. Once, during Pomeroy's tenure managing the Oilers, a team from Pueblo, Colorado got so involved fishing for kings, it overlooked its baseball obligation.

"They just didn't come back for the game," said Pomeroy.

And forfeited.

There was little doubt the small but big-thinking town was excited to have its own baseball team. Pomeroy said he was made to feel very welcome right away—he was even presented with a key to the city before coaching a game.

Just how ready Kenai was for baseball became obvious on opening day. The Oilers made a bigger splash than a world-record king salmon. They beat the Goldpanners in their first game, spreading a David-triumphs-over-Goliath glow of emotion through the region. About three thousand fans turned out and it seemed to Pomeroy that they all descended on the field to celebrate afterwards.

"It took us a half hour to get out of the dugout," he said.

Don Dennis remembers his team losing the first two games to the Oilers. But then reality arrived. A barrage of Goldpanner home runs followed, fourteen of them in the next two games, as Fairbanks slaughtered the Oilers.

Jim Dietz, the most accomplished manager in Alaska baseball history, ran the Goldpanners then and said the home runs were like a July 4 fireworks exhibition. It was something to see, he said. But he remembers one other aspect of that first series with the Oilers equally well. It was freezing. He retains a picture of his team filling metal buckets with wood and burning it, the players huddled around the fires trying to keep warm.

Even in summer, Alaska has been known for the Big Chill.

As soon as the Goldpanners departed, said Pomeroy, the Oilers' booster club trooped to the outfield and heightened the fences.

Even if the Goldpanners flexed the muscles that sometimes reminded fans of the 1927 Yankees, the Oilers had exacted their price and won over their crowd. Subsequent games with the Goldpanners and Glacier Pilots were huge community events. The rivalries were fierce. It was a big deal, a major social event, when Fairbanks or Anchorage came to town. And when the Oilers traveled to those cities, fans made an occasion of it.

"They would fly us to the games and half the town would go with us," said Pomeroy. "The airport was jammed with fans."

You might say the Oilers had struck bingo.

Soon enough the Oilers attracted really first-rate players. One guy who went on to the majors was Rich Aurilia, currently shortstop for the San Francisco Giants. Aurilia grew up in Brooklyn, New York, as city as you can get. For Aurilia, spending a summer playing baseball in Alaska was almost as exotic as a trip to outer space. He had never spent time in the wilderness, and he had never fished in a place like the Kenai River—especially not after playing a night baseball game.

"It was a different type of lifestyle," said Aurilia, who coincidentally ended up marrying a woman with Alaska ties, whom he did not meet while playing for the Oilers. His wife, Raquel Garcia, was a volleyball star for Alaska Pacific University.

Everything was so foreign for Aurilia, but Don Pearson and his family hosted him and made him feel so welcome that they have maintained contact for more than a decade and they visit at spring training.

The first week on the Kenai, Aurilia couldn't sleep because of the late-night light, but then the scenery and wildife blew his mind.

"There were moose roaming the street," he said. "There were bears on the river when I was fishing. It was kind of like being at the zoo, but the wildlife was running free. The day seemed to last forever."

The baseball was good for Aurilia, but that was the least of his experience. When he reflects on his time spent in Alaska, it is the non-baseball aspects that seem most vivid.

"A lot of good things came out of Alaska for me," said Aurilia.

Aurilia is one of the many, many Oilers who made it big, but you didn't have to be a young man just starting out for the Oilers to play a unique part in your life.

Pomeroy managed the team for only the 1974 and 1975 seasons, but collected memories that remain special for him a quarter century later. Some of those memories were rekindled regularly.

For years, Pomeroy had a rendezvous with Seymour at the annual college baseball coaches winter convention. Seymour usually brought the same gift for him: canned salmon.

6

ON THE ROAD

Bear bites and tornado warnings

THE BEAR helped put Alaska baseball on the map of amateur baseball nationwide.

It was 1964, before the Goldpanners or Glacier Pilots ever won a National Baseball Congress title, before there was an Oilers, a Miners or a Bucs team in existence.

Of course, Red Boucher was the ringleader in the scheme.

After their eye-catching debut at Wichita in 1962, Boucher knew that his Goldpanners made friends and an impact. Fans were wowed by the Alaska flavor and impressed by the runnerup finish.

Boucher knew his 1964 team was skilled and could go all the way, but he didn't want the Alaska novelty to wear off, either. So Boucher rounded up a small black bear, tranquilized it, and transported it to Wichita.

Boucher had the foresight to get clearance from NBC founder Raymond "Hap" Dumont for his bear, named "Midnight," to claim a bonus roster spot. Dumont was a kindred spirit, a promoter with flair who knew what was good for the gate. Hall of Fame sportswriter Bob Broeg wrote a book about Dumont titled "Baseball's Barnum." He was clearly the type to be sympathetic to Boucher's bizarre plan.

Dumont created the NBC as a Kansas-only tournament in 1931 and took it national in 1935. The Most Valuable Player that year was Satchel Paige, thirty years before his visit to Anchorage. Pitching for the Bismarck, North Dakota, team, Paige was guaranteed $1,000 to appear and he made it worthwhile for Dumont at a time when that price was higher than a new car. Paige won four games. His sixty tournament strikeouts still stand as the record.

Regarded as an innovator for his quirky speed-up rules, Dumont introduced a limit of twenty seconds between pitches and ninety seconds between half innings, as well as a mercy rule if one team was too far ahead. Dumont had a microphone pop up from the ground to broadcast player-umpire disputes, allowed patrons in pajamas in free to a 5 A.M. game, and invited women to umpire. He called them "wumps."

If the NBC was Dumont's grand baseball legacy, his most memorable societal legacy when he died of a heart attack at age sixty-six in 1971 was his color blindness. Paige made his first showing at Wichita twelve years before Jackie Robinson broke the Major League color barrier with the Dodgers. And teams with black players were always welcome at the NBC.

So, truth be told, were teams of any kind that might sell tickets.

Bring a bear? Sure.

The bear accompanied the Goldpanners to their hotel, causing a bit of havoc. Some claim the bear broke a lamp or two. Some say the bear demonstrated a lack of familiarity with flush toilets. Boucher remembers the bear best for the fact that it nearly removed a few layers of his skin.

"I can still see the bear biting my butt," he said.

And probably feel it, too.

The bear was a bigger hit at the ballpark. When the Goldpanners emerged from the clubhouse, the bear joined the players, albeit on a chain. Boucher tied the bear to the dugout during warmups and the fans went crazy. His players were wary. Most hung out in the bullpen for safety.

Boucher got the publicity he sought. A bear! People were astonished. People laughed. And people talked about that team from Alaska, all right.

They have played a lot of high-quality, championship baseball in Wichita since 1935, but the bear very much lives on in NBC lore.

Less so in Alaska. That's because no one from the state ever saw the bear again. When the Goldpanners left Wichita, Midnight was left at the local zoo.

"I put him on waivers," said Boucher.

Alas, the Goldpanners just missed winning their first national crown, losing to Wichita Service Auto Glass, 6-1 in the championship game. Runners-up again. Tom Seaver gave up three runs in the game.

The symbiotic relationship between Wichita and Alaska was established. The ties only grew stronger in future years. The Pilots certainly did their share to cement that tie when they were victorious in 1969. What started as the Goldpanners' domain in the 1960s, though, expanded to a general feeling of warmth extended to all Alaska teams.

From unknowns, Alaskans swiftly became fan favorites. From being viewed as extreme outsiders, they became adopted sons.

NBC Commissioner Larry Davis also credits Boucher and the early Goldpanners for changing the focus at the tournament to college players.

"It turned our program from the sandlotter and ex-pro to the college-aged kid," said Davis. "Red never met a stranger. His 1964 team, that sent seven kids to the big leagues. Seaver was the headliner."

Davis became so fond of the Alaska teams—and the NBC and the Alaska Baseball League became so intertwined—that he twice made pilgrimmages north to view regular-season action first-hand. The first trip was in the early 1970s. More than twenty-five years later, Davis still remembers staying at the Polaris Hotel in Fairbanks. But his most vivid memory matches a common one among travelers from the Lower 48.

"I was amazed," said Davis. "It never got dark."

The initial NBC-Goldpanner relationship broadened and now the participation of any Alaska team translates into good box office. Lance Deckinger, the associate vice president of the NBC, said Alaska teams have built-in fan support now because of their history.

"A lot of it came from Fairbanks and the Pilots," he said. "When they came in with college players and they were beating the ex-pros, the fans were rooting for the hustling guys."

It didn't hurt any that the Alaskans won a lot.

"They win championships and you start following the teams that win," said Deckinger. "There's a feeling of, 'Boy, it's the Alaska League, we've got to go out and see them.' Wichita State players play for those teams, too. It makes it nice. Now it's gotten to the point where they know that they play about the best baseball."

When Kansas sportswriter Bob Lutz wrote the historical pamphlet on the NBC's first fifty years, he included a personal observation about Alaska baseball.

"I was curious to see just what Alaska players looked like and was surprised to see that the players from Alaska looked just like the players from Kansas and other states," wrote Lutz. "Except perhaps those from Alaska were a little better. I didn't realize the players I thought were Alaskans really were mostly college students from California."

Lutz noted that, "Baseball is big in Alaska, of all places." But it was no longer a secret, since he also noted, "Alaska baseball has produced big leaguers by the truckload."

Three hundred and counting now.

The famous poet Robert Service once wrote that strange things happen in the Land of the Midnight Sun, but it became apparent that sometimes strange things happen when Alaska teams take road trips to Wichita, Kansas. For better or worse.

Perhaps it is best that a limited number of details be released about the Goldpanner mid-1960s incident with the lady of the evening. Names will be withheld to protect the guilty parties.

The story told is that Boucher ran the club with the iron hand of a Marine drill sergeant during the regular season in Alaska, but that once players were in Wichita and reached the quarterfinals, he loosened the rules a bit to cut the tension.

Which may account for the time that a play-for-pay lady set up shop in a hotel room and bestowed her sexual favors on the entire team, one player at a time, while a team official sat outside the room with a stop watch to determine just how long it took her to "get the whole team off."

The lady, named Wanda, went home with a Goldpanners team jacket. Wanda, it seemed, founded her own fan club chapter.

Another time, Boucher became enraged at the behavior of his club. He went out to dinner with Larry Davis and when he returned to the hotel about 11 P.M., he was furious to see a pile of beer cans outside the window of one player's room and several items of furniture floating in the pool.

In those days, Boucher carried a football coach's whistle with him.

"I got the whistle," said Boucher.

And he blew it. Loudly. Boucher went door-to-door and rousted the players, yelling insults at the top of his lungs on the order of, "All right you assholes, up and at 'em!"

Boucher dragged his sleepy and somewhat drunk team to a nearby field and made players run windsprints, punctuating each dash with a blast of the whistle. It was Wichita in summer, so it was about a million degrees, too. But he ran the Goldpanners until 2 A.M.

There was little doubt the punishment made the players feel worse than the crime.

Teams entering the NBC World Series do play for a first-place cash prize. Alaska teams always make a good run at it, but even with a $10,000-plus payoff, the sheer cost of traveling to Kansas, then feeding and housing the team for two weeks, often guarantees a loss.

"It becomes more of an ego thing than a make-sense thing," said Jim Dietz, the long-time Goldpanners' manager who also managed the Pilots for a few years. "You win the whole thing and you lose money. We used to play our way there because the air fare was so prohibitive."

What price do you put on being the national champion, though?

The title is priceless, but the Goldpanners did make a habit of stopping in such places as Kamloops and Kelowna in British Columbia, in Washington, Oregon, and in Boulder and Grand Junction, Colorado, to pad the coffers. Somebody always watched the purse strings.

Once, Dietz said, general manager Don Dennis informed him of a good-news, bad-news scenario.

"You've got two days off," said Dennis. "But I've got a pickup game. We can make $1,500."

On one tour leading to Wichita in the 1970s, Dietz remembers playing the well-respected Liberal Bee Jays at the race track on a fairgrounds. It was not a precisely laid out field.

"You could score from second base on a wild pitch," said Dietz.

But that was hardly the most memorable part of the excursion. The Goldpanners were so late arriving for the game they did not take infield practice and changed into uniforms in team vans.

Why so late?

"We ran out of gas in a small town," said Dietz.

A very small town. Late at night.

The Goldpanners undertook a commando raid to solve the predicament. Skulking through backyards, players found a garden hose. They cut it into small sections, then by filling borrowed buckets, they siphoned off eight-to-ten gallons of gas from a car in order to get the vans back to civilization.

"If somebody had lit a match, they would have found us in orbit," said Dietz. "One kid did the siphoning wrong and the rest of the night he was spitting."

By now the statue of limitations has probably run out on the Goldpanners in rural Kansas.

Another time in Wichita, the Goldpanners were eating dinner at a restaurant when very loud sirens blared. The players looked at each other as people scattered. The waitress saw them sitting still and said, "Aren't you coming?"

It was a tornado warning. The Goldpanners joined fleeing patrons and the twister hit the area. It missed their location by about a half mile, but took out some small farms nearby.

The NBC is a double elimination tournament and one of Dietz' Goldpanner teams committed the sin of losing its opening game. That put them a game away from going home. So after the loss, the team packed its suitcase, ready to leave on short notice. The Goldpanners won. Next game, same thing. Pack the suitcase, win the game.

"After that we left them alone," said Dietz.

Events had moved into the realm of superstitution. The crazy notion took hold that if the team unpacked, it would be jinxed and surely lose.

Once the Glacier Pilots made off with the 1969 trophy, they had their own Wichita fan base. The Anchorage-NBC connection is very strong. A local bank takes a particular interest in the Pilots.

"Every time the Pilots come to town, they put on a picnic," said Ron Oklerlund, the team's current general manager and an official with the club since 1972.

There came a stretch of time when the Pilots were broke, but still determined to journey to Wichita. Current Los Angeles Dodgers pitcher Darren Dreifort was a Pilot on his way up. His brother Todd not only played for the Pilots, but was an assistant coach. The Dreifort family was well-disposed towards the Glacier Pilots, so mom Carol organized an effort to house the players in private homes.

The money-saving device helped the team when it was financially down, but the arrangement posed one difficulty.

"It was a transportation problem," said Okerlund. "You had to go all over Wichita to round up the team for the game."

Displayed on a wall in the basement room at Pilots coach Jack O'Toole's house is a handmade, crocheted license plate that reads, "Glacier Pilots, No. 17." That is his uniform number. Inlaid in the plate is a picture of three youngsters. The words "NBC Wichita Fan Club, '86" adorn it.

The kids, Dan, Katie and Chris, are from one Wichita family. Years ago, O'Toole met the kids and paid them a dollar to retrieve foul balls. O'Toole's birthday is in August, usually during the NBC tournament, so he also took them out for ice cream to celebrate.

It became an annual ritual. The kids were roughly between ten and twelve years old when O'Toole first met them. They became known as "Jack's Kids," and for years received the ice cream treat.

By 1995, though, the kids were grown up.

"We went out for beers," said O'Toole.

Red Boucher's great Goldpanner clubs never quite attained the goal of winning a National Baseball Congress title. He laid the foundation, but his reign as manager ended in 1969. After that, with Don Dennis calling the shots, an even better era of Goldpanner glory began.

The Goldpanners triumphed in Wichita for the first time in 1972 and won again in 1973, 1974, 1976 and 1980. The NBC decade at Wichita belonged to the Fairbanks Goldpanners.

7

SALMON, MOOSE AND BEARS

The players encounter the wilderness

DAVE WINFIELD was glum. He played his heart out, hitting and pitching for the Fairbanks Goldpanners in the 1971 National Baseball Congress tournament. But the Goldpanners lost the title game, 5-4, to the rival Anchorage Glacier Pilots.

For the Goldpanners, it was an especially bitter loss, because the upstart Anchorage team, only three seasons old, now had two championships to their none.

To Winfield, the 6-foot-6 supremely talented player representing Fairbanks in his first of two seasons in the far north, it was more personal. He just hated to lose. At the Wichita airport, as the teams were breaking up for the season, Winfield was toting a huge NBC runnerup trophy under his arm when he bumped into Pilots coach Jack O'Toole.

O'Toole was sympathetic.

"Winnie," he said, "that's a tough one for you to lose."

Winfield, frustrated with the Pilots' victory on a two-out double in the ninth inning by Larry Corrigan, said, "I hate this game."

Winfield, an all-around natural athlete, said he was going to give up baseball in favor of football or basketball.

Clearly, words spoken in the depression of the moment. Winfield, from the University of Minnesota, did play college basketball. He was drafted by the San Diego Padres in Major League baseball, the Atlanta Hawks of the National Basketball Association, and the Minnesota Vikings of the National Football League.

But he stuck with baseball. If Seaver was the greatest player in Alaska Baseball League history, Winfield may run second in career achievement. He played in the majors for more than twenty years and collected 3,110 hits and 465 home runs. He almost surely will be the second Alaska leaguer to make the Hall of Fame.

For the Goldpanners, Winfield, who became a sterling outfielder with the Padres and New York Yankees, was mostly a pitcher. He had the size and strength to throw more than 90 mph.

"He was awesome," said O'Toole.

Winfield was one of those guys who had never been away from home when he joined the Goldpanners. He grew up in St. Paul, Minnesota and Fairbanks seemed far, far away. Years later, Winfield called playing in Fairbanks "one of the challenges of my life.

"I went with an open mind. It was just a pleasant surprise. It was kind of rustic, kind of small town. It was the best baseball I was exposed to. I was enthusiastic about playing there."

Winfield was 9-2 for the Goldpanners during the 1971 season, and everyone who saw him pitch thought of him as a rare commodity.

"Winfield is easily the greatest athlete who has ever been through here," said Don Dennis, years after Winfield played.

Lowell Purcell, affiliated with the Goldpanners since the 1960s, said he knew Winfield's power would pay off.

"I thought Winfield would be a great hitter," said Purcell.

There is some debate over whether or not Winfield clubbed a shot onto that curling club in the adjacent block. Dennis said Winfield blasted a home run over Growden's left-field wall, still soaring at about the 325-foot mark. He said it hit the curling club across the street on one bounce.

Similarly, as part of his Alaska baseball story repertoire, Purcell tells people that Winfield's bomb took one hop and clunked against the building.

Meanwhile, when Winfield returned to Alaska during the off-season in 1984, he visited the park for old-time's sake. His wife, accompanying him, asked, "Is that the building you used to hit the balls off the roof?"

Well, all's fair in love and war. A guy can't be blamed for trying to impress a date, can he? No matter. Winfield's other baseball feats were impressive enough.

On that same return trip to Fairbanks, in winter, Winfield posed for pictures wearing a fur coat and swinging a bat while standing on snowshoes. The Goldpanners turned the photo into a baseball card and sold it as a souvenir.

In his autobiography, *A Player's Life,* Winfield spends many pages discussing his days in Alaska. It was apparent from the book and his off-season visit, a rarity among active ballplayers, that Winfield considered his time in Fairbanks to be an important part of his life.

When he first landed in Anchorage in 1971, the mountain scenery dazzled Winfield, but as the plane continued to Fairbanks he was spellbound by rivers, glaciers and the vast expanse of undeveloped territory. He does admit wondering for a minute where the heck he was going.

Winfield stayed with a married couple and their two kids four miles out of town in the woods and had a part-time job in a furniture store. Winfield said playing for manager Jim Dietz was quite an experience. Dietz was a tough taskmaster who maintained tight discipline, but also wanted his players to develop into future pros and have a good time in Alaska.

Dietz, now in his sixties, coached a few years at the University of Oregon, but the bulk of his collegiate coaching career has been at San Diego State, where he tutored the great hitter, Tony Gwynn, among others.

Dietz's players pigeonholed him as a straitlaced guy. Then the next thing you knew, he was playing a practical joke. Dietz's scary bear stories on a wilderness trip kept Winfield from venturing to the outhouse.

The Dietz version is more detailed.

The late John Butrovich, a renowned Alaska state legislator, was a big fan of the Goldpanners and sometimes took Dietz and players into the forest to his family cabin. Winfield was one of the chosen. Traveling to the cabin via river in a small boat, they rounded a bend in the river, only to approach a large grizzly bear.

"Dave stands up and John grabs him with one hand and slams him down," said Dietz. "A bunch of blue language comes out. This crusty, old guy is just chewing him out. 'Goddamn, you're going to tip us over.' "

The next day, the group was sitting around camp playing a game of hearts. Suddenly, Butrovich cursed, jumped up, grabbed a large revolver and started blasting away at an unseen target. Turns out there was a bear right outside the cabin, nosing into the food cache.

"He shot this thing off the front porch," said Dietz.

Well, that did it for Winfield. He was terrified the rest of the trip.

"I don't think Dave went to the bathroom for two days," said Dietz. "We couldn't get him to go grayling fishing."

All Winfield wanted to do is get back to town in one piece.

Bruce Robinson, later a Major League catcher with the Oakland A's and

New York Yankees, and a four-year player for the Goldpanners in the 1970s, said he shared a borrowed house with Winfield and they couldn't get over the contents of the family's freezer—moose burgers and moose steaks.

"That was pretty funny," said Robinson.

Robinson said he and Winfield once took a fly-in fishing trip, going after northern pike, which are known as vicious fish with an impressive collection of teeth.

"They look nasty," said Robinson.

Winfield landed one and was bragging about his fishing prowess when the fish flopped off the hook and bounced all over the boat.

"All of a sudden, this thing's loose," said Robinson. "It looks like a shark."

Another time, a story also addressed in Winfield's book, Dietz may have saved his player's future with quick thinking and quick feet. During his second summer in Fairbanks, Winfield worked as a groundskeeper at the ballpark. One day Winfield was cutting the lawn, driving the big tractor mower in the outfield.

Dietz looked up to see the large vehicle veering from side to side. Then, as he watched in horror, the mower picked up a little speed and set a steady course for the outfield wall.

A stunned Dietz realized Winfield had fallen asleep driving the mower. Dietz swore and sprinted for the fence. When he caught up, he shouted until Winfield woke and cut the engine.

"I saved your life," said Dietz.

"No, no, I wasn't asleep," was Winfield's answer.

Dietz said the mower was about fifteen feet shy of the outfield fence.

In 1972, when Winfield came back for a second season, he was nursing a sore arm. He wondered if the Goldpanners would even want him, but Dietz told him to come on up, anyway. Why wouldn't he? Dietz saw the pure talent.

"I knew instantly Dave Winfield was something special," said Dietz.

Winfield became an everyday player. He hit .315, with 15 home runs and 52 RBIs, and was named the team's Most Valuable Player.

By rejoining the Goldpanners, Winfield had the distinction of being part of the first-ever Fairbanks NBC champion. Twelve years after Red Boucher formed the franchise and just a year after the tough loss to the Glacier Pilots at Wichita, the Goldpanners got their title. They also got revenge, besting the Pilots, 3-2, in the championship game. Winfield hit two homers in the tournament.

Winfield is the biggest, most enduring name from that team, but others spent some time in the majors. Jim Sundberg and and Dave Roberts were the best-known among them.

On his 1980s trip to Alaska, Winfield made a speech at an athletic banquet in Anchorage before touring his old stomping grounds in Fairbanks. Winfield said he enjoyed himself so much in Alaska as a young man that he commissioned a painting of an Alaska baseball scene.

"I am a product of Alaska baseball," he said.

Nearly thirty years after Winfield's last playing sojourn in the north, the Goldpanners still consider him a special friend, too. Any Goldpanner history talk quickly turns to Winfield. His name comes up in the first paragraph. Whether he ever hit a home run off the curling club roof or not.

There is always going to be a special place in the fans' hearts for that first championship team. Once the first title was banked, though, the Goldpanners took off. If they were Wichita curiosity in the 1960s, in the 1970s they—with help from the Pilots and Oilers—made the name "Alaska" a brand of excellence.

8

THE SEVENTIES

Anchorage and Fairbanks rule the world

DON DENNIS was the sports editor of *The Daily Sentinel* in Grand Junction, Colorado when he met Red Boucher in the 1960s.

The Goldpanners were coming to town, playing their way to Wichita, and Boucher felt it was his patriotic duty to promote the heck out of his team to the young sportswriter. Dennis was a willing audience, intrigued by the flashy Boucher's patter, and receptive since he was also business manager of the Grand Junction Eagles.

"In those days, barnstorming was what it was all about," said Dennis.

The Eagles got interested in the Goldpanners after Dennis saw a small item in the *Omaha World-Herald* noting that the Wichita Dreamliners played in the 1963 Midnight Sun game.

The Goldpanners came to Grand Junction, were treated well and Boucher made a speech about Alaska. Dennis said the town fell in love with Boucher and his team. This happy rapport lasted a few years and Boucher began lobbying Dennis to come north and be part of the Goldpanners. Dennis resisted.

In 1967, Dennis, now approaching sixty years old, was accepting a job for the Associated Press in Denver. The persistent Boucher talked him out of it. Dennis decided he'd try Alaska—for two years.

The 1970s ushered in two years of dominance by the Goldpanners, witness this championship sign at Growden Park. LEW FREEDMAN

"There were two pros and twenty cons," said Dennis. "But one was more money. The other was adventure."

Like so many before him wooed by the mystique of Alaska, Dennis signed on for adventure. Dennis went to work for *Jessen's Weekly,* but the paper folded nine months later. Then he hooked on with the *Fairbanks Daily News-Miner.* He shifted careers and from 1979 on worked for a local Native corporation, the Arctic Slope Regional Corporation.

His true love was always the Goldpanners, though. When Boucher stepped aside, Dennis became the club's main man and he presided over the fantastic run in the 1970s. Basically, the Goldpanners had a winning team off the field before it put a winning team on the field.

Dennis was the astute leader. Jim Dietz was hired to manage. And banker Bill Stroecker, who has served a series of one-year terms as president since 1965, had key community ties.

"It's a hobby," said Dennis after more than thirty years on the job. "I wouldn't be doing this if it wasn't fun. I am a lot more taken by great people than great players. But most of those who succeed are good people. Just to get to this point, these players have left tens of thousands of players in their wake."

Although Fairbanks' reputation was well-established by the early 1970s, the tremendous stretch in Dennis' first years at the helm of the organization set a phenomenal standard.

Beginning in 1971, the Goldpanners appeared in the NBC title game six years running. They lost to the Pilots in 1971, won their first crown in 1972, then took the titles in 1973 and 1974, lost the championship to the Boulder Collegians in 1975 and swept to another title in 1976.

The 1972 gang was the second Winfield year. The 1973 repeat was sparked by Gene Deylon's three-for-four night in a 10-6 victory over Liberal, Kansas in the championship game, and the .500 hitting by Most Valuable Player Lee Iorg.

The Goldpanners beat Boulder, 7-5, to win their third in a row in 1974. The man of the hour was Steve Kemp, on his way to a first-rate career with the Detroit Tigers and other teams. Kemp had an astonishing season for the Goldpanners, one of their best ever. The outfielder batted .425, a mark which stood as the team record average for twenty-one years, until Adam Kennedy hit .434.

The graying and balding Dennis, a large man who looks as if he could still take a few cuts in the batter's box, loves reminiscing about Kemp.

"Hands down, he was the most exciting player," said Dennis. "He was ferocious when he hit it. He would drag the bat up to the plate like he was totally disinterested. Then the first cut was always full out. He swung from the heels. He electrified the crowd."

The Goldpanners lodged an early recruiting foothold with UCLA, the University of Southern California, and Santa Clara, especially the latter two schools.

"Some years I would have six players from Southern Cal and six from Santa Clara and fill in around them," said Dennis.

Then Dennis turned the talent over to Jim Dietz.

There is little doubt Dietz is the greatest manager in Alaska Baseball League history. After one season as an assistant coach, Dietz took over as Goldpanner field leader in 1971 and managed the team through 1977. He left, spent 1982 and 1983 managing the Glacier Pilots, then returned to the Goldpanners for four seasons ending in 1993. In his eleven years running the Fairbanks team he won 486 games, or about seventy percent of the time. Dietz led the Goldpanner teams which won in Wichita in 1972, '73, '74 and '76.

Much of Dietz's Alaska success coincided with his early years at San Diego State, where he has coached since 1972 and where he has won more than 1,000 games. Among players who competed under Dietz for the Aztecs are Mark Grace, Kevin Kennedy, Bud Black, and Chris and Tony Gwynn, all of them major leaguers.

When Dietz coached summer ball in Colorado in the 1980s, before returning to Alaska, such future major leaguers as Mark Langston and Joe Carter came under his tutelage. When he ran the Glacier Pilots, he coached future home-run great Mark McGwire. Dietz's fingerprints are all over the careers of dozens and dozens of players who reached the highest level of baseball.

The Goldpanners were already a known quantity by the time Dietz arrived, but he lifted them to a perpetual championship level.

"They had Seaver and Kingman, so the Alaska league always got a lot of publicity," said Dietz. "It was the league to go to. We were just besieged. The biggest thing was sorting out who to take."

Although his hair is graying, with his tinted glasses, solid build and well-maintained tan, Dietz still looks like the prototypical skipper. And whether he is at the ballpark, or vacationing in Soldotna, Alaska at the home he shares ownership of with Tony Gwynn and Grace, Dietz loves to talk about baseball and the ABL.

It is pure coincidence that Dietz's wife Carol is from Fairbanks. He met her in Oregon. When they were dating near the end of a school year, he told her he had to go to Alaska for the summer. She said, "You're going where?" Dietz left his mark in her hometown.

Dietz played baseball as a young man. He tried out with the Detroit Tigers' organization, but said, "I didn't get very far." He got a lot farther in Alaska.

"It is a unique place," said Dietz.

That was the thing about Dietz. He coached the highest caliber summer baseball in the nation, but he wanted to ensure the players took a piece of Alaska home with them in their memory banks.

Sometimes he played tricks to teach them lessons about Alaska. Dietz found time for the Goldpanners to make a side trip to nearby Portage Glacier when they played the Glacier Pilots in Anchorage. Portage Glacier is one of the most beautiful natural phenomena near Alaska's biggest city.

On one visit to Portage Glacier the mosquitoes were so fierce Dietz had players jogging around the sightseeing venue the whole time. A southpaw pitcher, whom Dietz can't remember, didn't seem to be the sharpest knife in the drawer. Glacial ice looks blue in the water and one evening Dietz and other players touting its rareness and special qualities, snatched a piece and gave it to Mr. Left-Hander.

"We convinced him if he wrapped it in a newspaper and put it in a cardboard box, he could mail it to his folks in Los Angeles," said Dietz. "We got him all jacked up."

Early next morning, rapping on his door awakened Dietz. The pitcher was very upset.

"Somebody stole my ice," he told Dietz.

Dietz contained his laughter, but rather than inform the young fellow that of course his ice melted, he ordered the whole team out of bed, lined up the players and began an "investigation" by shouting, "Somebody stole his ice! His box is empty!"

Goldpanner players are introduced before a game at Growden Park. LEW FREEDMAN

Players' eyes began rolling back in their heads as they tried to stifle laughter. Then someone guffawed. They roared. The player stormed out of the room.

"We didn't see him for a day," said Dietz. "It took him a week, a week-and-a-half, to get over it."

Dietz said he played one of his riskier practical jokes on Harold Reynolds, a future Major League second baseman. Dietz said he didn't discover until later that moose can really be dangerous. The team came upon a moose standing in a field of fireweed in Anchorage and stopped to admire the animal. Moose can grow to more than 1,200 pounds and may be quite territorial. Which means they charge, kick out with their front feet, and can knock people into the next area code.

Dietz told Reynolds that moose were docile and that the moose would eat out of his hand.

"I said, 'C'mon, we'll get a picture,' " said Dietz. "We'd tell the rookies they were tame. We'd go, 'Moosey, moosey, moosey.' "

The naïve Reynolds stepped up, ready to befriend the moose. The moose turned to face him with a gunfighter look in its eyes. The player quickly surmised that things weren't kosher and the suddenly wiser ballplayer threatened the world record for the fifty-yard dash as he sought safety. As Reynolds dived into the van, Dietz and the other players rolled with laughter.

Nobody sold Alaska like Red Boucher when he managed the Goldpanners in the 1960s.
COURTESY OF RED BOUCHER

"We got pictures of him in terror, running back to the van," said Dietz. "His eyes were the size of fifty-cent pieces."

Bruce Robinson, whose Goldpanner service coincided with the 1972-75 run, almost got himself killed on one of these impromptu, learn-about-Alaska field trips. According to Dietz, anyway.

The Goldpanner bus stopped by the side of the road on a thinly populated area in Palmer. Parked by a dirt bank, the players were admiring a distant glacier when they noticed two little black bear cubs perched on a mailbox. Robinson was fascinated and announced to the assembled that he was going to catch one.

"I don't know what possessed him," said Dietz. "He goes running out of sight."

Baby bears may be small and cute, but they do not make good pets. And most often if there are cubs around, so is a very protective, more cantankerous mother.

The main action took place out of view, but all of a sudden there was a loud yell from the other side of the embankment and the Goldpanners heard fast footsteps churning on gravel.

"The mother was coming," said Dietz. "We never saw her, but she saw Bruce. He couldn't get over the bank. He was like a madman getting up that dirt bank."

The cubs squealed like pigs and Robinson's clothes were coated with mud.

"Sounds like a good story," said Robinson from his home in San Diego many years later. "I don't remember it." He suggested Dietz cooked it up for its "creative appeal," or confused him with someone else. "He is known for his exaggerations."

Dietz insisted it was Robinson.

"A lot of these guys will do a disclaimer," said Dietz. "But that's B.S."

Robinson, now in his mid-forties, is a true-blue Goldpanner. Not only did he compete four years, but in 1993, on a visit to Alaska at age thirty-nine, he worked his way back in the lineup for a one-night stand in an exhibition game.

Robinson grew up in San Diego, Dietz's town, and that helped gain him an invitation to play in Fairbanks after his senior year in high school.

"They were the best years of my life," said Robinson.

That's saying something from someone who played parts of three years in the majors. Robinson, a catcher, had his share of fun in Alaska, though. One season, said Robinson, players routinely drove to nearby Harding Lake after night games for water skiing and beer drinking.

"We had five guys going 90 mph out to the lake," he said.

One time the beer drinking barely stopped and Robinson hardly slept before showing up at the ballpark for a double-header.

"I was so hung over," he said.

However, he strode to the plate late in the first game and swatted a home run.

"We won the game based on that home run," said Robinson. "I hit home plate and went over to the third-base fence and just puked."

Between games, Dietz lectured the players, told them to stop partying so much. He turned on Robinson and reamed him out. "Robinson," he yelled, "you're just killing us."

Killing them? Robinson's hit had just won the game. The players broke up.

After his third year of college, Robinson was drafted by the Oakland A's. He thought about signing right away, but negotiations dragged. Then he decided after three years he would try playing for the Glacier Pilots. Dietz got wind of it and telephoned.

"They would just boo you all the time," said Dietz.

So Robinson joined the Goldpanners for a last year. Only when he reached Alaska, they were on a road trip on the Kenai Peninsula, staying at what seemed like a remote barracks.

"I didn't know where they were," said Robinson. "I was walking down a dirt road with a baseball glove, a guitar and suitcase when the bus pulled up."

The Goldpanners were in Pueblo, Colorado, on the way to Wichita, when Robinson and famed A's owner Charlie Finley finally agreed on a contract. Robinson was at the hotel pool when Finley called. His roommate, Doug Jenkins, was wakened by the jangling phone. When the caller said it was Charlie Finley, Jenkins said, "Yeah, right," and hung up. This happened a couple of times before Robinson was allowed to turn pro.

Instead of going to the NBC, Robinson reported to the A's minor league affiliate in Modesto, Calif. A couple of years later, he was in the Yankees' chain, at Columbus, Ohio, when an auto accident injured his throwing arm. He didn't think it was a big problem, but the damage worsened, limiting his play for two seasons and ultimately ending his career.

Then Robinson became a hitting coach back at Modesto. Among his first pupils were Mark McGwire and Jose Canseco, two of the sport's great sluggers of the 1990s.

In-between, Robinson retained Fairbanks ties by investing in a local sporting goods store. Now the father of three, he is vice-president of business development for a health care firm that is based in Atlanta.

Of course, Robinson and Winfield were hardly the only Goldpanners who went fishing. You can't come to Alaska and not fish at least once. Many city-bred players didn't know much about the sport. They were just game to try it. Dietz found he had to educate them a little bit. Salmon travel thousands of miles to reproduce. They return to the river or stream of their birth to spawn and then they die. The deteriorating carcass floats downriver out to sea.

"The kids didn't realize spawned-out red salmon weren't any good," said Dietz. "They wanted to filet them."

Yuck.

Sometimes the Goldpanners zipped over to Anchorage's Ship Creek after a night game. The sun was still out and the fishing was good for king salmon on the creek located in the heart of the city.

Dietz sometimes drove the van. Once, a Goldpanner hooked into a large salmon. It was about two o'clock in the morning. The player fought and fought, but couldn't land the fish. He wasn't about to give up, so Dietz went for a snack. When he returned the battle still raged.

"It's 4 A.M. and it's a Mexican standoff," said Dietz, who was getting irritable hanging around. "I'd been up all night waiting for this kid."

Ship Creek's shores are very muddy, very slippery. In places, the mud resembles quicksand and fishermen regularly get stuck. Well, the player started

Panners Manager Red Boucher poses with a Japanese team manager during a 1969 tour.

COURTESY OF RED BOUCHER

walking up the bank, leading his fish, and he slipped. He dropped the rod and away swam the fish. The player fell face-down in the mud and couldn't get up. The more he flailed and tried to free himself, the more deeply imbedded he got.

"Coach, help me!" he yelled.

Dietz carefully descended the bank and tried to give the player a hand. He reached and pulled. No luck. Dietz turned himself into a human mudball. Both of the players' hands were stuck so deeply into the mud he was unable to raise himself at all.

"He was a mud angel," said Dietz. "Like a snow angel. That's what he was."

Dietz got a rope and tried to haul the player out. No go. Finally, Dietz called the police. Their combined efforts brought the player up, but not before everyone stripped down to his underwear.

For all the joking around, Dietz was a stickler for rules. The bus left on time, in Alaska or on a barnstorming trip in the lower forty-eight. Dietz didn't care who you were, you had better be on it or you had to find your own way to the next town. Once, Dietz left his wife behind.

"She was ticked," he said.

One season, Red Boucher's son Johnny, aged about twelve, was the bat boy. The team was in Washington and headed to Portland, Oregon. When the bus was ready to roll, Johnny was absent. Carol Dietz told her husband, "You can't leave him." But Johnny showed Dietz.

"When we get to Portland, there's Johnny," said Dietz. "He's already beat us down. I don't know how he got there to this day."

Robinson has a different Johnny story, one that didn't turn out as well for the youngster.

Robinson and his roommate, Kurt Wittmayer, got into an on-the-road, hotel-room battle with Steve Swisher, another future Major Leaguer, and his roommate, Randy Rasmussen.

"They trashed our room," said Robinson. "So we wrecked theirs. They came back and ripped up our clothes."

Johnny Boucher was staying with Swisher. Expecting retaliation, Swisher and Rasmussen left strict orders for Boucher not to open the door to anyone. The inhabitants went to the pool. Robinson, mimicking Swisher's thick southern accent, conned his way with Wittmayer past Johnny, who was shocked at being fooled.

Robinson and Wittmayer trashed the room, and for good measure waved out the window to Swisher at the pool. Swisher and Rasmussen charged upstairs and confronted Boucher. He told them the maid let the other guys in. But hiding nearby, Robinson and Wittmayer started giggling and that gave Boucher away.

Swisher and Rasmussen stripped the poor bat boy to his undershorts, bound him in athletic tape, put a gag in his mouth, and loaded him on the elevator. Then they pushed the button for the first floor.

"Wouldn't you know it, a group of ladies is there going for tea," said Robinson.

Presumably the hotel manager rescued the youngster.

Dennis considers the early 1970s to be his all-time favorite Goldpanner period. Not only because the Goldpanners were great. The Pilots were, too, and the rivalry was frantic, intense, and of such unbelievably high quality it transcended Alaska and had its final seasonal chapter played out each season in Wichita.

Stunningly, the Alaska teams owned not only the 49th state, but the other forty-nine states. The Glacier Pilots materialized virtually out of the mists to win the national championship in 1969. In 1970, they were runnersup. In 1971, Anchorage won again. In 1972, the Goldpanners beat the Glacier Pilots for the title. In 1976, Fairbanks topped Anchorage in the finale.

If more seemed at stake on distant territory, emotions were sometimes wild in Alaska.

"It got vicious at times," said Lowell Purcell. "With fistfights at Growden Park. We sent busloads of fans both ways."

At the 1971 NBC tournament, Red Boucher awards the first place trophy to the Anchorage Glacier Pilots, while his old team, the Panners, looks on. COURTESY OF RED BOUCHER

In Fairbanks, when Pilots coach Jack O'Toole walked out to the first-base coaching box, noise came over the loudspeaker, Crunch, crunch. Godzilla-like sounds. He'd take a step and turn around, wondering where the sound emanated from. Steve Dennis, Don's son, started the joke. It took a while before O'Toole caught on.

Robinson, who played in his share Goldpanner-Glacier Pilot confrontations, said it is tough to convey just how hard-fought they were.

"That made the whole Alaska atmosphere," said Robinson. "It was like the World Series. Dietz played that to the hilt."

So many years later, Robinson still loves and misses Alaska. His children, Scott, Kelly, and Tommy are good ballplayers. Robinson is already lobbying Dennis to choose Scott for the Goldpanners in a couple of years.

"I'd love for him to have that experience," said Robinson.

And if Scott is as good as the old man was, it doesn't seem likely the Goldpanners will turn him away.

9

LOCAL COLOR

Cigars in batting practice and tavern trips during games

FROM THE BULLPEN to the bar to the bullpen. The players thought the coaches never knew.

Alaska was a freewheeling place in the early 1970s, and Jack O'Toole was a live-and-let-live kind of guy. He was also an Anchorage bar owner. Which meant that he knew other Anchorage bar owners. Which is why the bartender at a certain establishment told him some of his Anchorage Glacier Pilots players were sneaking off to have a few beers—in mid-game.

The bullpen for the home-team Pilots is located far down the right-field line at Mulcahy Stadium. Once the game begins, a bunch of relief pitchers are shipped to that far corner of the ballpark. In case of fire, they are supposed to put it out.

Well, how often is a reliever needed early in the game? You've got to have faith in your starters, don't you?

So some of the guys kept a car parked nearby. They slipped out of the park and zipped over to the nearby Irish Setter. They listened to the game on the radio.

"They would follow the game," said O'Toole. "They'd say, 'Looks like so-and-so is getting in trouble. We'd better get back.' "

O'Toole got the tip, but he took no action.

"I didn't say anything," said O'Toole. "As long as they got back."

Imagine such a laissez-faire coach today.

Oh yes, O'Toole said Roger Schmuck, one of the 1970 team's power hitters, took batting practice smoking a cigar.

It really was a different era.

"I've seen different phases," said O'Toole. "Back in 1969 and the early 1970s, there were more throwbacks. The hard-nosed players who drank a lot of beer. They were not out of a ballgame just because of a sore leg, either."

High jinks aside, the Pilots of the 1970s were nearly the equal of the Goldpanners. The Pilots finished second at the NBC in 1970, won the championship in 1971, fell to Fairbanks in the title game again in 1972, and were runners-up in 1976. It is generally believed the 1971 team was the best Glacier Pilots squad of them all.

"The 1971 club," proclaimed O'Toole. "The 1971 Pilots were the best we ever had."

That team sent a platoon of players to the majors. Guys like pitcher Randy Jones, who won the Cy Young Award for the San Diego Padres and these days sells sausages outside the park there and has an in-season radio show. Guys like Bump Wills, Doug Ault, Dave Oliver, Ron Pruitt, Bruce Bochte, and Larry Corrigan, all Major Leaguers.

O'Toole loved Jones, a small southpaw hurler with a limited fastball, who out-smarted everyone.

"A soft left-hander who knows how to pitch," said O'Toole. "He got a lot of ground balls."

O'Toole is hardly alone among long-time Pilot employees in labeling the 1971 team tops. Broadcaster Dick Lobdell flat-out said, "The 1971 team was the best." And statistician Dave Foreman, not easily impressed, said, "You have to argue that's a pretty impressive team."

Look at the record book. That national championship team is still remembered in a big way by the numbers. Highest team slugging average, .556. Most runs scored in a season, 409. Most individual runs scored in a season, 60 by Pruitt. Most individual home runs in a season, 19 by Pruitt. Most individual runs batted in in a season, 62 by Corrigan. And second place on that all-time list is the 61 by Pruitt that year.

Ballplayers love to talk about the level of "pop" in their bats. That whole team had pop. If 1971 was clearly the defining Pilots team of the decade, it was also symptomatic of the kind of clubs Anchorage put on the field.

"It seemed like it was four or five guys every year who were in the big leagues in five years," said Lobdell.

In Foreman's mind, the Pilots of the 1970s were like Class A minor league professionals. Now the best Pilots are more likely to be rookie league beginners, he said.

Jack Brushert, a very popular player, chose not to turn professional when he was drafted by the Oakland A's in 1970. He was married and minor-league salaries were about $600 a month at the time. He moved back to Anchorage and from 1973 to 1979 served as the Pilots' general manager. It was enjoyable, but demanding and, as it turned out, not terribly lucrative, either.

"You had to be a one-man show," said Brushert. "You had to sell the billboard ads and tickets. You were responsible for putting the players in the homes and their travel. You're always trying to do it with not enough money. It's great. It's a lot of fun. But then there's a reality check. You've got to get a job."

Brushert said he was disappointed by "prima donna" players who complained about their jobs being too hard or not getting the use of a car. While O'Toole was tolerant, as GM Brushert was supposed to care if players whooped it up too much.

"They were in the topless bars and the bottomless bars," said Brushert. "It was the wild, wild west and they were away from home for the first time. After the games it was hard to keep them out of the bars."

Brushert didn't sign because he didn't think he was a Major League prospect. But later in life he second-guessed the decision because playing in the minors might have led to a minor league coaching career. These days Brushert, in his early fifties, is the national sales manager for a Hawaiian hotel.

The Pilots did do a marvelous job preparing young players for the majors. But one alumnus from the 1972 team who took a different route to the top was Lee Pelekoudas, a pitcher from Arizona State. Pelekoudas went into the administrative side of the game and for more than twenty years has been part of the Seattle Mariners' organization. He is now a vice president, in charge of negotiating contracts, among other responsibilities.

Pelekoudas, who played a season in the Basin League before spending a summer in Anchorage, said the Alaska accommodations were a welcome change. There was no family host program in the Midwest.

"We stayed in the basement of an old Alcoholics Anonymous office," said Pelekoudas.

Pelekoudas knew Alaska life would be different the moment he disembarked from his plane in Anchorage. Arriving with Bump Wills, a future big-leaguer, the newcomers were interviewed for broadcaster Steve Agbaba's "Deese's Dugout" TV show.

One problem.

"It was my first day in town," said Pelekoudas. "I didn't have anything to say."

The way Alaskans so warmly greeted visiting summer ballplayers made an impression on Pelekoudas that still lingers.

"It's incredible to think a family would take a stranger into the house and give him a key and a key to the car and let you come and go," said Pelekoudas.

In Alaska, Pelekoudas took a couple-hour float plane ride that enabled him to see glaciers, bears and moose, and the flight between Anchorage and Fairbanks to play the Goldpanners offered a breathtaking view of Mount McKinley. He dined at a high-rent cabin near Mount Alyeska. And he got a road trip to Hawaii. What more could a young player ask for?

Well, a trip to Wichita might have been nice. Pelekoudas missed out on the post-season roster. He thinks he can trace his downfall in the eyes of manager Paul Deese to the exact moment.

Involved in a tense game with the Goldpanners in Anchorage, Pelekoudas remembers his buddy Wills smashing a three-run homer for a late-inning tie. Pelekoudas pitched the top of the ninth and then the tenth. The feared Dave Winfield was the first batter.

"I hit him with an 0-2 pitch right in the elbow," said Pelekoudas. "I thought he was going to die."

A succession of those little, seemingly fated batted balls followed, including a grounder just past the reach of shortstop Roy Smalley, another budding big-leaguer. It was a bases-loaded situation when Deese walked to the mound. Steve Swisher, also headed to the majors, was due up and Deese warned, "Don't hang your slider."

"First pitch, I hang the slider," said Pelekoudas.

Swisher hit the ball into orbit. Grand slam.

"I hear this yelling," said Pelekoudas, "and I see Deese in the dugout. He took his glasses off and was jumping up and down on them. That may have sealed my fate for Wichita."

At that time the local sporting scene was defined by Pilots-Goldpanners matchups. It was chic to hate the other guy, to hold a grudge.

"It was very intense on the non-baseball side," said Foreman.

Hardcore fans put their money where their mouths were. We're better than you. We're better than you.

"A lot of money changed hands over the Pilots-Panners games," said Foreman.

Peledoukas, who appeared in 13 games for the Pilots, with a 3-1 record and three saves, remembers that aspect of Alaska ball well.

"There was a lot of betting," he said. "I always thought a good thing up there would be a dog track."

He meant greyhound racing, not Iditarod Trail Sled Dog racing.

For every offbeat, off-the-field adventure Jim Dietz remembers about life with the Goldpanners, Pilot authorities can offer an equally telling tale.

Just for starters, Pelekoudas said he saw the amazing Jack O'Toole put a cigarette out on his tongue. Yes, said O'Toole, it is a trick he has perfected.

Ron Okerlund and his wife Dee first became involved with the Pilots as summer parents when he was in the Air Force, stationed at Elmendorf Air Force Base. He saw an article in the paper asking for help.

"I said, 'Let's do it,'" Okerlund recalled.

He hardly imagined that more than twenty-five years later he would still be a critical man in the Pilots organization.

Like Dietz, Okerlund doesn't mind playing a prank or two on the young men naïve about Alaska. He figures during the course of the season they will get him back with heartburn, aggravation, or just by being big kids. So he has no guilt about the time he and other Pilot officials offered a special snack at a welcome meeting.

Okerlund and helpers passed out little "chocolate nuggets" to each player and said not to eat them until given the word. Then he gave them the word, all right.

"You're all holding moose turd," he announced.

The players went nuts.

"You'd be surprised how fast those things went on the floor," said Okerlund.

Creative Alaska souvenir sellers have managed to invent weird trinkets out of the same substance. They sell moose nugget swizzle sticks and other, shall we say, tasteless gifts.

Okerlund was not a direct party to what befell a player on a return trip to Anchorage following a game against the Peninsula Oilers.

The Pilots traveled in groups by automobile and one carload of players stopped to fish at the Kenai River. One player fell in the water. The water in Alaska is chilly, even in summer, so this soaked player had to strip off his clothes or sit in the car shivering. He was riding nude with his teammates when nature called in a different manner.

"He had to get out and take a leak," said Okerlund.

So what did his friendly teammates do next? They slammed the car door and floored it. Picture the look on this guy's face as the car pulled away. He was standing by the side of the road, buck-ass naked. Fifteen minutes later the perpetrators returned to pick him up.

Okerlund, an expert accountant by trade (skills sorely needed by the team), has served more than one term of office in high Pilot management. To a large degree, though, the 1970s were the Joe Armstrong years.

Armstrong, a fiery, gravel-voiced leader who bled Pilots blue, was born in Everett, Washington, in 1916. After moving to Alaska in 1950, for many years he worked for the city of Anchorage. But he also had strong ties with the local

In 1967, Don Dennis agreed to move to Alaska—for two years. He's been there ever since, a guiding force behind the Fairbanks Goldpanners and the expansion of Alaska baseball.
LEW FREEDMAN

electrician's union. Armstrong was a member of the Pilots' board of directors when the team won the 1969 NBC crown.

Red Boucher said Armstrong never let him forget that the Pilots beat the Goldpanners to a championship.

"Joe would say, 'Hey Boucher, who's the champ?' " Boucher said on the occasion of Armstrong's death in 1990. "And I'd say, 'Joe, go stick your head in the mud.' "

Armstrong said, "Second place is for losers."

Armstrong became president of the Pilots in 1972 and held that job until 1980. His health was weak that year, so he stepped down, but within a year he was back in a major role, as general manager. He held that post for two-and-a-half years, though when he died at age seventy-three, Armstrong was living in Las Vegas.

Armstrong resembled several other Alaska Baseball League leaders. He was fiercely protective of his club's interests, vocal in their defense, and it was sometimes tough to penetrate his bluster to find the human being inside. It was almost as if Armstrong, as gregarious as he could be sometimes, wanted to project a tough-guy image. It may have been that the union politics he knew on the Last Frontier were rough-and-tumble and he felt all negotiations had to be combative.

When Armstrong died, in fact, Red Boucher, who was quite fond of him, said, "He was an aggressive, rough-hewn man. He was a very worthy opponent."

Armstrong, not a particularly tall man, came off as a gray-haired fireplug, but he could laugh and he dearly loved baseball.

Don Dennis said he never saw eye-to-eye with Armstrong philosophically, but he always had fun with him.

"I thought Joe was a character," said Dennis. "He had lots of colorful phrases."

Meaning he swore a lot and wasn't ashamed of it. Armstrong sounded as much like a sailor as Boucher when he chose. Fitting enough, since during World War II, Armstrong worked for the 13th Naval District. Dennis still chuckles over a message Armstrong left for him that was probably eight parts cuss words to two parts other words.

Some people are friendly to the world on the outside and it's really phoniness. Some people tell you what they think, even if it hurts, but neither are they bad people. Armstrong was more like that. To get to know him, you had to peel back layers.

"He's one of those guys you had to judge from the interior," said Dennis.

Dennis, who has seen a lot of Alaska baseball officials come and go, considered Armstrong a stand-up guy. He based that view on a twenty-year-old financial mistake.

In 1978, the Pilots and Goldpanners banded together to start an event called the World Crown Tournament. There were four teams from Alaska by then, including the Valley Green Giants of the Mat-Su Valley, and they competed, along with Team USA and foreign teams from Japan and China. Four individuals, including Dennis and Armstrong, signed the bank note for a loan to cover expenses. The tournament lasted two years, but the losses were big, $30,000 per sponsoring team. What impressed Dennis was that regardless of any other differences over league matters, Armstrong never tried to shirk the debt.

"The Pilots worked off their share," said Dennis. "They stood up to the fact that we failed."

Lou Sinnett, another prominent Pilots executive, came aboard in 1982, at Armstrong's urging. Sinnett was also a union man and while the two weren't close, they knew of each other from that mutual tie. Sinnett, then forty-eight, was commissioner of the Anchorage senior hockey league when recruited. He had just taken early retirement and had an interest in sports, so Armstrong figured he had time on his hands. Sinnett was interested, he just didn't want to be general manager. He became assistant general manager, and somewhat reluctantly became GM years later.

Armstrong was really the public face of the Pilots in the 1970s.

"He was devoted to that team, heart and soul," said Sinnett.

Sinnett believes Armstrong liked to be seen as a gruff guy. Even when he was fundraising—a big part of the job all the time—Armstrong wasn't the kind of man who came to you hat-in-hand for a donation. His style with a hat was slightly different.

"He would walk into a bar," said Sinnett, "and take off his hat, hold it out, and say, 'We need to play baseball.' "

The idea was for patrons to fill it up, and often they did.

Armstrong was very much a baseball fan. Probably his favorite Pilot was Mark McGwire. He just really enjoyed the kid, felt strongly that he would make it, and was pleased he got to see him succeed in the majors.

"Joe Armstrong saw McGwire being where he is before anyone," said Boucher, who said he sat with Armstrong in the stands for a 1982 game watching McGwire play and listening to Armstrong gush about him.

McGwire has always been grateful for the opportunity he got to play the field regularly in Anchorage. When Bob Broeg researched his book on Hap Dumont, he talked to McGwire and the player told him, "Joe Armstrong became a life-long friend."

Armstrong died of lung cancer. After his death, Lefty Van Brunt took Armstrong's ashes and scattered them on the mound at Mulcahy Stadium. Armstrong always enjoyed watching from behind home plate and now his view of the pitcher would be unobstructed by the backstop fencing.

By the 1973 NBC tournament, the Pilots were a known quantity. Scouts scrutinized Anchorage players closely. Deals were cut at the tournament, and players signed the moment it ended.

One player sought that year was Warren Cromartie. Cromartie was from Florida, out of Dade Junior College in Miami, and Florida A&M. He blistered pitching late in the season and scouts hovered around him. It seemed to O'Toole that the Montreal Expos wanted Cromartie more than anyone else and he steered him to Bob Oldis.

Cromartie approached O'Toole and said, "Jack, they want to sign me."

O'Toole told him to listen and that he would stay down the hall and be available for advice.

Oldis, a former Major League catcher with the Pittsburgh Pirates and other teams, made Cromartie an offer. Cromartie returned to O'Toole, who asked, "Are you going to sign?"

Cromartie told O'Toole the Expos were willing to pay him $38,000 a year and pay for two years of schooling. This was before the days of million-dollar bonuses. O'Toole told him it sounded like a good deal.

Cromartie signed and the deal worked out well for everyone. Cromartie became a well-respected Major Leaguer, playing nine years for the Expos and recording a career batting average of .280 before playing in Japan. He later wrote a book about his experiences.

Oldis became a regular habitue of Alaska, taking an annual scouting trip to the north.

And O'Toole became an Expos scout. Except for one year when he worked for the Florida Marlins, he maintained that allegiance for the rest of the century.

When Sinnett joined the Pilots he was not a baseball expert, nor was he an expert on Pilot history. His first trip to the NBC was in 1982, soon after the Glacier Pilots' glorious 1970s, and he couldn't believe how much the tournament officials and fans loved his team.

"They got treated like they were already the champions," said Sinnett. "It was amazing."

Of course, the Pilots had given the locals some very special memories.

One of the best came in perhaps the greatest-ever NBC championship game. In 1976, the title game pitted the Goldpanners against the Glacier Pilots—after they split two previous games in the tournament. During the season-long series, tournament included, the Pilots defeated the Goldpanners fifteen times and lost five.

But it seemed this game might end in a tie. After nine innings, it was 0-0. Fairbanks pitcher Greg Harris, winner of three games in the tournament already, was superb. He was throwing a two-hit shutout. Anchorage pitcher Dan Boone was superb. He was throwing a two-hit shutout.

While others who have spent an adult lifetime watching the Alaska Baseball League differ, some in the lower forty-eight say this was the best amateur baseball game ever played.

In the tenth inning, Fairbanks catcher Dan Cowgill—who in the 1990s would become the Goldpanner manager—stroked a single to right. It helped start the rally that gave Fairbanks a 2-0 victory. Cowgill had faced Boone many, many times, and had little luck against him.

Cowgill was an iron man catcher that year, behind the plate for fifty-six games. He probably felt as if he could barely stand up by the end of that night. But his hit was a big one.

"I had seen Boone a hundred times in college," said Cowgill. "I was only one-for-a-hundred. But that was the one that counted."

If it was difficult to see the future well enough to envision Cowgill skippering the same team he helped win a national championship, it was perhaps more incredible to envision the twists and turns Boone's baseball life took.

Not only did he make the majors, but Dan Boone became the most amazing player in Alaska baseball history. He was a Pilot who became a Goldpanner, who in a league designed for collegians returned at an age when his teammates were young enough to be his children.

10

DAN BOONE

A knuckleballer who just wouldn't quit

NEVER MIND Satchel Paige: Dan Boone was the man who might pitch forever. Some pitchers burn out fast, their arms as limp as noodles before they turn thirty. Other pitchers stay fit with age and persevere with their wiles as they lose mph off their fastballs.

And then there are the Dan Boones of the world. Or perhaps it should be said, then there is Dan Boone. He may well be one-of-a-kind.

In a league designed for college players, Boone tried a little bit of everything, starting and relieving, at just about every age. In a league designed for players during their college years, where a four-year appearance was rare in the old days, and any kind of multiple-year appearance has grown more unusual, Boone is a record-holder. He played eight summers in Alaska.

Not consecutively, either. Not hardly.

"No one has had an ABL career like Dan Boone," said the Pilots' Dick Lobdell.

Boone was a normal recruit when he joined the Anchorage Glacier Pilots in 1974. He met a girl he liked and that was some incentive to return in 1975. Same in 1976. He and Marge got serious and they married.

Boone finished pitching at Fullerton State. He went on to the minor leagues, and briefly made the majors. Then he was released by the Milwaukee Brewers. Always up for the chance to visit Alaska and see relatives, Boone signed on for a return engagement in Anchorage in 1985.

Still dreaming of the majors, Boone hooked on in the minors again and got another stab at the big time. When he didn't stay with the Baltimore Orioles after the 1990 season, pitching was not out of his system.

Just because he was pushing normal baseball retirement age, Boone had no desire to retire. He stunned old-time Alaska baseball fans by showing up as a short reliever for the Fairbanks Goldpanners in 1993, craftily employing a knuckleball to baffle a younger generation of hitters.

It was something to see college guys meeting a well-executed knuckler for the first time. They swung at air so many times they might as well have been shadow boxing.

Boone returned to the Goldpanners in 1994, 1995, and 1996. By then he was forty-two. He didn't look tired, or seem to be faltering, either.

"He could still come back and pitch," said Jack O'Toole a few years later. "He's just as good now as he was at twenty-two. He was always scrawny and lean. A couple of years ago when I saw him I said, 'Goddamn, Dan, you're putting on some weight . . . a couple of ounces.'"

Boone was an up-and-comer during his first Pilots stretch. Slightly built at five-foot-eight, and one-hundred-and-forty-five pounds, Boone always looked as if a strong breeze could knock him over. And his thick, brown mustache seemed as wide as his face. He could throw reasonably hard, but his fastball would never win a contest against, say, a Randy Johnson. Guile always played a part in Boone's ability to get hitters out.

"I remember seeing him pitch when he was with the Pilots the first time," said Mat-Su Miners general manager Stan Zaborac. "Strictly control."

Boone generally had good stuff. One year he was 6-3 with a 1.70 earned-run average. And he was the man on the mound that fateful day in August, 1976, going head-to-head with Greg Harris in the Pilots-Goldpanners NBC showdown.

"Oh, boy, what a heartbreaker," said Boone. "We were battling and battling. It was unbelievable. There were just some wild plays."

The only reason Boone was even in Wichita that year was Marge. Despite being drafted by the California Angels, he chose to play another season for the Glacier Pilots because of her. But nobody thought they'd see Dan Boone in Alaska again, except for vacations.

In 1981, Boone made the majors. He found what seemed to be a niche coming out of the bullpen for the San Diego Padres. That season he was 1-0 with a 2.86 ERA and two saves in 37 games. The next year he was traded and with San Diego and Houston he went 1-1 with two saves.

Then it was back to the minors, looking for a job, and finding himself out of one, with time on his hands. The second Alaska coming of Boone, in 1985, was a cameo, something to do while he made contacts for a Major League comeback. He was thirty-one, but did pitch for the Pilots in the NBC for the first time since the famous 1976 game.

Somewhat incredibly, eight years after his last Major League appearance, Boone was a late-season call-up of the Baltimore Orioles in 1990. Throwing a seven-inning no-hitter for the Rochester Red Wings in AAA at age thirty-six got the parent club's attention.

Although his record was 0-0 with the Orioles, and he had no saves, Boone was quite effective in four showings with a 2.79 ERA. There was a lot of talk, nationally—and in Alaska—about what Boone might do the next season.

But there was no next season. At least not in the majors.

"Most guys, by the time they go through the majors, they're pretty well through," said Zaborac. "Hell, the way he pitches, he could be pitching in his sixties."

Boone returned to his El Cajon, California, home and started a construction company. He stayed active pitching in nearby San Diego leagues, and when a quixotic group formed a seniors baseball league in Florida, Boone was part of it. The league went belly-up in eighteen months.

However, Boone was renewed. He was experimenting with a knuckleball, the floater pitch that seems to have a mind of its own. Some call it a pitch of last resort. Few pitchers master it and catchers go crazy handling it.

"I knew if I was ever going to get back to pro ball, I had to do something," said Boone.

He did not for a moment think "something" would be returning to Alaska, never mind for the arch-rival Goldpanners. But the Lord works in mysterious ways.

A member of Boone's church was a next-door-neighbor of Don Dennis in San Diego, where the Goldpanner general manager had a winter home. Ann Dennis, the team executive's wife, got a recommendation from the neighbor on some carpentry work. The person endorsed was Boone.

When Boone got to the house, Don Dennis remembered him. Boone mentioned that he was still pitching, had recently finished throwing in a big event held at San Diego State's stadium. Where Jim Dietz coached. Dennis phoned Dietz and asked how Boone looked. Dietz told him Boone was the best pitcher in the tournament.

"Don gives me a call and asks, 'What do you think of going to Alaska?' " said Boone.

"For what?" answered Boone.

Dennis thought Boone might make a good pitching coach, and he apparently could still throw. You could never have too many arms. So he promised Boone he could do some pitching. Good thing. Boone said he wouldn't have taken the position if it was coaching only.

And good thing for the Goldpanners. Make that great thing for the Goldpanners. During the third coming of Dan Boone to Alaska, he was virtually unhittable, a relieving machine who proved you can fool everybody all of the time.

In this relief-pitching-happy era, teams kill for a closer, the guy with the knock-'em-dead outlook who can stride in from the bullpen with little warming up, and set hitters on their butts. Mostly, managers look for speedballers to do the job, but they'll take any proven commodity.

There are hardly any knuckleballers in the majors because the pitch so often does what it wants to do against its owner's will. Those who use the pitch, though, usually have long careers. Hoyt Wilhelm pitched in relief until he was almost fifty and made the Hall of Fame. Phil Niekro rode the knuckler to the Hall as a 300-game winner. His brother, Joe, won more than 200 games using it.

Boone's knuckler could place him in an Alaska Baseball League Hall of Fame. During his 1990s tour of the north, he threw it eighty percent of the time. During the summer of 1993 alone, he saved 15 games, won five, and posted a 2.28 ERA. Not bad for a coach. He was just about that good the other years, too.

Boone did everything but parade around ballparks wearing "I'm available" sandwich signs, but there were no Major League takers. So in 1995, Boone prepared to be a replacement player during the strike. He knew he might be labeled a "scab" by pro-union forces, but said his family came first. He just hoped he didn't have to cross a picket line.

Boone went through spring training with the Padres, but then the players settled with the owners the day before the regular season was to begin. It might not have been the same, but it would have technically put him back in the majors for the first time in five years. As a fallback, he wanted a minor league contract, to be sent to AAA Las Vegas, but the Padres offered nothing.

Finely honed from a good spring's work, Boone went back to Alaska and confusing young players. Astounding them is more like it.

During one Pilot-Goldpanner game that year, Boone was summoned from the bullpen with one out in the bottom of the ninth. The home Pilots had a runner on first. Pilot batter Travis Wyckoff worked the count to 2-2. Boone's next offering came up sweet, it seemed. Then it dipped. Wyckoff swung and hit a grounder to third. Double play. No more trouble. The knuckler ruled.

"He sure shut us down," said Pilots' outfielder Jon Macalutas. "If it moves real good, you're going to ground out or strike out. It's harder to hit because it's unorthodox."

In the 1993 championship game of the Bucs Invitational, Boone lifted the Goldpanners to a 6-5 win with a save.

"Good ole Dan Boone," said Bucs manager Mike Garcia. "Shoot."

Garcia felt like shooting Boone.

Another time, Glacier Pilot slugger Steve Carver, who was the ABL's player-of-the-year in 1994, came to the plate while a Stanford University teammate, Dusty Allen, then with the Anchorage Bucs, sat in the press box.

Carver swung and missed at a Boone pitch. Allen chuckled and tapped on the window. Carver glanced up. Allen nodded and Carver grinned. Yep, it was all true. Allen had been telling Carver about this senior-citizen Goldpanner reliever nobody could touch.

"He could hit spots," said O'Toole. "He kept the ball low, out of the hitting zone. It looked like a balloon coming up."

Not every pitcher has the makeup to be a finisher, to come in with men on base, take the inherited mess and make order out of chaos. Boone did.

"He had the mentality of a closer," said Dave Foreman, the Pilots official. " 'If they hit me, tough. I know what I can do.' "

The old man just kept throwing and the young guys, many of whom would one day reach the majors and not see a knuckler again till then, kept swinging. Players would march into the batter's box convinced they could crush Boone's slow-moving tosses, then meekly walk back to the dugout, trailing their bats. For the Goldpanners, Boone was the sure-thing safety valve.

Who ya gonna call? Ghostbuster Dan.

"It's a luxury we have," said Stacy Parker, the Goldpanners' manager at the time. "We know if we get in a jam, we can go to him. You don't see a knuckleballer, hardly ever. And he can throw it for strikes whenever he wants."

It only seemed that way. Not even Boone could impose his will on a knuckeball with that kind of certainty. Still, when knuckleballers get hot, as the Boston Red Sox' Tim Wakefield has shown in recent years, they can be amongst the best pitchers in baseball.

"When it's working, it's no fear," said Boone.

All knuckleballers have a peculiar relationship with the pitch that is their career-maker. On the whole, they'd rather be like everybody else, a fastball-throwing strikeout artist. The knuckler is such a quirky pitch, it is of them, but not truly theirs. They are pleased when things go right, but they also know they might not have an explanation if the knuckler deserts them in a crucial situation.

"The knuckler is a real advantage," said Boone. "If it's working, it's so hard to hit. I know I wouldn't want to have to face it. I know guys hate to hit against guys like me. It's embarrassing if I get them out."

Knuckleballers are fond of saying they don't even know where the ball will land once they fling it. That's why poor catchers use over-sized mitts to block the plate when they're working with a knuckleballer.

Former Pilots manager Steve McFarland said the knuckler is just an incredible weapon, and it's a tricky task to track it without radar, especially when it's used by a master manipulator like Boone.

"Everything he does throw moves," said McFarland. "And it doesn't move in the same direction two pitches in a row."

Boone made them all marvel. At his tireless arm. At his assortment of slow stuff. At the way this little guy bossed around big sluggers, as if he were a lion tamer with just a whip and chair for protection against wickedly sharp teeth and claws.

It seemed like he could pitch in Alaska indefinitely. Then, at the very end of the 1996 season, Boone was horsing around with Goldpanner teammates, tossing a football. The ball broke the middle finger of his left, throwing hand. He couldn't throw a knuckler at all. It took more than a year for the fluke injury to heal and in the interim Boone went to work for a major construction company.

When the 1997 season arrived, Boone stayed home. In 1998, no Alaska. Ditto in 1999. The pattern has all the appearances of retirement, even if Boone can't outright admit he won't ever throw in Alaska again.

"I sure have missed it," he said in 1999. "Every time June and July rolls around, I miss it."

Maybe Dan Boone will return in 2000. That would make him the first ABL player to compete in four different decades.

11

THE VALLEY GREEN GIANTS

Competing with cabbages and mosquitoes

THE VALLEY Green Giants. The Valley Green Giants?

That was the name of the Alaska baseball team formed in 1976 to compete with the Goldpanners, Glacier Pilots and Oilers—and who would win their first NBC crown in 1977. And even if the name sounded silly, given the area's ties to farming and agriculture, there was logic in it.

In 1935, during the heart of the Great Depression gripping the United States, a large group of optimistic settlers arrived in Palmer, Alaska. They came from the Midwest for a promised opportunity to farm the fertile soil of the Matanuska-Susitna Valley, some fifty miles north of Anchorage.

Notwithstanding the oddity of producing the world's largest cabbages, regularly honored in competition at the Alaska State Fair, the agricultural opportunities never quite lived up to the hopes of those who took the long train trip, nor the governmental entities which encouraged the migration. Yet over time the area gradually grew into a major commercial and population center, albeit one that generally revolved around Anchorage.

By 1976, the trans-Alaska Pipeline was opening, the state's population was expanding, so why not expand the ABL?

Sitting outside the team Winnebago in 1978, Charmaine Smith, wife of club president Chuck Smith, sells season tickets for the Valley Green Giants. CHUCK SMITH

The Valley Green Giants' name made the club instant attention-getters. It didn't hurt any that the Jolly Green Giant was a staple of television ads, selling canned corn and other vegetables. The Valley Green Giants were a clever play on that cartoonish, greener-than-broccoli pitchman.

Stan Zaborac, whose Alaska league involvement began as a board member for the Valley Green Giants, said "its catchiness" sounded good at first.

Catchy it was, but people snickerered when they first heard the name. Even Elmer "Chuck" Smith, at first team vice president, then president. Smith said Don Dennis deserved credit or blame for bestowing the name.

"I used to laugh," said Smith. "I said, 'Where the heck did you come up with a name like that?' At first it was a joke. The fans wondered what it was, a garden show?"

The novelty didn't hurt, though. Whoever heard of such a name for a baseball team? So at least people remembered the Valley Green Giants.

If Dennis was the behind-the-scenes organizer, Smith evolved into a community point man. At one time or another, Smith sold tickets from a recreational vehicle parked near shopping areas, sold ads, wrote a baseball column for the local *Frontiersman* newspaper, and worked the park's public address system. He also physically helped build the field.

Smith, now in his early seventies, was an Alaska educator and administrator with a deep background in baseball. He grew up in Puyallup, Washington, where he was a football, basketball and baseball star and was captain of all

The uniforms of the '78 Valley Green Giants players were as green as their namesake. CHUCK SMITH

three teams. If he was better in basketball, he gained more notoriety as a shortstop in baseball.

But Smith finished high school in 1945, during World War II. He went right into the Army and was heading to Iwo Jima when the war ended. He made it as far as Whittier, Alaska, before being stationed at Fort Richardson in Anchorage. While in Alaska he became friendly with another soldier. Richie Ashburn would soon be on on his way to a Hall of Fame outfielding career with the Philadelphia Phillies. Smith played on base teams with Ashburn. Later, after Smith played some third base for Pacific Lutheran University in Tacoma, Washington, his contacts with Ashburn led to an opportunity to join the Detroit Tigers' organization.

Smith, sandy-haired and trim more than a half century later, is still built like the infielder he was. In 1948, he signed for a $1,000 bonus, but resisted when the Tigers wanted to ship him to an East Coast minor league club.

"I bargained with them," said Smith.

So he was sent to Great Falls, Montana. He has a strange memory from his brief time with the Montana club. One of the names shouted at roll call was that of Steve Agbaba. He was a no-show. Smith remembered the name because it was unusual, never dreaming he would later become friends with the man in Fairbanks.

Injury cut short Smith's stay in the Pioneer League. He was playing second base when a hard liner hit a rock and ricocheted into his face. The impact cost him several teeth and broke his cheek bone badly.

Giants outfielder Wes Clements warms up on Hermon Brothers Field in Palmer. CHUCK SMITH

"It was a grisly thing," said Smith.

After a rushed rehab stint, Smith was sent to Jamestown, New York, in the Pony League. He wasn't really ready to play yet.

"I couldn't eat," said Smith. "The only thing I had all summer long was soup."

Smith retained his batting stroke, if not his appetite. He always hit well, in the .300 range. But it was hard to regain comfort in the field.

"I hate to admit it," he said, "but I was becoming gun-shy."

Red Rolfe, a former Major League star, was the director of the Tigers' minor-league system and he encouraged Smith.

"He kept telling me, 'You're going to make it,' " said Smith.

It was clear he was not going to make it that summer, however, and after struggling a few months, Rolfe sent Smith home with the order to "Get healed."

He did so. But Smith also enrolled at Western Washington University, where eventually he earned an undergraduate degree in public education and a masters in public administration. When the 1949 season loomed, the Tigers offered a typically low minor-league salary of $200.

Smith rejected the offer and instead joined a relative who had a truck, driving gravel on the new Alaska Highway to Fairbanks. He stayed for the construction season and one day wandered down to the ballpark and approached a guy about playing.

It was Mike Stepovich, a member of one of the community's most prominent families. Before statehood, Stepovich was Alaska's territorial governor. When Smith stayed through the winter, he lived in a basement apartment with George Sullivan, later mayor of Anchorage and the man for whom that city's major indoor arena is named. Smith made good contacts with influential Alaskans.

There was barely room for pencil erasers in the Hermon Brothers Field pressbox in the early days. CHUCK SMITH

Smith married his wife Charmaine in 1952, had three children, and in 1953 began putting his degrees to work with a job at the old Anchorage High School. Ultimately, Smith taught or served as an administrator all over Alaska, from Allakaket to Hope to Kenai to Dillingham to Chugiak to Fairbanks. When he retired from school service in 1977 he was superintendent of schools in Fairbanks, where he got to know Dennis.

A member of the Goldpanners' board of directors, Smith knew he was going to retire and move back to Southcentral Alaska, so he was one of a handful of original investors when the Valley Green Giants were formed. Five supporters put in $5,000 apiece, Smith recalled. Two years later he was the boss.

Although Don Dennis was one of those backers (and if not for him there wouldn't even have been a team), a public relations fiasco hurt the Giants' outlook from the beginning. Dennis retained the title of general manager. That was probably a tactical error, since he was based in Fairbanks. Dennis normally scoured the country seeking ballplayers for the Goldpanners. In 1976, he did the same work for the Valley Green Giants, too. With different results.

It might be said that the green uniforms with yellow stripes down the pant legs gave the Giants the look of giant vegetables, but that would be unkind. More unkind was the assessment that the team often played like giant vegetables.

The real problem was that the Goldpanners were very good and the Valley Green Giants were not. That produced a backlash.

"Palmer people weren't happy with Dennis because they thought he was taking the cream of the crop," said Smith. "The feeling in Palmer was pretty clear. They felt they were getting the short end of the deal. They were just getting shellacked."

To this day, Dennis insists the conspiracy theory is baseless. He said the

A tiny set of bleachers sufficed for the Giants fans. CHUCK SMITH

resentment was quite real, but unfounded. The Valley Green Giants did play a brutal schedule, he said, and that didn't help. For one thing, he points out, the year previously, the top three teams in the nation were the Oilers, Goldpanners and Pilots, the Green Giants' main foes.

"Unfortunately, Fairbanks dominated them that year," said Dennis.

The Valley Green Giants were of respectable quality, but had a losing record from the start. Fans became testy, said Smith, usually taking it out on him. The *Frontiersman,* the local newspaper, ran an editorial, the gist of which was that it was Fairbanks' fault the Mat-Su Valley didn't have a competitive team.

"They always struggled," said the Pilots' Dick Lobdell. "I used to kid them. I said, 'You guys would rather beat the Glacier Pilots than get a good crop.' "

Besides Smith, the other most visible and prominent team official was John Sweeney. Sweeney, fresh out of San Diego State, was hired by Dennis to assume the title of assistant general manager.

Young Sweeney was thrilled to be working for a baseball club as his first job out of school. Little could he imagine that at forty-nine in 1999, he would still be associated with the Alaska Baseball League as director of the Bucs Invitational tournament. In-between, Sweeney worked for the Valley Green Giants, the Goldpanners and the Bucs. He wrote baseball for the *Fairbanks Daily News-Miner* and the old *Anchorage Times.* And broadcasting—his true love—provided him with more adventures than all of the other jobs combined. Or at least it seemed that way.

Sweeney grew up in Southern California listening to Los Angeles Dodger and California Angel broadcasts. He admired and revered Vin Scully, Dick Enberg and others.

In 1976, he was the Valley Green Giants' official scorer and public address announcer. But the visiting teams arrived with radio crews.

"I'd see these guys come through and think that's what I wanted to do," said Sweeney. "I was like the guy in Hollywood. I wanted to direct."

By 1978, Sweeney broadcast seventy games a year. Despite switching teams, jobs, and cities, he has broadcast some baseball every year since.

However, when Sweeney came to Alaska—he whips off the date, May 12, 1976, with no prompting—the Valley Green Giants' pressing need was not who would become the next Red Barber, but where this fledgling ball club would play. The start of the season was a month away and the Valley Green Giants had a major problem.

"We had no field," said Sweeney.

What transpired next is one of the great, enduring legends of the Alaska league. Over the next few weeks, a field was carved out of a stand of trees next to the site of the Alaska State Fair in Palmer. Never mind a cornfield in Iowa, this was the field of dreams. Only Shoeless Joe Jackson didn't come to play in Palmer, a whole new team of collegians did.

Through the industry and dedication of a construction company operated by a local family, the field was created in almost no time. Bulldozers rolled, volunteers worked, and what were once trees became Hermon Brothers Field, named for the clan who made it happen.

"In early June we played our first game, with a grass infield," said Zaborac. "It was quite an accomplishment."

Improvements have been made, lights installed, but essentially, the field as it was manufactured, almost out of thin air, remains in use today.

Of course, as a new team, the Valley Green Giants faced other challenges. Like how to establish an identity.

Seattle is credited—or blamed, depending on your point of view—with inventing The Wave, the fans' arm-raising gesture of support. Given the exposure of the Jolly Green Giant, it was thought a Valley Green Giants gimmick might become popular. It was perfectly logical to assume that a fan-friendly Ho, ho, ho cheer would catch on.

But it didn't.

Neither did the Green Giants.

Smith said attendance was a lowly hundred-and-fifty to two-hundred fans a game and the Green Giants' roster was stocked with good guys who didn't necessarily swing good lumber or have good arms.

"We didn't have much," said Smith.

One player with a famous name, anyway, was Cam Killebrew, the son of Hall of Fame slugger Harmon Killebrew, who is a member of baseball's elite 500-home-run club.

Yet it wasn't as if the team was bereft. The Valley Green Giants did grow some major leaguers alongside the giant cabbages. Only in Alaska, where other clubs produced them by the bushel, might it be said that the Giants "didn't have much." That was true in comparison to the talent-rich Goldpanners, Pilots and Oilers, but the team did graduate seven guys to the majors.

Pitcher Dave Schmidt, lifetime 54-55 and twice a ten-game winner for the Baltimore Orioles, had a twelve-year career. Tom Niedenfuer pitched in the 1981 World Series for the Los Angeles Dodgers. Floyd Chiffer and Dave Rucker also threw in the majors. Outfielder Ron Roenicke spent several years in the National League and Paul Zuvella was up for nine seasons. Cliff

The 1979 Valley Green Giant CHUCK SMITH

Pastornicky had a ten-game cameo with the Kansas City Royals. They all can always say they were Valley Green Giants.

Besides extra-large vegetables, one other thing the Valley became known for was an infestation of mosquitoes. It could be crazy during games, with swarms of the aggressive flying bloodsuckers harassing players, coaches, or anyone else who sat still for more than a minute.

"We had some good laughs up there in the mosquito zone," said Glacier Pilots' broadcaster Dave Foreman. "They didn't have money to spray back then."

The bugs were legendary.

Jim Dietz, the old Goldpanners' manager, tells a vivid tale.

Growing up a Vin Scully fan in Southern California, John Sweeney later became immersed in Alaska baseball, working for the Valley Green Giants, the Goldpanners and the Anchorage Bucs; writing about baseball for the *Fairbanks Daily News-Miner* and *Anchorage Times;* and broadcasting just about every game he could. He is now director of the Bucs Invitational tournament.

LEW FREEDMAN

"We had to wear mosquito nets," said Dietz. "The players who weren't playing wore them. We looked like we were from outer space, or an exterminating company."

The Valley Green Giants may have been the weakest of the four Alaska clubs at the time, but they had at least one terrific moment of glory. The World Crown Tournament that was a financial backbreaker for Dennis, Armstrong and the others, was an artistic success for the Valley Green Giants. Infielder Brian Hurley hit a grand slam homer to win the 1978 championship and shock the older Alaska teams.

"It was the shot heard around the Valley," said Sweeney.

Maybe so, but it did not produce a long-term fan boost.

The way Smith remembered it Sweeney took as much guff as he did from unhappy fans simply because he was seen as Dennis' agent.

"If he hadn't been connected with the Goldpanners, he would have gotten along great," said Smith.

Sweeney, though, said the people in the Valley were terrific. "I thought it was Mayberry RFD."

Smith promoted the Valley Green Giants everywhere he traveled. He carried literature that hyped the league and he found that fans knew about Alaska baseball.

"But they never heard of the Valley Green Giants," he said.

Soon enough, no more would be heard of the Valley Green Giants at all. Zaborac, though, emerged as a savior of Palmer baseball.

12

THE MAT-SU MINERS

Local ownership makes the difference

THE PROUD people of the Mat-Su Valley, whose parents and grandparents came north to make new lives, were independent by nature. So perhaps they bristled more than expected at what they took to be long-distance overseers connected to the Goldpanners.

Nonetheless, it was apparent that if the Valley Green Giants franchise was to survive, local leadership was critical.

Stan Zaborac took over as general manager, the Valley Green Giants were consigned to history, and then reborn in 1980 as the Mat-Su Miners.

John Sweeney said the Giants were founded with the goal of someday being managed locally. But he thought the flashy name would stick.

It didn't.

"The Valley Green Giants. Not too many people remember them now," said Zaborac.

In a league in which almost all teams have strong-minded front men who zealously protect the interests of their clubs, Zaborac is the man who assumed that role for the Miners. He has shepherded them through two decades of operation. Without Stan Zaborac, the Mat-Su Miners would be long gone.

A worker installs new field lights at Hermon Brothers Field for the Mat-Su Miners 1981 season. CHUCK SMITH

Zaborac, who turned sixty-five in 1999, has roots in Alaska that date back to the 1930s. His grandparents came to the territory in 1937 and they owned the old Talkeetna Hotel, then quite remote, but now an hour or so trip by car from Palmer on the Parks Highway. Zaborac visited Alaska for the first time at age seven in 1941 and his family planned to move to the state soon. Except World War II intervened, delaying the migration until 1948.

As a young man Zaborac loved baseball. He grew up in Anchorage and played first base in American Legion and in the Anchorage city league.

"I played whenever I could," he said.

Zaborac's playing days pre-date the Alaska league, but he was active when the recreational leagues were more than just recreation.

"We used to have quite a few fans," he said.

Although nursed along by the Goldpanners' support, there was no doubt the time had come to cut the Valley Green Giants' strings and establish a fresh start.

"People here in Palmer decided they wanted their own identity," said Zaborac. "They were our team instead of Fairbanks' team. There was a lot of feeling that the Valley Green Giants were a farm team."

These days, Zaborac has gray hair, with a thick, gray mustache. He is over six feet tall, but seems a little stoop-shouldered. He has a large build, and once weighed more than three hundred pounds. A series of heart attacks convinced him to lose about a hundred of those pounds. Over the years, people around the league have worried about the general manager's health and his team's, almost as if they are one. To some extent, they are. Zaborac is rarely seen at games, or anywhere in public, not wearing his kelly-green Miners' jacket.

If the Giants had difficulty competing with the top-echelon teams, Zaborac remedied the problem by hiring good managers and recruiting better talent. The Miners are clearly the on-field equal of the other clubs.

In 1987, the Miners won their first National Baseball Congress championship, a glorious moment for the team. In 1997, the Miners won the national title again.

Looking on from afar at what Zaborac accomplished, Chuck Smith offered a bow.

"I picked up a lot of respect for him," said Smith. "When he came on the quality of the team improved. He did a lot for that team."

The Miners not only joined the other established Alaska teams in manufacturing bigger-name players, they seemed to have a knack for signing up lesser-known collegiate players who blossomed into Alaska stars in a single summer.

Still, no one can deny Zaborac bragging rights in playing a role in the rise of such big-league guys as long-time pro Mike Devereux, a highly respected hitter; Steve Trachsel, the Chicago Cubs starting pitcher; power-hitting Jeff King; Marvin Benard, a .300 hitter for the San Francisco Giants now; and Craig Counsel, who played a significant part in the Florida Marlins' 1997 World Series triumph. Not to mention the most traveled Alaska league player of them all, Tom Niedenfuer, who played for the Valley Green Giants, returned to Palmer to play for Mat-Su, and also played for the Glacier Pilots in Wichita in 1980. Niedenfuer did everything but receive a Permanent Fund Dividend check as an official resident.

Zaborac relishes the memory of Devereaux smashing the ball all over Hermon Brothers Field.

"He could play," said Zaborac.

And he waxes rhapdsodic about the hard-hitting King.

"King had one of the nicest swings I've ever seen in baseball," said Zaborac. "Even at eighteen or nineteen."

Benard, now San Francisco's regular leadoff man, experienced his Major League breakthrough during the 1998 summer. What seemed like a temporary hot streak became a normal performance level for him. Bernard went from a short-term fill-in to starter because the Giants couldn't afford to leave his bat out of the lineup. In one game against the Philadelphia Phillies, Benard opened eyes with four hits, a walk and a stolen base.

Benard had kind words for the Mat-Su Miners.

"I enjoyed it up there," he said. "I had a great time. Beautiful country. It was the first time I saw snow."

The Mat-Su Miners turned to the community for fund-raising support. Club president Chuck Smith is on the left.
COURTESY OF CHUCK SMITH

No, it did not snow at Hermon Brothers while Benard, a warm-weather guy by upbringing, was playing. But snow remains visible on the surrounding, high mountains year-round.

Although Hermon Brothers Field was constructed hastily, the view over the left-field wall is one of the most picturesque in the nation. Pioneer Peak, a 6,000-foot mountain, looms in the distance, above the road to Anchorage. It is an impressive, craggy peak that looks even larger than its measurements because of the open spaces beneath it.

Over the years, improvements were made in the initial ballpark structure. Lights were installed in 1980, an important addition to accommodate night games. It gets dark enough in Palmer to make it hard to see a swiftly pitched ball. One thing is certain, though, the Miners will never come up short on parking. Having the yard located adjacent to the state fairgrounds means there are thousands of available spaces.

If Benard was pleasurably surprised by his short stay in Alaska, perhaps no one had more fun in the Mat-Su Valley than Rich Amaral, later a reliable hitter for the Seattle Mariners and the Baltimore Orioles.

Amaral was a member of the Miners in 1982, the same year Mark McGwire and Cory Snyder played for the Pilots, Wally Joyner for the Anchorage Bucs, and Shane Mack for the Goldpanners.

"There was great talent up there," said Amaral.

Amaral had just finished his freshman year at UCLA, and was serious about baseball, but he was still anxious to enjoy himself.

"I loved it," said Amaral. "I had no idea what to expect. I knew nothing about Alaska. Palmer was a real small town, but I stayed with a nice family. It turned out to be a great summer. It was a blast."

Until then, Amaral was used to spending summers on the beach. Amaral wasn't kidding when he said he was ignorant of what Alaska would be like. He guessed it would be freezing, so just before he got out on the plane, Amaral went shopping. He invested between $200 and $300 in a heavy coat sure to protect his thin blood.

"It was a big, old fur coat," said Amaral. "It was like one of those the Marlboro man wears."

Of course he didn't need it. Later, though, Amaral briefly got some use out of the coat while skiing. Eventually, he tucked it away in a closet and thinks he might still have it.

"Somewhere," he said.

One reason Amaral had such a great time was the motorcycle his host family loaned him for wheels. The Miners had no clubhouse at Hermon Brothers, so Amaral dressed at the home and jumped on the bike in full uniform. He rode dirt trails through the woods, exploring the forested area while he commuted.

"I remember how pretty the countryside was," said Amaral much later. "That was something for a guy from California. I was able to check out all kinds of places."

When he completed his grand tour of the neighborhood on the two-wheeler, Amaral roared into the park. It was James Dean as baseball player.

There was other sightseeing, some by accident. Like the time the team bus stopped to admire a moose in the road on the fifty-mile ride to Anchorage. Amaral also did his share of fishing and nearly two decades after the fact he is loyal to the oath he swore never to reveal the location of the hot spot.

"Top secret," he said. "It was a mucky stream that came out to a crystal pond. Every time I threw a line in I hooked a salmon. I ended up getting them smoked."

Once it became apparent that the Miners were a team of their own, fans in Palmer embraced them. One long-time fan is Jack Niggemyer, who is better known as race manager of the Iditarod Trail Sled Dog Race, the man who makes sure the trail to Nome stays open in blizzards for each March's event.

Growing up in Ohio and Wyoming, Niggemyer was a huge baseball fan. He played the game as often as he could, went to games wherever he was. But as he aged, he drifted away from the sport. The Miners brought him back in the 1980s and now he shares the passion with his family.

"It's just wonderful," said Niggemyer, who as a resident of Sutton lives perhaps sixty miles from Anchorage, making it unlikely he would ever zip into the big city to see games. "You spend three bucks and you get to watch good quality baseball. It just revived my interest."

Niggemyer is devoted enough to say that if the Miners ever need rescuing financially he would try to form an operations group to keep the team alive.

The Alaska teams are non-profit organizations, but many times have faced

After nursing the Valley Green Giants through their painful and brief existence, Stan Zaborac, now general manager of the Mat-Su Miners, emerged as a saviour of Palmer baseball. LEW FREEDMAN

crossroads money crises. And indeed, the Miners seem to be a shoestring operation even in their finest years.

Former Goldpanner manager Jim Dietz does not retain fond memories of team visits to Mat-Su when he said his club was put up in "cubicle housing. They seemed like cardboard. Street people have better housing. Everything was to save the dollar."

Everything was to save the dollar. The Miners built up debts that almost broke the franchise. It is one thing to be a non-profit organization, and another not to produce revenue. But Zaborac and helpers persevered.

In the 1980s, the Miners developed a certain cult following among fans who picked the bleacher seats on the left-field side to congregate. The deep-throated band of irreverent harassers gave fits to visiting players and umpires. The group became known around the league as "The Bleacher Creatures." They could be funny, and they could be mean, but at all times they were loud supporters of the home team and loud detractors of the enemy.

One woman made a habit of shouting at the visiting pitcher constantly. Her favorite insult was "Weenie Arm!" because the player would no doubt serve up easy-to-hit "meat." Fans were also known to call players "Oscar," as in Oscar Mayer meat products.

Once, proving their quick-thinking adaptability, fans zinged an umpire by detouring through one of their own players. When Miner shortstop Dave "Opie" Cunningham made an error just after a conversation with the base umpire, the cry rang out, "See Opie, you get close to him and you stink, too!"

One of the most outspoken Bleacher Creatures, a man who could enervate the troops, was a big guy with a beard who wanted to be known simply as Bill. Just Bill. Bill, however, was an analytical guy. The way he told the story, the Bleacher Creatures actually helped young ballplayers' careers because of the hostile environment.

"If they can't take it here, they'll never go anywhere," said Bill.

Maybe so, but the fans' pet target one season disproved that theory. The fans thought the young man playing shortstop for the Anchorage Bucs was a prima donna. They decided the player, whose first name was Jeff, had rabbit ears and was easily bothered. They thought his manner was quite cocky and that irked them, too. So he was serenaded with "Jeff-rey," the entire game.

"Jeff just gets what he has coming," said Mr. Bill.

The fans had their fun, but "Jeffrey" had the last laugh. Jeff Kent is now an all-star second baseman for the San Francisco Giants.

No one got more satisfaction than Zaborac when the 1987 Miners won the NBC title. It was validation. As national champion, the Miners matched the top achievement of the older teams.

The Miners of that summer were a comeback team, high-scoring and persistent. That might well be when the enduring, Miner-identified phrase "Rally in the Valley!" was pronounced for the first time.

"The 1987 team was a team that if we were within four or five runs after the seventh inning, the chances were we were going to win," said Zaborac.

The irony was that when the season began the Miners had no idea what to expect. Manager Jim Fleming, from Pima Community College in Arizona, pieced together what he thought would be a fine team. But then two players signed professional contracts and three players joined Team USA, the national team made up of the top amateur prospects in the country that is often the core of the next Olympic team.

"It's a mess," said Fleming at the beginning of the season. "We've lost so many guys, we've had to scramble to pick up some."

Compounding the confusion, 1987 was a year that the Alaska league decided to downsize from twenty-four to twenty-one-man rosters. That meant players had to be more versatile. Typically, teams that summer went with a dozen fielders and nine pitchers.

"I think almost every one of our position players can play two positions and do it adequately," said Fleming.

By the time Fleming finished scrambling, he had enough guys who could do it all. The Miners led the league's old Continental Division from opening day. By July, the Miners were 17-4. Although they later lost eight straight games and saw their lead over the Anchorage Bucs shrink to a half game in the standings, they righted themselves and qualified for their first-ever trip to the NBC. They went to Wichita unseeded, an Alaska team nobody really knew.

Although neither player ever made the majors, Mat-Su did have some heavy-duty weapons in first baseman Ken Kremer and designated hitter John Byington, who both were All-Alaska first-team selections. Kremer was the Most Valuable Player, rewarded for a season in which he hit 15 home runs and drove in 64 in just forty-three games.

Kremer came out of Rider College in New Jersey and was one of Fleming's late pickups. The player knew the Alaska league's rep in advance and said he wondered how he would fare.

"I thought, 'Wow, this is gonna be tough,' " said Kremer.

Instead, he made swinging the bat look easy.

After their late-season stumble, the Miners got hot in the always-hot late-summer climate of Kansas. The team scratched for runs in many ways and Kremer hammered pitching as he had done all season. The Miners bested Santa Maria, an NBC regular, and beat a Nevada club. A loss to the perennially tough Liberal Bee Jays dropped the Miners into the losers' bracket, and they were in jeopardy of being sent home, but they fought back from that. A convincing, 18-4 win over Red Oak, Iowa, put the Miners in the title game, fooling the seeding experts.

On championship game night, devoted Bleacher Creatures huddled forty strong at the Pioneer Bar in Palmer, sharing enthusiasm and beers as KABN radio broadcast the game. Fans shouted their usual taunts at umpires on the radio as if they could hear them. They chanted their favorite sayings, especially the famous "Rally in the Valley!" staple.

The Miners met the Wichita Broncos for the title, and the sweetest part of winning it all for Zaborac was how his club hung together in the face of possible doom.

"The way we won...," said Zaborac, smiling at the memory years later.

The Miners took an 11-8 lead into the ninth inning. Then the first three Wichita hitters loaded the bases against reliever John Hudson. Crisis time. The tension was extraordinary. Hudson fanned Wichita's leading tournament batter, Scott Childress, on a called third strike, and then wiped out the next hitter on a double play.

Now that's a relief pitcher who deserved the reward of a save.

In Palmer, champagne was served on the house and fans shouted their allegiance: "Miners!"

The Miners were the champs, making it to the top with balance more than superb individual talent. In a league where players head to the majors routinely, the Miners excelled without future stars.

"Not one of those kids made the big-time," said Zaborac.

On that August night, though, the Miners did.

13

THE NORTH POLE NICKS

They were more real than Santa

SANTA CLAUS swinging a bat. When the T-shirts appeared in the early 1980s as a promotional item for the North Pole Nicks, they produced chuckles. Who else had Santa Claus for a mascot?

If baseball fans laughed when they heard about the Valley Green Giants, they merely shook their heads in disbelief when they heard about the North Pole Nicks. They play baseball at the North Pole?

Of course, the North Pole Nicks were not located at the North Pole. The North Pole Nicks were located in North Pole. North Pole, Alaska, a genuine community with something on the order of a thousand-plus people, situated roughly fifteen miles from Fairbanks' Growden Park. Although the mythical Santa Claus did not reside in this North Pole, there was a famous Santa Claus House that enticed tourists to the neighhorhood with the aim of convincing them he really did. It was the grandest landmark in town.

The Nicks (short for Saint Nick, naturally), like so many of the Alaska teams, were the brainchild of Don Dennis. The more teams the growing population could support, the better for all, was the notion. And if the people of the Mat-Su Valley found long-distance management distasteful, at least in the case of North Pole, it would be right-around-the-corner management help. The Nicks would play their home games at Growden, sharing the field with the Goldpanners. That meant many fewer dark nights at the stadium during the height of the busy summer season. Though given the fact that it was Fairbanks in summer, dark may not have been the proper word.

North Pole Nicks. You had to give the founders points for cleverness. Even if the place was real some baseball fans didn't believe it. Still, when they asked, "North Pole?" there was great satisfaction in being able to reply, "Yeah, that's where we're from."

John Lohrke came to North Pole from Santa Clara University in 1980 to help get the new club going and ended up becoming general manager, a year-round resident of Alaska, and everything from a radio voice to the statistician for the team. Now president of the Peninsula Oilers, Lohrke said the North Pole Nicks' name got attention wherever the team went.

"Especially when we went to Wichita," said Lohrke. "We played it up. Santa Claus as our mascot and our colors were red and green in 1985. We were voted best-dressed. It's hard to match the nickname."

Baseball was big in the household when Lohrke, who now works for a car dealership on the Kenai Peninsula, was growing up. His dad, Jack, was a Major League infielder with the New York Giants and Philadelphia Phillies between 1947 and 1952.

"My dad knew enough about baseball and summer ball and college ball that he felt it was great this kid who just graduated from college was going to do something in the game," said Lohrke.

Lohrke's involvement in Alaska baseball stemmed from his involvement with Jerry McClain, then the Santa Clara coach. McClain was the Nicks' first coach and urged Lohrke, who worked in the school's sports information office, to join him for the adventure. It didn't matter what his title was supposed to be, the thinly staffed Nicks needed help on all fronts, so Lohrke did everything from handle the public address system to color analysis with play-by-play man Lowell Purcell, the long-time Fairbanks broadcaster.

Lohrke roomed with one of the team's assistant coaches, so he knew all the team signs. That made for some slick broadcasting prognosticating in key situations.

"I had Lowell thinking I'm a genius," said Lohrke.

It was a fun time, starting something from scratch, building it. Dennis really made it all happen, though. He ordered the uniforms and provided the gear so the Nicks could play. He planned their initial schedule, booked them in the ballpark.

"The first year we helped guide the development of the team," said Dennis.

Ralph Seekins, a prominent Fairbanks businessman, shifted from the Goldpanners' board of directors to the Nicks' board of directors. Dennis recruited McClain to manage because he'd already managed in the league with the Miners.

"They started on a shoestring," said Dennis, who sounded wistful about that period of Fairbanks-area baseball. "Those were the wonder years. We had a game out here every night."

The Goldpanners operated the concession stands and gave the Nicks thirty-five percent of the gross.

"We could mother hen them when they were here," said Dennis.

Originally, when all games were at Growden, the Goldpanners had a season-ticket offer that included Nicks' season tickets, too, for just $15 additional.

Purcell can vouch for the feeling of operating day-to-day without much money. His wallet kept reminding him that he was not employed by IBM.

"We were totally underfunded," said Purcell. "I was hoping I'd get paid at the end of the season."

The first Nicks team gathered in San Francisco and played some games against the Humboldt Crabs. The players had a sense of amazement that they were on their way to an honest-to-goodness place called North Pole. Repeatedly, anyone affiliated with the club had to assure doubters that North Pole was indeed a real town, not just a patch of ice squeezed onto the very top of maps. Santa Claus was a help in his own way, sort of a symbol that everyone could identify with if they believed the place existed or not.

"It was 'North Pole?' " said Purcell. " 'Oh, Santa Claus.' There is a North Pole."

The first season went well. The Nicks were pretty solid, but like the Valley Green Giants before them, they couldn't cope with the Goldpanners most nights.

"The Goldpanners won the national championship," said Lohrke. "We played them fourteen times and lost ten of fourteen. But the first night we played them and beat them."

McClain coached the Nicks for two years and was succeeded by Dan Cowgill, who years later took over the Goldpanners. In 1983, Mike Gillespie assumed command. Gillespie ran the club through 1985, then became head coach at Southern Cal, where he won the NCAA title in 1998.

Lohrke, who came to North Pole on somewhat of a lark, was approached by Dennis near the end of the 1980 season and offered the job of general manager. He returned to California at season's end, then moved to Alaska March 1, 1981, and has been a resident ever since. He was twenty-four years old and giddy.

"You get to run a baseball team," said Lohrke. "I just had seven or eight years of bliss."

One of Lohrke's tasks was helping to recruit against the better-known Goldpanners, Glacier Pilots and Oilers, as well as the Giants-turned-Miners. Another Alaska team, the Anchorage Bucs, was forming, and also about to start crowding the marketplace. College coaches knew the older teams' reputations, but the North Pole Nicks? Lohrke sold the Nicks as being part of the league with those other teams.

That made it OK, he said.

And the Nicks did more than OK. Although the Nicks' run ended after the 1987 season, there are still some former North Pole players in the majors. Chicago Cubs' all-star first baseman Mark Grace is the Nick who has done the greatest things. But Todd Zeile, Eric Karros, Luis Gonzalez (who had an all-star season in 1999), Steve Finley and Chad Kreuter were all still active in the big-time as the century turned. Kreuter, a catcher for the Kansas City Royals, married Gillespie's daughter.

Kreuter, who played for the Kansas City Royals in 1999, was given a summer job as a pro at the par-3 Arctic Acres golf course. Gillespie told him his kids were coming for a visit and asked Kreuter to give them putting lessons. Kreuter thought he was being drafted into a babysitting job and wanted to duck it. But when he slyly approached one of the little brothers and asked to see a picture of his sister, he was sold. Turned out Sis was about twenty years old, roughly his age, and he liked Kelly's looks so well he suddenly became eager to help her with her swing.

Nice little romance story there, but more amazing was that North Pole had a place to play golf.

"We called it the North Pole Country Club," said Kreuter.

Heck, when he and other players first were told they were going to play baseball in North Pole, they wondered if people even lived there.

"People don't think there is such a place," said Kreuter. "You say it's near Fairbanks and you build from there."

Kreuter played two seasons for the Nicks. His second summer he and several other players were assigned the task of building a duplex that was to be auctioned off to raise money for the team.

"By the end of the summer, we knew how to handle hammers and saws," said Kreuter. "We called ourselves "The Hammer Crew."

In fact, the carpentry lessons continue to pay off for Kreuter. Not so long ago he built his own deck using the skills developed in Alaska.

Gillespie signed on to manage North Pole after being prodded by Cowgill, whom he knew from California.

"I knew nothing about it," said Gillespie, speaking from his Los Angeles

When the North Pole Nicks were new at Newby, longtime broadcaster Lowell Purcell supplied the play-by-play. He still does play-by-play and PA announcing for the Goldpanners. LEW FREEDMAN

office fifteen years after he journeyed to Alaska for his first North Pole season. "I felt like a pioneer."

When he was told the team was called the North Pole Nicks, Gillespie said, "I thought they were kidding." Gillespie found that any time he mentioned his Alaska team people were skeptical about the name.

"They'd go, 'Sure,' " he said.

Even in 1985, when the best Nicks team showed up for the NBC tournament, a place where Alaska teams were known and appreciated, it was the same old thing. People didn't think the name was serious. Of course the way that team competed it didn't take long to recognize those guys were more serious than the IRS.

"That was a good club," said Gillespie. "It was an outstanding team. That team played defense anybody would have been proud of."

The 1985 Nicks put such players as Zeile, now with the New York Mets, Grace, and Andy Stankewicz, another future Major Leaguer, on the field and advanced to the NBC championship game.

Grace, then attending San Diego State, swung a mean stick. He batted .367 with 52 RBIs in the regular season and was even better at the tournament. That summer he was called "Amazing Grace," or "Saving Grace." Then a centerfielder, Grace joked about the Wichita heat and humidity, even when the Nicks played late-night games.

"It must be ten o'clock at night and I'm still hot," said Grace, who missed the point. He was hot all of the time that season.

Glacier Pilots coach Jack O'Toole, doubling as a scout for the Montreal Expos, adored Grace's swing.

"I fell in love with Mark Grace," said O'Toole. "I got on the phone and said, 'There's a guy here who could be in the majors right now.' He made a little splash in Wichita."

Before one NBC game, when the managers met at home plate, they were blessed with a visit from a pro-Nicks Santa Claus.

"We thought that was pretty funny," said Grace.

Purcell said Grace was the true standout of the era.

"We'd just marvel at his power," said Purcell, although Grace is not known for hitting home runs in the majors. Purcell loved Stankewicz's desire, too. "He always impressed me. I never saw Andy walk anywhere. He would run up to the plate. He would run back to the dugout. I thought, 'This kid is going to make it somewhere.' "

Stankewicz did, playing third base for several big-league organizations.

Gillespie remembers the 1985 bunch very fondly.

"That was a fun group to work with," he said.

Dennis was impressed with how Gillespie motivated the Nicks, using the pretty-much-true angle that the Nicks were underdogs against older, richer franchises.

"Gillespie was good at playing the chip-on-the-shoulder," said Dennis. "The Big Bad Pilots. The Big Bad Goldpanners. He sold the poor, country cousin beating Fairbanks."

One of Lohrke's favorites was Steve Finley, now in the Arizona Diamondbacks' lineup, and he stayed in North Pole only half of the 1986 season.

"A great kid," said Lohrke. "He loved living with the family he had, he was leading us in hitting. And then he got a call from the national team to play for them. He said, 'I can't pass it up.' "

Zeile stayed a lot longer. He played two years for the Nicks and said Grace, Kreuter, and Gonzalez remain good friends from those days. Playing in Alaska also helped mature him and polish his talent.

"It was definitely a good baseball experience for me," said Zeile.

And like so many of the young men who go off to the north for what amounts to baseball summer camp, it was a pretty playful time, as well. Zeile went fishing, and took pictures of moose and caribou. He traveled to Denali National Park and was impressed by the major red salmon run in the area.

"They were stacked on top of each other," said Zeile.

Zeile also saved a souvenir Nicks jacket and hat. The hat features an 'N', the jacket, Santa Claus.

In two seasons with the Nicks, Zeile had two jobs, park maintanence and bus driver. He much preferred driving the bus. The bus was called The Blue Goose and Zeile's job on the day of home games was to drive house-to-house picking up the players.

"It was an easy job," said Zeile.

After the early years shakedown, the Nicks sought more independence from the Goldpanners. Up went Wright Field at Newby Park. Or Newby Field, as the place was commonly called.

Most stories about Newby are not flattering. Newby was never going to be mentioned in the same breath as Camden Yards or Safeco Field, the new Major League gems of the 1990s. For that matter, Newby was not going to be mentioned favorably in comparisons with any other park around the Alaska Baseball League.

Dave Foreman, the Pilots official who can be blunter than Howard Stern, summed up his view of Newby: "All the rain water drained to the infield. The fences were like a half mile out there. I think they built the mound out of sand. They had a Little League backstop."

Steve McFarland, a several-season Pilots manager, said two things stand out in his mind about road trips to North Pole. The players always went to the Santa Claus house for a little side tourist trip, and merely finding the field required a map and compass.

"I just remember driving out there in the middle of nowhere and there was this field in a forest of trees," said McFarland.

When the field was built, the outfield fences were apparently accidentally measured from the bases rather than home plate. That factored an additional ninety feet into the distances, making the distance for home runs more-or-less impossible. Hence the impression left with Foreman that the fences were a half mile away. They almost were. Pretty soon adjustments were made.

Lohrke gently admitted Newby beginnings were "funny and embarrassing." But he was also struck by how much local pride and excitement there was when the Nicks had a field to call their own and how thrilling it was when the Goldpanners came to their park for the first time.

Fans and team management were loath to let any victory over the "big-city" Goldpanners get away from them, thus resulting in a strange scene at one rain-drenched 1986 game. It was a close game in the sixth inning when a rain delay was declared.

"The Panners took their cleats off and got in their vans," said Lohrke. "We go, 'Wait a minute.' We poured some gasoline on the field and lit it. We scorched that field. We just had a bonfire for twenty minutes. We dried it out. We had to rake it like crazy. It wasn't pretty, but it was playable. They had to put their cleats on and we ended up beating them."

Newby may not have been a palace, but it was home and Purcell claims that in its heyday it was a nice place. That heyday has passed, though, and when Purcell, still a major sports broadcasting figure in Fairbanks, traveled the short distance to Newby for a high school game a few years ago, he felt a little sad. The scoreboard didn't work. The press box he used in the past was a concession stand.

Lohrke always maintained a wry perspective.

Once the Nicks and Pilots had a misunderstanding over the starting time of a July 4 game. Lohrke was sure the game was scheduled for 7 P.M., so he sent the team off on the bus early in the morning with the idea they'd arrive in Anchorage in plenty of time. The phone rang at 11 A.M. It was the Pilots calling, asking where the Nicks were for the soon-to-start afternoon game. Somebody goofed.

"I said, 'I can't get them there any faster,' " said Lohrke.

Lohrke was doing radio when Newby opened and the team president threw out the first ball. Lohrke was amazed to see the ball thrown from the plate to the mound and he blurted over the air, "Are we a rinky-dink operation, or what?" Then they cut to a commercial. Players and coaches stared at the backwards scene and shook their heads.

Lohrke evolved into the Nicks' one-man gang. The on-field season lasted about two months, but his season was never ending. He oversaw everything, which was a blast. As he reached his thirtieth birthday, though, Lohrke began thinking he needed a career that offered a little more money.

"With non-profits, it's usually a few people doing the work," said Lohrke. "I don't want to sound selfish, but with North Pole it was me."

Simultaneously, the Nicks ran into financial trouble. The team had a great run at the NBC crown in 1985 and returned to the tournament in 1987. Perhaps they shouldn't have gone. The Nicks lost two straight on the very costly excursion.

"They let emotion get in their way," said Dennis. "The last trip to Wichita they were out of there in sixteen hours."

Lohrke tried to arrange a smooth management transition. He hired a manager, recruited a team. Everything was set.

"We would have been all right in 1988," said Lohrke. "We got to within six weeks of the season and the people of North Pole said, 'There's no way we can afford to field a team.' "

That was the most tumultuous summer in Alaska baseball history. Money was tight all over. In the end, the Anchorage Bucs, the Anchorage Glacier Pilots, the Mat-Su Miners and the North Pole Nicks fielded no squads in 1988. The Goldpanners and the Oilers played a schedule against non-Alaska teams.

All of the other franchises returned to the league, strengthened, in 1989. The North Pole Nicks went out of business.

"Unfortunately," said Gillespie, who still laments the club's passing and said with nostalgia he still checks the weather reports for the area. "It was a monumental effort on the part of a few community members. John Lohrke was kind of the guts of that team. Trying to shoestring it together, it was a battle."

Lohrke went to work for Ralph Seekins, who owns Alaska car dealerships, and moved more than five hundred miles south to the Kenai Peninsula. Once established in his professional life, he rekindled his connection to Alaska baseball and by 1998, at forty-one, he was president of the Oilers.

The Nicks, though, will always occupy a special place in his heart.

"It was just a hobby and I had a ball," said Lohrke. "I dearly loved it."

He doubts the same kind of run-the-whole-show, take-a-team-from-paper-to-the-field experience of North Pole is in the cards for him again.

"I have no desire to start the Alaska Indians or the Barrow Bruins," said Lohrke. He paused. "You never know, though."

Especially not in Alaska baseball.

14

THE ANCHORAGE BUCS

They wouldn't take "no" for an answer

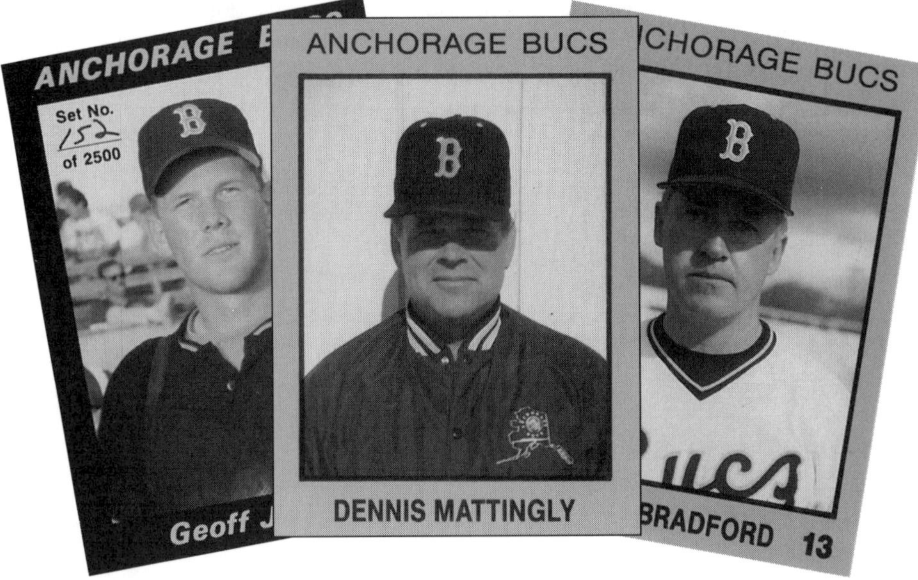

THEY SHOULDN'T have made Dennis Mattingly mad.

That might be the biggest mistake the Anchorage Glacier Pilots ever committed. But the Pilots' loss was Alaska baseball's gain.

The Anchorage Bucs were formed because Joe Armstrong wouldn't take Dennis Mattingly seriously, wouldn't even treat him politely. Armstrong's worst nightmare was not even in Mattingly's head in 1980 when he sought to pit his Anchorage Adult League team against the Pilots for a few games. He wasn't planning to grow into a full-fledged in-town ABL competitor. But he didn't like being snubbed and what began as let's-see-where-we-stand-against-the-big-boys curiosity quickly turned Anchorage into a two-baseball-team town.

In 1979, Mattingly was catcher and coach for a very good team playing in Anchorage's rec league. Growing up in Missouri, Mattingly loved baseball and loved the St. Louis Cardinals. He introduced his sons to the sport and in the 1970s he coached West and Bartlett among Anchorage American Legion teams.

Short but strongly built, Mattingly is ruddy-faced and plainspoken, with a whipsaw arm. Now in his early fifties, he still enjoyed pitching batting practice for the Bucs when he was well into his forties. By the end of the 1970s, though, Mattingly's knees were wearing down from too much time behind the plate and he joined the everyday lineup primarily when his team was shorthanded.

"I didn't want to kneel down anymore," said Mattingly.

Mattingly's team was so good that it had no genuine competition in the city league. He talked it over with his sponsor, Lanny Siegel, a sporting goods store owner whose son Wade played on the team, and Mattingly decided in 1980 to try and schedule games with the Oilers and Pilots.

When Mattingly approached Armstrong, the Pilots' president, Armstrong went ballistic.

"What are you trying to do, young man?" said Armstrong.

Mattingly wasn't trying to do anything except provide his team with better games, and he said so.

"I guess he thought I was trying to move in and take over," said Mattingly.

Armstrong's intransigence irritated Mattingly. Max Swearingen, then the general manager of the Oilers, said sure, the Oilers would play the Bucs. Mattingly approached the Mat-Su Miners and they agreed to play him, too. Good enough.

The Bucs, or Buccaneers, were named by Wade Siegel. They had black uniforms and the name and outfits matched. The roster was made up mostly of homegrown Alaska players and a few junior college players from the lower forty-eight who had friends on the team. Mattingly, then thirty-one, was the oldest player by far. Satisfied with games against the Oilers and Miners, Mattingly hyped the matchups. Then, two days before the Bucs were scheduled in Kenai for a doubleheader, Swearingen called.

"Dennis," he said, "I can't play you these games. The league decided they're not going to honor you."

Then Mat-Su pulled out.

Mattingly was furious.

"It really upset me," he said. "It made me look like a fool. Later on it was admitted to me that 'they didn't want to give you exposure.' "

Who? Clearly, the Pilots were the only ones who cared about such a thing.

Mattingly pursued another avenue. Fairbanks and North Pole agreed to play the Bucs. So the Bucs, featuring the locals, abetted by the junior-college guys, formed a three-car caravan for the long ride north.

"I bought the gas," said Mattingly. "I put up the meal money."

The nobody Bucs split with North Pole, which royally ticked off coach Jerry McClain.

"We went out to McDonald's and when we came back they were still running in the outfield," said Mattingly.

The Bucs did not beat Fairbanks, but they came close, falling 17-13.

"We stayed with them," said Mattingly. "We were just tickled to death."

The Goldpanners won the NBC title that year, so it truly was a moral victory. The trip made Mattingly believe that the Bucs, who won the Adult League championship and finished 17-2 at that level, could become something more. Wade Siegel assured Mattingly he could find several collegians willing to pay their own way to Alaska to play.

The Bucs took the plunge. At about that time the first major schisms appeared in relations between Alaska league teams. Disagreements were rampant over how to run the league. The Goldpanners and North Pole Nicks wanted an ally in disputes with the Miners, Pilots and Oilers. So the Bucs were accepted by the northern teams, who didn't care if the Pilots were disenchanted or not.

Mattingly was a baseball man. Jack Powers, the team's early president, offered just the spark the club needed off the field.

Powers grew up in Pittsburgh, a big fan of the Pirates. He sold hot dogs at Forbes Field as a youth, worked the midway for the circus and worked on the boardwalk at Atlantic City. He is not kidding when he calls himself a carnival man. Powers had great promotional instincts and a love of the game. He was intrigued by the Alaska league scene and was friendly with Joe Armstrong. But the Pilots were a closed shop, he said.

"I was never invited to be part of the Anchorage Glacier Pilots," said Powers.

Powers, now in his late fifties, said a group of five Bucs supporters met at a restaurant and while drinking coffee talked about what type of commitment it would take to lift the Bucs from the Adult League to the Alaska Baseball League. Armstrong's vehement reaction to their initial league petition made a huge impression on Powers.

Sitting with Armstrong at the bar at Club Paris, Anchorage's best restaurant, the Pilots chief became enraged.

"He said, 'I'm gonna bury you guys,' " said Powers. " 'I'm gonna bury you guys before you get started.' "

That only motivated Powers and the partners to work harder. At that time Powers worked for the local telephone company, but he handled the team presidency for a half dozen years and then spent five more years as promotions director: eleven years in team management in all. Some people think Powers designed the Bucs uniforms because of his devotion to the Pirates, but the team already had the name.

As the pace quickened approaching opening day 1981, and the vastness of the task became a reality, there was a pervasive feeling of excitement, but also fear that the small group of Davids had taken on too much work and too many Goliaths.

Founder and general manager Dennis Mattingly has always been a driving force for the Anchorage Bucs—and an occasional batting practice pitcher. LEW FREEDMAN

"Our original program, it was done with a borrowed copy machine and we stapled it ourselves," said Powers of the first Bucs printed souvenir lineup card. "We had no office, not even a telephone number."

Using the name Cook Inlet Bucs, the team played a full ABL schedule under the direction of a young manager named Jim Coveney. Coveney, then twenty-six, and the head coach at Scottsdale Community College in Arizona, heard the Bucs needed a field boss and called Mattingly.

Just as Armstrong feared, the Bucs were now a viable property, moving into direct competition with the Pilots.

"He resented me very much," Mattingly said of Armstrong many years later. "I didn't understand it. They thought we were going to come in and steal the Pilots' thunder."

Mattingly thought that statement over and realized he had eventually done just that.

"I'm not saying we didn't steal some of the wind out of their sails," he said.

For two seasons there was a feeling amongst Bucs officials that they might be in over their heads. When would they win? When would people come?

Then, in 1983, the Bucs blossomed into a first-rate team and qualified to go to Wichita as one of two Alaska Baseball League representatives at the NBC tournament. It took a doubleheader victory over North Pole on the season's last night, but it was a thrill for the young organization.

Wichita? The NBC? The Bucs hadn't given it much thought, but they had earned the right to play for the national championship.

"I heard a lot about it," said Mattingly. "That seemed to be the big thing to do."

There was just one problem. The team didn't have the money for the trip. Powers said they "were tapped out."

A meeting of more than a dozen Bucs officials and key supporters was convened at a private home. How can we afford to go? How can we afford not to go? Jim Hayes, the owner of the El Toro Mexican restaurant in downtown Anchorage, was a club benefactor. It was also conceded he loved Dennis Mattingly like a son.

"Jim Hayes reaches down and brings up a paper bag," said Powers. "He says, 'Here's $10,000. Take the team to Wichita.' "

Mattingly took the team to Wichita. But it was a horrible experience. He worried about money every second. The Bucs won just enough (finishing tenth) to stay around too long.

"We stayed at the Holiday Slum Inn," said Mattingly, disparaging the cheap hotel the Bucs used. "Four guys to a room. My nerves were shattered just to get us there and back. We didn't have enough money, not even close. I had to come up with my own money, out of my own pocket, about $9,000."

Powers said team officials maxed out their credit cards to get everyone home when the team was eliminated.

The team's success brought credibility in the community, though. More experienced managers were hired, more prestigious players brought in. The Glacier Pilots were seen as the establishment team. At a time when oil money flowed and brought younger people to Alaska, the Bucs were seen as a hipper operation. Newcomers didn't know the Pilots were supposed to be the real deal and the Bucs the upstarts. All they knew was that the Bucs gave away free tickets, or two-for-one deals, and always seemed to have fun activities.

The Pilots believed the ballgame was the thing. Period. But the Bucs operated on the theory that it was OK to have a good time because of a promotion, and next time a fan might come just for the ballgame.

"I was always busy giving away groceries, or picking the Fan of the Day," said Powers.

Powers believed in co-promotions, selling the house to a business and letting it give away tickets. That's how the owner of a home furnishings store happened to throw out the first pitch one night.

"We packed the ballpark and it didn't cost us a dime," said Powers.

Powers rarely had time to get to know the players or even see the action. He scanned the grandstand looking for a likely suspect to receive a bouquet of flowers as Fan of the Day.

"I would look through the stands and pick people who just weren't happy about life," said Powers. "People who looked like they needed to be cheered up. Once, I picked an older lady and it turned out she was just out of the hospital the day before. She's crying and saying, 'You have just made my day.' You can't buy public relations like that."

Powers didn't know what to call it when Jerry Vasquez, an assistant coach, told him about his experience staying at a low-rent hotel in the downtown area. Vasquez was convinced the maid was stealing from him.

"These are college coaches, right?" said Powers. "Intelligent people. So Vasquez deliberately leaves his wallet and money on the dresser to prove it."

He returned to the hotel, and guess what? The money was gone.

"I said, 'You sure proved it,' " said Powers. "Just leave a $10 bill or something. I still think of it. He proved his theory all right."

Powers hosted up to four players a summer at his home in the team's early years, and Mattingly had more than that staying with him.

"It was like the Pennsylvania Railroad Station at Dennis' house," said Powers. "They were sleeping everywhere."

Although he did not maintain contact with players who ascended to the majors, Powers was surprised by an envelope he received years after hosting David Klipstein, a player who did play in the minors.

"Ten years later I received a piece of mail from his grandfather with a brand, new $10 bill in it, thanking me for being so nice to his grandson," said Powers. "I found that touching."

Powers didn't mind mixing humor with promotions. One year, Domino's Pizza was a sponsor and Powers was listening to the Bucs game being broadcast in Hawaii. Powers got on the phone and found the Domino's closest to Rainbow Stadium. Soon after, long-time broadcaster Ken Garland exclaimed on the air, "Hey, we've got a pizza from Jack Powers. That's one heck of a delivery from Anchorage, Alaska."

The pizza was hot. It made it within the parameters of the thirty-minute delivery guarantee, too.

Rarely did Powers stray into baseball business, but once a friend in Michigan tipped him about a pitcher who was both talented and would be good box office because he had only one hand. Powers tried to sell Mattingly on the player, but couldn't do it. It was Jim Abbott, the young man who won an Olympic gold medal and had a top-flight Major League career while inspiring millions of people.

"I remind Dennis of that," said Powers.

Although the people closest to the league knew that the Cook Inlet Bucs were based in Anchorage, any time the Bucs traveled, the geographic description did the team no good. Where is Cook Inlet? Is that a town? Cook Inlet is

Jack Powers served as president of the Bucs and came up with the marketing strategies that let them compete for Anchorage fans with the Glacier Pilots. Lew Freedman

the body of water that Anchorage is located on, though it extends for more than a hundred miles to the Kenai Peninsula. Mattingly said the Bucs were always supposed to be known as the Anchorage Cook Inlet Bucs, but when the incorporation papers were filed, a mistake was made.

By 1984, the team was pretty well recognized as the Anchorage Bucs and they were beginning to become well-known in college baseball circles. One great word-of-mouth advocate of the Bucs program is Chris Bradford, who first joined the club as a coach in 1983 and spent the 1984, 1986, 1989 and 1990 seasons in Anchorage, too.

Bradford, a high school teacher and baseball coach in Mountain View, California, got his introduction to Alaska baseball early. In the mid-1960s his California team played a series of games in Fairbanks and he never forgot his first flight to Alaska. The team flew from San Diego to Los Angeles to San Francisco to Portland to Seattle to Sitka to Anchorage to Fairbanks.

"I wrote it down," said Bradford. "People don't believe me. It was horrible. We got the major puddle jumper. It was an ocean jumper."

To ensure that the visitors had a good time and were no doubt perky for the games, they were whisked from the twelve-hour flight by bus to dorms at the University of Alaska Fairbanks, then shuttled directly to the Riverboat

Discovery for a tour that lasted four hours. No sleep was budgeted. The Goldpanners whipped them seven straight nights. Of course, the Goldpanners might have done that anyway since during that period Fairbanks was sending about ten players a year to the majors.

Bradford was with the Bucs when North Pole's Newby Field was unveiled and he said the description of the fences being in a galaxy far, far away is accurate. It was probably five hundred feet to the center field wall, he said.

"They were not really ready," said Bradford.

Driving back to Anchorage from another northern exposure, Bradford, the equipment manager, and other coaches hit a moose on the outskirts of Fairbanks. The collision resulted in about $1,500 in damage.

Bradford was on the Bucs bench for the inaugural appearance at Wichita and remembers the mood when the Bucs qualified and had no ready cash.

"It was mad panic time," said Bradford.

In the early rounds at the NBC tournament the schedule runs long. The Bucs had an 11:30 P.M. starting time against a team from St. Louis and the game went into extra innings. By the time the game wrapped up, it was 4:30 A.M. and there was no transportation handy.

"It was 102 degrees when we started and it was still 93 degrees at 4:30 when we finished," said Bradford. "We walked a mile-and-a-half back to the hotel."

It was the Wichita trip, Bradford is sure, that hastened the need to bury the Cook Inlet name.

"People started telling Dennis, 'You've got to call it Anchorage,' " said Bradford.

Soon enough, the Anchorage Bucs were on the map of amateur baseball in a big way. They went head-to-head successfully with the Glacier Pilots on the field and at the gate. Later, the Bucs invited Team USA to town and played the nation's top non-professional team tough. They also hosted the Silver Bullets, the all-women's team. The pattern was set. Play good ball against all comers and have a good time.

"I'm very proud of what I've accomplished," said Mattingly, almost two decades after the Pilots first suggested he take a hike. "We're equal, if not better. We think we do things pretty right around here."

Powers, who has slicked-back gray hair and blue eyes, remains a devoted baseball fan, but has gone on to other things. He runs a very large, popular bingo parlor. In the late 1990s, Powers found himself buying advertising in both Bucs and Pilots yearbooks. It was a circumstance he admitted was ironic: Jack Powers supporting the Pilots with his bankroll.

"I wouldn't have bet money on that," said Powers. "I'm wishing both teams well. It's good for the city of Anchorage."

15

STEVE AGBABA

Famous for his walkabouts and Wallbangers

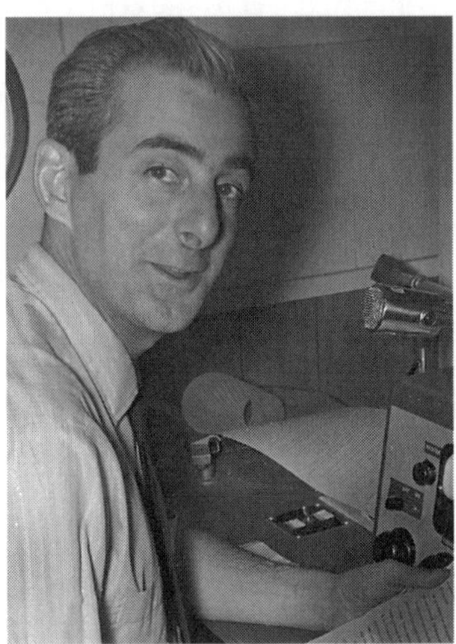

STEVE AGBABA'S nickname was "Agblabba" because he never shut up. He was a man of a million words who called himself a loudmouth. Fittingly, he made his career in radio, where a thousand words are worth one picture.

But simply characterizing Agbaba as a broadcaster would be like summing up Babe Ruth as merely an outfielder. Both descriptions would be true, but sorely lacking in details that round out the whole man.

Besides, if Ruth was the most important baseball player who ever lived, then Agbaba's Alaska Baseball League influence spread far beyond the sound of his own voice. For better or for worse, and some would most assuredly lean towards the latter, he was far more than just a guy speaking into a microphone.

Before he died in 1992, run down from diabetes, arthritis, and other ailments, Agbaba made his mark with quirky broadcasts, by nearly bankrupting the Anchorage Glacier Pilots in a single year as general manager, and by amazing fans, ballplayers and even the most casual observers with bold, brazen, but not always perfect promotional schemes.

Born talking. That was Steve Agbaba. He had joy in his heart and a gleam in his eye, and maybe a little larceny, too, though not in a mean-spirited way. He loved radio, baseball and poker, in addition to his wife Delphine, though nobody asked him to rank his devotions. He cut a path through life unbound by any rules that authorities wished to apply.

If he grew bored, or if someone set stricter boundaries than he was willing to abide by, he simply walked away. He was talented enough to be hired again somewhere. And sometimes hired again in the same place. It's said that one Alaska radio station hired and fired Agbaba seven different times. Absolutely possible, though the story may be apocryphal.

Agbaba was born Oct. 14, 1927, in Fairbanks and died just shy of his sixty-fifth birthday. In-between he had a rollicking good time, mostly in Alaska, periodically in Seattle. If his physical description of white hair and white beard fit an older man, in demeanor and outlook he probably more resembled a high school prankster.

"Too many people worry about their image," Agbaba once told a newspaper reporter. "I've never done this. I think we should laugh and giggle and have fun. People take life too seriously."

Dick Lobdell lived in Fairbanks in the early 1960s and that's where he first crossed Agbaba's path in 1961.

"I had heard about Agbaba," said Lobdell. "I heard of this legendary wild man Agbaba. I was told, 'You'll like him right away, but don't lend him any money.' He liked to play cards. He owed everybody in the state of Alaska money."

Indeed, Chuck Smith, who shared a city league basketball backcourt with Agbaba in Fairbanks in the 1950s, said he was once told a story that hinted at Agbaba's perpetual indebtedness. The way the story went, an Agbaba friend was headed to Juneau. Agbaba gave him ten dollars, with instructions to hand it to the first person he saw when he got off the plane.

"That doesn't make any sense," the man protested.

Agbaba said, "I owe everybody in the town money."

That tale may or may not be true, but Agbaba had so much charm that people hated to refuse his financial requests.

There were generally accepted rules governing broadcasting, but Agbaba set his own. He went on walkabouts while on the air, leaving his partner wondering whether to resume play-by-by. Agbaba might mosey off to the men's room and return an hour later. Smith said Agbaba acted the same way with the basketball and baseball teams they played on in Fairbanks. Agbaba was the shortstop "when he was there," said Smith.

One walkabout affected Lobdell when he was first paired with Agbaba as color man on high school basketball in Fairbanks. Agbaba didn't come back until the third quarter was under way—and he was mad at Lobdell for talking on air while he was gone.

"He just chewed me out up one side and down the other," said Lobdell. "I

When the Bucs wanted a new mascot in 1998. a research firm suggested a giant parrot. Local schoolchildren gave it a name: "Beekmin."

never figured that out. After that, if a station wouldn't send him to a basketball tournament, he'd quit. He probably worked for every radio station in the state of Alaska—twice."

According to Lobdell, Agbaba once stayed at a downtown Anchorage hotel for a week, running up an $800 bill on credit simply by repeatedly saying his radio station would cover everything. In the 1960s, $800 was a pretty serious hotel bill.

One of Agbaba's most memorable walkabouts occurred at the NBC in Wichita. Alaska listeners were stunned when a strange voice came on to call the action. Agbaba fled in mid-game, leaving the play-by-play to a teen-age boy in the vicinity.

"We had no idea what happened to Agbaba," said Lobdell. "There was no indication. Was he sick? Did he die? No one knew."

It turned out Agbaba discovered a hot poker game and couldn't wait to be dealt in.

Like Lobdell, Lowell Purcell was a newcomer to broadcasting in Fairbanks when he first met Agbaba, also in 1961, when he was seventeen.

"He took me under his wing," said Purcell, slender and dark-haired and now in his mid-fifties.

Purcell grew up in Sacramento, California. Inspired by the Pacific Coast League Solons' radio reports, he decided that describing ballgames was what he wanted to do for a living. By the age of six or seven he wrote out his own scripts for practice. At nineteen, Purcell was program director of his own station in Fairbanks, a station, he noted, that repeatedly hired and fired Steve Agbaba.

His baptism by Agbaba came two years before.

"We had done about four games together," said Purcell. "It was my job to read the commercials. We're in the middle of the fifth inning and all of a sudden Steve goes, 'Now with the play-by-play, here's Lowell Purcell' and he walks out! He wanted to break me in. He thought the best way to do it was to let me flounder. And boy, did I flounder. To this day it has to be the worst broadcast in the history of Alaska."

Agbaba gave up drinking March 4, 1966 (he readily reeled off the date), but if there was one thing he loved more than baseball on the radio, it was the sound of his own voice on the radio. He read personal messages and if they got in the way of the action, so be it. If he hadn't finished reading the messages and the game ended, he wouldn't sign off.

Off the air, Agbaba published "The Agbaba Gazette," more tidbits of gossip. He kept printing that newsletter for years, right up until his death.

"It was everyone from up and down the highway," said Jack Powers, the former Anchorage Bucs president who was a subscriber. "His private fan club."

Or private fun club. Worked both ways.

After all his years handling games, after all his years schmoozing, Agbaba was well known around the Alaska league. When the Pilots shopped for a general manager in 1984, they chose him. They faced a challenge from the Bucs and they were looking for creative ways to put butts in the seats.

That was Agbaba's pledge. And when the season began, the Pilots had nearly doubled their box-seat sales. They also had mascots (for lack of a better word) galore.

Agbaba tried to live up to his image as the king of promotion. So he introduced Wizo the Magic Clown. Wizo's job was to blow up ballons and do back flips for the amusement of youngsters. Agbaba also introduced Tyrone Wallbanger. Wallbanger's job was to dress as a super hero in a helmet and cape, then whenever a Pilot hit a home run, race all out down the right-field line and bash his head into Mulcahy Stadium's outfield fence.

It is doubtful any promotion as weird or baffling has ever occurred at another ballpark. Anyone who witnessed Wallbanger's stunt was agape.

Years later, San Francisco Giants pitcher Mark Gardner, who was a member of the Pilots that summer, remembered Wallbanger well.

Dick Lobdell, who in the 1950s played on the first Alaska American Legion team to travel outside the state, has been a broadcaster for both the Pilots and the Panners and is a board member for the Pilots. In his time, he's seen it all, from Steve Agbaba walkabouts to Tyrone Wallbanger. LEW FREEDMAN

"We thought it was pretty funny," said Gardner. "It was amusing."

Wallbanger's act did not wear well. Seeing him smash head-first into the wall left fans cringing as often as applauding.

Dave Foreman, a Pilots board member, grimaced every time Wallbanger banged a wall. He called Wallbanger "a nut case. That was the perfect, Agbaba over-the-top promotion. That pretty much stands alone. That was about the stupidest thing I remember."

Agbaba said there were more than a hundred complaints. Some fans said Wallbanger stood in their way during the action and others were annoyed by the way he beat his tambourine, never mind his head.

Agbaba admitted the mistake by firing Wallbanger less than a month into the season. "Tyrone's head has not been in the right place," Agbaba announced. "Tyrone hit his head eight times against the fence (behind home plate) and really frightened the fans sitting down there. He just got too obnoxious."

Wallbanger did not take his dismissal well. He picketed outside the ballpark. But there was no second chance for Wallbanger. Agbaba, apparently still not convinced the original concept was flawed, allowed a second, mysterious Wallbanger, wearing a mouse costume with a white dove on the shoulder, to assume the wallbanging for a time.

However, since 1984, anyone who hit his head against the outfield wall did so accidentally.

"What an episode," said Don Dennis, who watched from afar in Fairbanks.

Dennis Mattingly, the Bucs' long-time general manager, who believes in mascots as a way to make ballpark visits more of a family experience, couldn't get over Wallbanger's actions.

"Now there was a character," said Mattingly. "That was a creature. I thought he had a spring loose."

There was some general admiration for Agbaba's ways, though.

"In a lot of ways, old Steve was a visionary in getting into some of the promotional stuff he tried," said Stan Zaborac of the Miners.

Agbaba was hard to read if you worked for him, though.

Steve McFarland, the Pilots manager who later took the club to an NBC championship before moving into professional ball, called 1984 "a carnival atmosphere. Tyrone Wallbanger wanted more money because we were hitting too many home runs. He was a unique character."

McFarland, who in the summer of 1999 was a coach with the minor-league Lansing Lugnuts in Michigan, paused for a moment, then added that so was Agbaba.

During the 1984 season, the Pilots played the rival Goldpanners thirteen times. On the first trip to Fairbanks, the Pilots got smoked.

"We fell flat on our face," said McFarland. "When we came back Agbaba wouldn't talk to me."

During a four-game Anchorage series over July 4 weekend, the Pilots swept.

"Agbaba was sick and couldn't come to the games," said McFarland. "He told me to come over, and he goes, 'Here I am on my deathbed and you didn't even bring me a bowl of soup.' "

Tyrone Wallbanger notwithstanding, Agbaba got points for showmanship and over the years Anchorage baseball has had its flirtations with mascots and madmen, human performers and anthropomorphic creatures. No one felt there was anything wrong with trying to spice up a baseball game, as long as it did not detract from the sport.

Max Patkin is the most famous of all acts who have worked the baseball circuit, from the minors to the majors, from Florida to Alaska. He played Mulcahy Stadium and Growden Park in the 1980s.

Patkin, who died in 1999 at the age of 79, performed at ballgames for more than fifty years. He wore a uniform which featured a "?" on the back in lieu of a number. As The Clown Prince of Baseball, he did 3,500 shows and traveled about five million miles. The rubbery-faced and rubbery-armed Patkin teased umpires and players, made fun of himself and fooled around on the sidelines and at selected moments, on the field. He was sort of a one-man Harlem Globetrotters.

"The crowd treated me great," said Patkin in a 1998 interview of his Alaska sojourn. "It's the longest trip I ever took in my life. I enjoyed my trip there. It was wonderful."

Patkin was paid $1,000-plus for his trouble and was savvy enough to realize he wouldn't be snowed on in summer. That did happen to him once, though, in Lethbridge, Alberta. Although Patkin claims to have met just about every ballplayer who has played since World War II, his appearance in Alaska was fresh.

"They didn't know who I was up there," said Patkin. "I was new. I came in, rested, and went to the ballpark. I bragged about playing Alaska. No one knew they had ballclubs up there."

It was not professional baseball, either Major League or minor league. But that didn't stop "The Chicken" from coming, either. What came first, the chicken or the Ted? Actually, that's about as tough to answer as the original riddle. The Chicken was birthed as the San Diego Chicken, affiliated with the San Diego Padres. Performer Ted Gianoulas proved so popular he went out on his own and became known as the Famous Chicken.

The furry yellow Chicken did his funky dances and his umpire-baiting, player-teasing routines at Mulcahy on behalf of the Anchorage Bucs for the first time in 1982. He came back more than once. Sometimes The Chicken pulled out a foam-rubber umpire and swatted it around while the song "Whip it" played. Once he dressed four youngsters as baby chickens and used them to play follow-the-leader. The Chicken was wildly popular, drawing thousands.

"The Chicken cost $6,000," said Powers. "They (his board members) thought I was nuts. But we grossed $12,000. Is that nuts?"

Mark O'Brien, a Bucs coach during one fowl visit, participated in on-field routines with the Chicken, and he enjoyed it. O'Brien believes mascots of all types can serve a purpose and generate energy among fans.

"It's a transfer of electricity," said O'Brien. "He gives it to the fans, they give it to us."

After the Agbaba days, the Glacier Pilots steered clear of mascots and such gimmicks, but the Bucs plunged right in.

Actually, the Bucs featured Frenchy The Pirate as an "official mascot" in the early 1980s, a young woman who wore a pirate hat and carried a parrot.

Powers was never shy trying to sell the product. As a young teenager he worked the carnival midway for the Ringling Brothers Circus.

"I was a huckster, not a hustler," said Powers. "A hustler takes advantage of you. A huckster is just a good, good marketing machine."

Frenchy was the forerunner of Captain Bucco. For several years in the 1990s, the Bucs hired a local actor to play Captain Bucco, another pirate. Captain Bucco had his own theme song. The song suggested Captain Bucco would lead the team to victory and help the Bucs make history, even if he never threw a pitch or swung at one.

Captain Bucco wore a patch over one eye, a yellow bandana with black polka dots and a sword on his hip. He carried a bullhorn and yelled "G-o-o, Bucs. G-o-o, Bucs." He danced on top of dugouts between innings and hugged children between plays. Captain Bucco toted around a little cloth parrot, too.

Kids loved him. The players didn't mind Captain Bucco, either.

"He adds a little to the game," said Bucs outfielder Chad Alexander during the 1994 season. "He's great for the kids. I've only seen mascots on TV in the majors."

Sometimes, though, Captain Bucco was heckled by adults, like the time he wrapped up the famed lyrics during a "Take-me-out-to-the-ballgame" sing-a-long and a fan shouted, "I don't care if you ever come back." At least once an adult asked if he knew Captain Hook personally.

Captain Bucco also got the wave going at times, though once again that left him open to criticism from a heckler, who instructed "Wave goodbye!"

All hazards of the trade. There's no doubt Captain Bucco made more child friends than Tyrone Wallbanger did.

In 1984, when Agbaba dreamed up Tyrone Wallbanger, he was just winging it. Few teams had mascots. By 1998 when the Bucs replaced Captain Bucco, a scientific survey was involved. Bucs' executive director Brian Crawford consulted a Calgary, Alberta-based research firm.

"They suggested we go with some kind of animal, rather than a human-type character," said Crawford. "They faxed a drawing and it looked good."

Voila, off the drawing board to reality came an extra-large parrot. The red-and-purple parrot (operating with a human inside the suit) wore a giant pirate hat and carried a fuzzy sword. Some 20,000 Anchorage elementary-school kids were asked to vote on what the parrot's name should be.

The parrot was christened "Beekmin."

The sophistication of the mascot-choosing business has come a long way since Tyrone Wallbanger.

Life with Agbaba was always an adventure. He looked at life as a broad canvas and his own brush strokes pretty much amounted to an impressionist painting. Which was probably fine for entertaining on radio, but wasn't so hot for running a ballclub where he was supposed to pay attention to the bottom line.

Agbaba's tenure as Pilots' general manager lasted about a year, but he ran up more than $100,000 worth of debt, and it took the team several years to work it off.

"He had a smile on his face. He's one of those guys whose personable and likeable," said Dick Lobdell. "But boy, I'll tell you, he almost wrecked the Pilots."

Agbaba retreated to radio, and eventually to Washington. He never really left baseball, though. He was a fan and follower to the end.

"He was always real proud of the fact he'd done baseball for forty years," said Chuck Tozer, a former Bucs broadcaster. "I think the fondest memories I have of Steve are talking baseball. I never knew anyone who had as good a time."

That was a worthy epitaph for Steve Agbaba.

16

THE BUCS VS. THE PILOTS

Competition breeds quality

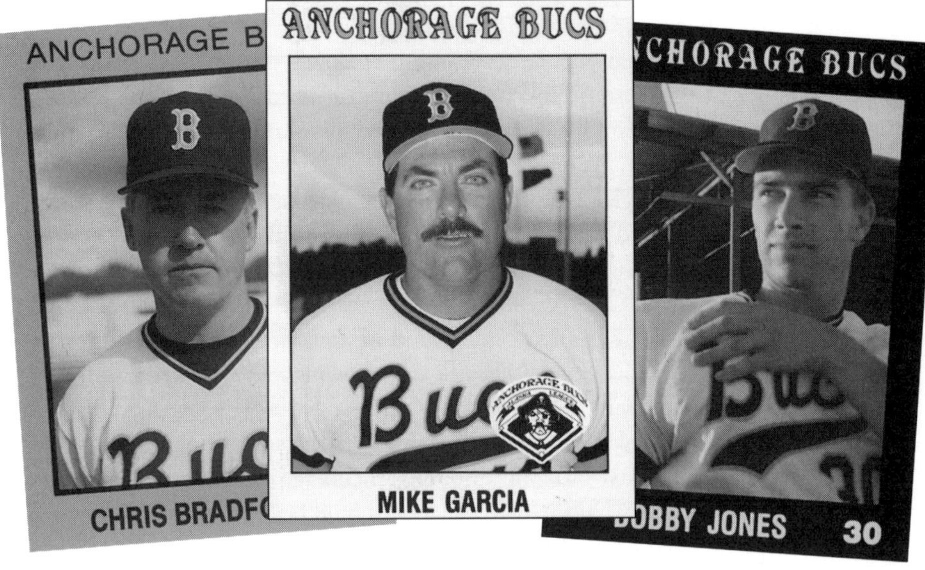

AS A PLAYER, Mark O'Brien was the second coming of his idol Pete Rose. The way he hustled on the field, running everywhere. The way he got his jersey so dirty the best detergents couldn't clean it without trouble. He couldn't hit like Pete Rose (who could?), but he was the type of guy other baseball people sagely described as great managerial material.

They were right.

He was also Mr. Buc. If general manager Dennis Mattingly is the founding father of the Bucs and the continuing inspiration, O'Brien is his most devoted disciple. He played for the Bucs, served as a coach, and when Mattingly needed a field boss a few years ago he turned to the man hungriest for the job.

On the June, 1996, day when O'Brien made his managerial debut, he posted his lineup on the third-base dugout wall of Mulcahy Stadium three hours before the game.

"That was the first lineup card I put up that I made," said O'Brien.

It was a proud moment. He was twenty-seven years old.

"I've been an assistant all my life," said O'Brien. "Now I get to do my thing."

Anyone who came into contact with O'Brien was sure he would do things with energy and ebullience. He is such an upbeat guy that he makes Ernie Banks seem like a grump. If you are looking for a spark, you can either rub two sticks together or call Mark "OB" O'Brien.

"OB is a fiery guy," said Pepper Arredondo, a two-year Bucs infielder. "He motivates you."

Players are embarrassed not to hustle in OB's presence. If Rose's nickname wasn't "Charlie Hustle," it would be applied to O'Brien. O'Brien always wore a No. 14 uniform jersey in homage to Rose and he even carried a biography of Rose with him on the road.

O'Brien played second base for the Bucs for two full years and part of another, served as a Bucs coach for two years, and then became manager.

The Bucs beat the Mat-Su Miners, 6-5, to make O'Brien's debut a pleasant one and he saved the ball that made the last out.

"I think I'm gonna remember this night," said O'Brien.

O'Brien had a memorable two-year run as field boss of the Bucs, and then after the 1997 season had to tell Mattingly he could not return because he was becoming the head baseball coach at DeAnza College, a good professional opportunity. It was with tremendous sadness that O'Brien faced the summer of 1998—with obligations in California instead of Alaska.

"I don't know what I'm gonna do," he said. "I'm gonna be going crazy. The Anchorage Bucs have done so much for me."

O'Brien did a great deal for the Bucs, as well. He played his high school ball for Chris Bradford, the former Bucs assistant coach, but he was a DeAnza student in 1990 when the Bucs stopped in the neighborhood to play some early-season games. O'Brien was on the other team.

"I had a great series," said O'Brien. "Eight for eleven, or something. They were looking for a second baseman. Two days later, Dennis Mattingly called me.'"

O'Brien became a regular on some of the greatest Bucs teams. The Bucs were awesomely talented at the turn of the decade under Mike Garcia. Garcia, a former AAA infielder in the Atlanta Braves' organization, is now athletic director and baseball coach at Canada College in California.

Actually, even before the great run that spanned 1989-1992, the Bucs featured players starting to make major marks in the Major Leagues.

Wally Joyner, later an impressive power hitter with the Angels and other teams, had a poor season in Anchorage, but was one of Mattingly's favorites.

"Wally is a great guy," said Mattingly. "He played Nintendo baseball with my kids. He had a pretty miserable year, though. He hit about .210."

Anthony Telford was a dominating pitcher for the Bucs in the mid-1980s and has had a successful career throwing middle relief with the Baltimore Orioles and the Montreal Expos.

"That's the only guy who made it to the major leagues who sent me an autographed picture," said Mattingly.

After the 1989-92 stretch, there would be other several other Buc major leaguers.

In 1989, the Bucs won the league title with pitcher Doug Tegtmeier of Nebraska going 10-0 and catcher Troy Buckley driving in a team record 75 RBIs. Buckley was from Santa Clara, where he is now an assistant coach. The team finished 42-17.

Garcia was matched with the Bucs by Bradford, who seems to know everyone in baseball. Garcia was a star player at Fullerton State and played for the Peninsula Oilers in 1976. He once described himself as "a Mark O'Brien," the type of guy who had to hustle his butt off in order to stay around. Garcia stayed around the Braves's minor-league system for six years.

In Garcia's first season at the Bucs' helm, there was one player who was a cancer on the team. When Garcia sent him home, the team won sixteen games in a row.

"He was killing team chemistry," said Garcia. "We had real talented people who were team guys."

Players like Kevin Jordan, now with the Philadelphia Phillies.

Jordan said there remains a bond among ballplayers who played in Alaska.

"When I talk to guys who said they played there, it's 'Hey,' " he said. "I had a good time. We went fishing on the Russian River at midnight. It was supposed to be midnight. It was like daytime."

It was a tremendous season, but then the Bucs got better after that.

In 1990, O'Brien's first season, the Bucs were 49-13, at one point winning seventeen straight. They went 10-0 against the Goldpanners. Outfielder Calvin Murray, called up to the San Francisco Giants in 1999, was not only the Alaska player-of-the-year, but the nation's summer player-of-the-year. Murray stole a team-record 42 bases, drove in 47 runs as a leadoff man, and hit .371.

Murray once said he was frustrated in college because he was sometimes reined in.

"At times I couldn't wait to get to Alaska, where they'll just leave me alone and let me do my stuff," said Murray.

Murray's stuff left fans screaming in appreciation.

That season, too, pitcher Bobby Jones, now of the New York Mets, struck out seventeen men in a game. Summer leagues are supposed to be for development, but Jones was so slick, not only did Garcia wish to avoid tampering with his motion, he wanted other players to emulate his style.

"His pitching mechanics were so good that I took him aside and said, 'You're the smoothest kid I've seen,' " said Garcia.

Bob Dickens has operated the "Dickens Den" concession stand at Mulcahy Stadium since 1981 as a way to help out the non-profit teams. LEW FREEDMAN

Garcia learned Jones' Fresno State drills and introduced them at his own school.

O'Brien, Jones, and another top pitcher, Dave Tuttle, took a social trip that summer.

"We're out in a boat having a couple of beers," said O'Brien, who said he was twenty at the time, but had an ID that read twenty-two. "All of a sudden, we look up and there's a lot of water in our boat. We're bailing with the ice chest. It was absolutely amazing. We were a hundred yards from shore. Tuttle waded ashore."

That was not O'Brien's only transportation misadventure. Another time he and Chad Dembisky, a Fullerton State pitcher, were dragging the infield on a small, motorized tractor.

"He decides he wants to drive up the Seward Highway right before a game," said O'Brien, who was on the back of the vehicle.

Dembisky puttered off towards the highway where cars travel fifty-five miles per hour.

"The national anthem is playing and I yell, 'Hey, where ya going?' " said O'Brien. "He takes us to the trails behind Mulcahy. He got the tractor stuck in a creek. We were full of mud. We were just a mess."

O'Brien knew little about Alaska when he arrived.

The fences of Mulcahy Stadium bear the insignias of Anchorage rivals the Bucs and the Pilots. LEW FREEDMAN

"I didn't think it would be as domesticated," he said. "I wasn't going so far as to think there were igloos, but I didn't think it would be that big of a place. Everything is so big there. Every flight I've ever taken to Anchorage, there's always guys with lures on their hats."

Sometimes, O'Brien and other players stayed at a remote lake cabin. He called home from there so he could say, "I'm in Alaska, water skiing." Relatives or friends couldn't picture it. So O'Brien obligingly took pictures. He was sure to point out that they were snapped at 11 P.M.—in bright light.

Those Buc teams featured sluggers like Geoff Jenkins, now batting over .300 for the Milwaukee Brewers, Brant Brown of the Pittsburgh Pirates, and slugger-pitcher Brooks Kieschnick, who played for the Cubs, and is now property of the Anaheim Angels.

Kieschnick, a 6-foot-4, 225-pound slugger from the University of Texas, was the Alaska player-of-the-year in 1991 when he hit a Bucs record 16 home runs and drove in 56 runs in 62 games. He also was 5-2 as a pitcher. The next year he was College Player-of-the-Year.

"I made a lot of good friends," said Kieschnick of his Alaska stay. "I have nothing but good memories."

Garcia has good memories about Kieschnick.

"He dominated," said Garcia. "He was one of those stop-and-see guys. You'd stop and see what he was gonna do. Whatever he did, he did with flair."

Garcia's three-year tenure ended with a 127-57 record (though he returned as skipper for the 1994 season). But the Bucs kept it up, going 44-13 in 1992 under new manager Ed Cheff. Kieschnick was 6-0 with a 1.26 earned run average and Texas teammate Braxton Hickman, who played professionally in the minors, batted .410. Hickman had a twenty-nine game hitting streak and was Alaska Player-of-the-Year, the third season in a row a Buc won the honor.

In 1991, the Bucs boldly invited Team USA to Anchorage for exhibitions. Team USA was returning from Japan and a few weeks shy of competing in the Pan American Games in Cuba. Loaded with talent, Team USA represented the crème de la crème of the nation's amateur players. So no matter how well the Bucs played in the Alaska Baseball League, they were supposed to lose.

More than 3,000 fans watched on July 2 as Bucs star pitcher Patrick Ahearne carried a shutout into the eighth inning. He couldn't hold it, though, and the Bucs lost, 4-1.

There were even more fans the next night when the Bucs made a statement for all underdogs. They upset Team USA, 6-5, in a dramatic game when Murray tripled with the bases loaded in the eighth inning and Jeff Foster drove Murray home with the game-winner.

"We proved to ourselves we can play with anyone," said Murray of one of the Bucs' finest hours.

Although overshadowed because of the magnitude of beating Team USA, the creation of a new Bucs-sponsored tournament in 1991 had more enduring value. The Bucs Invitational is now a season-ending staple of the calendar featuring all of the league's teams. The tournament director is John Sweeney, the same John Sweeney who worked with the Valley Green Giants.

When Sweeney started the 1999 campaign as Bucs broadcaster and tournament director, it marked his twenty-fourth consecutive year involved with Alaska baseball. At season's end he could claim viewership of about 1,400 games featuring Alaska teams.

Even though he spent considerable time in print journalism, Sweeney always worked his way onto the air for an inning here or there to keep his broadcast streak alive. In 1986 and 1987, Sweeney traveled to Hawaii to cover the Goldpanners. He broadcast play-by-play and wrote the game stories.

"I'd be on the air," he said, "then I'd switch hats and be a reporter."

Sweeney arrived on the Bucs' scene in 1991, the middle of the powerhouse years.

"My favorite Buc of all time, on the field and off, is Brooks Kieschnick," said Sweeney.

During the 1999 season, when Sweeney returned to the booth full-time for the first occasion since 1996, he included a regular trivia feature in his broadcasts, mentioning great moments in Bucs history. They were often events seen with his own eyes.

"He knows Alaska league history better than anybody," said Mattingly.

The Bucs Invitational in 1999 included five teams from Alaska, plus the Bay Area Stars. Coached by Mike Garcia.

Garcia brought his son on the eleven-day swing through the state to golf and fish, circumstances which prodded him to recall his first-ever bear sighting. While fishing on the bank of the Funny River on the Kenai Peninsula, a bear appeared four hundred yards away.

"We called it a day," said Garcia. "We packed our gear and went the other way."

From the early days keeping their fingers crossed when they brought in The Chicken, the Bucs were regarded as a hustling organization. Mattingly is a baseball man first, but he never shied away from promotional stunts, either. The Chicken. Team USA. The Silver Bullets.

By the early 1990s, leading all of summer baseball in attendance, and winning pennants and tournament championships, the Bucs claim they had surpassed the Glacier Pilots.

O'Brien believes so.

"In 1990, I think maybe the Pilots were still the number one team in Anchorage," said O'Brien. "In 1991, I think we overtook them."

Mattingly said promotions made a difference.

"All those things helped out along the way," said Mattingly. "I like flair. I like variety. I don't think it helped me recruit."

What helped the Bucs recruit, besides word-of-mouth from coaches like Chris Bradford and players who went on to stardom like Joyner and Telford, was an annual trip to Hawaii.

As philosophical differences split the Alaska Baseball League, the Bucs aligned themselves with the Fairbanks Goldpanners in welcoming aboard the Hawaii Island Movers in 1986. It was part of an attempt to embrace the Pacific Rim. Japanese and Korean teams showed up at Mulcahy Stadium for a time. The Bucs committed to finishing their season each year at the Island Movers' tournament in Honolulu.

To save money, the Island Movers played their games in Alaska all at once each summer. Some financially pinched Alaska teams hated the high cost of traveling to Hawaii. The Island Movers played good baseball, but were an awkward ABL fit. They always felt like a non-league opponent, here one minute, gone the next. When the Island Movers took a leave of absence in 1999, the team's ABL future was clouded.

Mattingly, though, always liked having Hawaii road trips on the schedule.

"I used Hawaii as a recruiting tool," said Mattingly. "It's attractive to a kid."

Alaska sold itself, too. Mike Macfarlane, later a major league catcher, was an inexperienced teenager almost in awe of competing against elite players in Alaska, until playing with the Bucs taught him he could compete.

"I took off my sophomore year," said Macfarlane. "The Alaska summer league had a lot to do with it."

Alaska, though, more than baseball, sticks in Macfarlane's mind. While

Team president Chuck Shelton (left) and general manager Ron Okerlund wear their Glacier Pilots loyalty on their chests. LEW FREEDMAN

teammates slept on buses, he kept his eyes open staring at the mountains and lakes.

"I just enjoyed the beautiful scenery," said Macfarlane, who played for the Oakland A's in 1999. "It's a memory I'll never forget. It was the highlight of my college career. Just a great experience and a fantastic summer. Portage Glacier, it was just phenomenal. I always praised how great Alaska was."

For his summer job, Macfarlane cut the lawn at an apartment complex.

"A moose came out of the thicket," said Macfarlane. "It was pretty close. It just kind of looked at me."

Lucky for him. That might have been rougher than any collision while blocking home plate.

Although Hawaii was a sexy road trip, committing to the Island Movers' post-season tournament left the Bucs out of the Wichita loop. It will never be known, but the Bucs of 1989, 1990 and 1991 surely would have contended for a national championship.

What took on increasing significance were intra-city battles with the Glacier Pilots. The Pilots-Bucs rivalry eclipsed the old Pilots-Goldpanners rivalry. Although for years the organizations barely spoke and did not even schedule each other, over time cooperation improved and a Mayor's Cup series was established. Sometimes Mayor Rick Mystrom threw out the first pitch, or presented the trophy. By the end of the 1990s, the teams routinely played during the regular season and contested three games as part of the Cup.

The 1996 Bucs on-field leadership: coach John Webber, who is scheduled to manage in 2000; Mark O'Brien, who managed in in 1996 and 1997; and Mike Oakland, who succeeded him in 1998 and 1999. COURTESY OF MARK O'BRIEN

Normally, the home Anchorage team could count on unanimous Mulcahy crowd support. At Bucs-Pilots games, Bucs fans congregate on the third-base side and Pilots fans root from the first-base side—Home Brew Alley.

"You want to be the best in town," one-time Bucs pitcher John Codrington said. "You've got the Bucs fans over here and the Pilots fans over there. It's definitely a different series."

There is extra electricity when the teams play and players' host families let them know how critical it is to beat the crosstown guys. In fact, one Pilot summer parent, Mac Shelton, wife of team president Chuck, will not allow the word "Bucs" to be spoken aloud in her household. In conversation, she routinely calls the other team "The B-U-C-S." Mac Shelton has told summer sons they won't get dessert if they don't beat the Bucs.

At century's end, the all-time series was tightening up with Pilots ahead 65-54. However, the Pilots owned eight-of-ten Mayor's Cup titles.

That only raised the stakes higher for the Bucs. Once, when O'Brien was a coach, he gathered the team before a Pilots game. He said when he played, his host family fed him steak or pizza. He paused. "Then we lost to the Pilots and they didn't feed me at all."

Point made.

In 1998 O'Brien became assistant coach at Stanford University, probably one of the top ten baseball schools in the nation. He may be a couple thou-

Mark O'Brien, hitting fungoes to his fielders, played for the Bucs before he became coach and then manager. COURTESY OF MARK O'BRIEN

sand miles removed from Alaska baseball, but the Bucs are never far from his thoughts. O'Brien had Hall of Fame mental skills, but his foot and bat speed were a little slow. Playing with the Bucs is the closest thing he had to a professional, play-every-day, travel-by-bus experience, and he cherishes it.

"That's why it's so special for me," said O'Brien. "I thought someone would sign me as a free agent. But I didn't run well. I was a below-average runner."

So as soon as OB stopped playing, he started coaching. He's been an assistant and head man at DeAnza, an assistant at Cal Poly San Luis Obispo, and now an assistant at Stanford.

"My number one goal when I started out was to be the head coach of the Anchorage Bucs," said O'Brien.

He reached that goal in 1996. O'Brien said he always talks about the

Mark O'Brien, a "Charlie Hustle" player, was known to lose his temper as a manager. COURTESY OF MARK O'BRIEN

Alaska Baseball League at coaching conventions and guesses that he fields as many as two hundred calls a year about Alaska, from other coaches who want to know what's it like, or from players who want to hook up with a team.

O'Brien has souvenir Alaska photos on his office walls and he saved scrapbooks from his Alaska days. He even has been known to wear his Bucs shirt to work.

O'Brien wants to be an NCAA Division I head coach some day, but said he also would like to manage in Alaska again.

"I'm an ambassador for the Alaska League," said O'Brien.

And, of course, the Anchorage Bucs.

17
THE MIDNIGHT SUN GAME

No lights, just an arctic glow

THERE WAS plenty of blue in the sky at 10:45 P.M. on June 19 in Fairbanks in 1998. Good thing. Things go more smoothly in the Midnight Sun baseball game on clear, sunny nights.

It was the biggest night of the season for the Fairbanks Goldpanners. It always is. The Goldpanners have a tradition like none other. In the third week of June each summer, in honor of the Summer Solstice, and as close as possible to the June 21 longest day of the year, the Goldpanners play a baseball game that begins in late evening and extends into early morning of the next calendar day.

And under absolutely no circumstances do they turn on the Growden Park stadium lights. The Midnight Sun game has been an institution since 1906. And it is always played by the glow of natural light. Even if that natural light gets a bit dim at times.

Unlike Barrow or other points north of the Arctic Circle, Fairbanks does not have twenty-four hours of daylight in summer. People are often confused about that, but technically, the sun does set. On June 19, there were twenty-one hours, forty-seven minutes of daylight. The sun set at 12:46 A.M. and it rose above the horizon once again at 2:59 A.M.

The billboard at Growden Park lets fans know the 1998 Midnight Sun Game will be on June 19th. LEW FREEDMAN

Nowhere else in the world does anybody attempt to play baseball at night without banks of lights shining on the field. This is an event unique to Fairbanks and one that over time has become world famous.

"That's crazy," said Jose Cruz, Jr., a former Goldpanner now with the Toronto Blue Jays.

That's one way to look at it.

Preparations for the Midnight Sun game begin in earnest a day early. The night before this game, Lowell Purcell was manning the public address system at Growden, and as the Goldpanners' game against the Kelowna Grizzlies of British Columbia dragged into extra innings, he stated, "I'd like to remind you that the Midnight Sun game will be starting in twenty-three hours, forty-three minutes."

Paul Lockhart, a Fairbanks player back for his second season, played in the 1997 game when it got cloudy.

"It seemed weird we were going to play at 10:30," said Lockhart. "It was a great atmosphere. Towards the end it was getting real dark. Only here in Alaska. I'm really not used to this."

Who is?

Nobody anywhere else. But they love the game in Fairbanks.

"It's just a community event," said Bill Stroecker, the banker who has been Goldpanner president since 1965.

Stroecker began one-year terms in the Red Boucher administration and at age seventy-seven in 1998, was at the front gate taking tickets, just to help out, as he put it.

Stroecker's father Ed played in the first Midnight Sun game in 1906. His father was a catcher raised in San Francisco who came north in 1900 for the

Gold Rush. In his father's day, the small town on the frontier virtually closed down for the Midnight Sun game. Ed Stroecker sailed from San Francisco to Dutch Harbor, Alaska, and immediately played a baseball game there. Stroecker, a distinguished, silver-haired man, owns a 1910 picture of his father wearing his uniform. Ed Stroecker was a trapper in the early part of the century and then became a banker, the career his son followed.

It was the ninety-third Midnight Sun game, so the tradition has legs. Fairbanks began regularly importing opponents in 1963. A year after the Goldpanners played the Wichita Dreamliners at the NBC, Wichita came to Alaska. Teams from Japan, Taiwan and Canada have been Midnight Sun foes.

Stroecker said his father was a pretty good ballplayer, and he once read a newspaper article that said Ed wanted to gather a bunch of Fairbanks players, take them to the Lower Forty-eight to test their abilities and promote Fairbanks and Alaska.

"And that's the way Red was," said Stroecker of Boucher. "Fairbanks was completely isolated. It was the game. It still is. It's the only place in the United States that could have one. I remember a National Geographic map. That's how they identified us."

Home of Midnight Sun baseball. It is a distinction.

Once, when he was managing, Boucher had his players don yellow, 3-D-type movie glasses, supposedly as a secret weapon.

"The idea was they would think our guys could see the ball and they couldn't," said Boucher.

That was hardly Boucher's best Midnight Sun game stunt, though.

In 1965, when the Goldpanners played the University of Southern California, Boucher made sure Tom Seaver played for his side rather than his college team. That year, by the seventh inning, the cloud cover was thick and the sky was starting to resemble true night. Tough to make out the white sphere. Boucher ordered Seaver to fake a pitch and told the catcher to pop the glove to improve the illusion. The umpire called "the pitch" a ball and Boucher stormed onto the field to protest the call.

"I'm arguing that it was right down the pipe," said Boucher.

A dumbfounded Rod Dedeaux, Boucher's USC buddy, came out of his dugout and asked, "What the hell is going on here?"

Meanwhile, Seaver tried to hide the ball, but the umpire searched and found it. Boucher was tossed out of the game.

"A little show business never hurt," said Boucher.

Any proof of a fan's attendance at a Midnight Sun game is coveted. Fans for the 1998 game received commemorative coins. On a counter behind his desk in his bank office, Stroecker has a commemorative mounted ball from the 1988 Midnight Sun game.

These days, Goldpanner general manager Don Dennis is keeper of the tradition.

"I've always toyed with the idea of starting at midnight," said Dennis. "Unfortunately, twelve to one is the darkest time. Besides, we don't call it the mid-morning game."

Every year in the days leading up to the Midnight Sun game, Dennis receives long-distance phone calls from newspaper and radio reporters. They wake him in the morning, seemingly unaware of the four-hour time-difference from the East Coast. And they wake him at night.

Dennis remembers one year that Goldpanner Bret Boone, now the second baseman for the San Diego Padres, gave an interview about the late-night light. Boone said, "It was weird playing with sunglasses and there's no beach."

Dennis may have the quaintest description of the quasi-twilight that sometimes makes picking up the fastball in the batter's box quite challenging.

"It's a lot like when you were a kid, fifteen minutes before your mother called you," he said.

On several occasions the lack of bright light has annoyed visiting teams, and even Goldpanner players.

Emmitt Wilson, the 1960s Goldpanner player, said the home team has waffled. Once year, when he was acting as an assistant coach, players worried they couldn't see the ball. Wilson told Boucher he had to turn the lights on for player safety.

"He wouldn't do it," said Wilson. "When it gets cloudy and you've got guys throwing ninety mph, it can get dark up there on June 21. It's hard to see. I played two or three games where I didn't see the ball. Of course, that was getting close to the time when I was going to need glasses."

Jim Nettles said he was there in 1967 when the Goldpanners pleaded with Boucher to flip the switch. A Japanese team named Kumagai-Gumi was the opponent. Dennis said the Asian teams approached the games "serious as death" and this crew was no exception. But Goldpanner players asking for the lights? That was tantamount to mutiny.

Boucher was incensed. He said, "It's never happened in a hundred years." He appealed to Goldpanner pride. The Goldpanners won, 5-3. The lights stayed off.

In the 1970s, when a team from Ponchatoula, Louisiana was the opponent, the Goldpanners lost, 5-4, at least partially because of an umpire's misjudgment in the dusk. A Goldpanner swatted a ball off the outfield wall and the ump didn't see where it landed. He called the hit a ground-rule double, holding Fairbanks runners at second and third, instead of allowing a run.

"We've had more balls lost in the lights than we've had lost in the Midnight Sun game," said Dennis.

Five bucks buys you a ticket to an event unique in baseball. LEW FREEDMAN

That observation did not pacify the Republic of China Olympic Team, the 1984 opponent. About the fifth inning it was getting fairly dark and the Taiwanese wanted to stop play. The umpire cajoled them into continuing, telling them to just try to make it to the seventh inning. When the game reached the seventh, conditions had changed—it was getting lighter, not darker. The Taiwanese were ahead, 2-1, and they demanded the game be halted. The ump refused, and Taiwan forfeited, the only forfeit in the history of the Midnight Sun game.

The Anchorage Bucs were the 1996 Midnight Sun foe and then-manager Mark O'Brien understood the light trend well. He said you'd best get an early lead because comebacks are unlikely.

"Get ahead by five runs," said O'Brien. "That's the strategy, because they're not turning the lights on."

Lowell Purcell said he remembers a new umpire in 1997 who was not really clued into the no-lights tradition. The umpire, who had never worked the Alaska league before, felt it was getting dark around the fourth inning.

"The ump wiggles his finger in a circle," said Purcell, who was upstairs in the press box behind home plate. "I shake my head. The scoreboard operator, though, goes running down like he's going to turn on the lights. I yell, 'If you turn on those lights, not only will I kill you, but Don Dennis will.' They finally got to the umpire and told him, 'We don't turn on the lights.' "

Before the 1998 game, Purcell pledged to make certain that the master breaker switch was inoperative.

By the time a player makes the majors, he has probably had just about every possible baseball experience. But only a small fraternity can say they swung at a pitched ball in the middle of the night without lights to help.

"Unbelievable," said Oakland A's slugger Jason Giambi, an ex-Goldpanner. "The light was pretty good until the eighth or ninth inning. Then I wondered if I could see the next pitch."

Tom Goodwin, now a Colorado Rockies outfielder who was also a Goldpanner, said he felt the same way.

"It was a little weird," said Goodwin. "But we made it through."

They always do.

The Goldpanners' team yearbook always devotes extensive attention to the Midnight Sun game. The team's boast in part reads, "Since the Goldpanners are the farthest north baseball club on earth, where in summer the sun rarely stops shining, the team annually takes advantage of its unique geographic location by staging the patented Midnight Sun game.

"With Fairbanks a mere one-hundred-and-sixty miles south of the Arctic Circle, the sun is just beginning to set in the north as the game gets under way, and, at its conclusion some three hours later, the sun begins to rise again—also in the north. It is a phenomenon ever-so rare."

Dennis said that when he mentions this oddity on live radio, the broadcasters start stammering.

"They're not prepared to deal with it," said Dennis.

Goldpanner managers make sure their players are prepared to deal with the conditions. Fairbanks manager Dan Cowgill played in the game himself, was an assistant coach in the game, and was managing in it in 1998, a cool trifecta.

"Though it's not like doing three Iditarods," said Cowgill. "There are some corners and cracks the players will have to deal with, but they'll have to figure it out. You need a batting helmet and a visor for protection."

Cowgill said having Stroecker around, and the direct lineage he brings to the Midnight Sun game through his father, is pretty special.

"It's more than just a game," said Cowgill. "It's really special for a lot of things. For the city of Fairbanks, for the Alaska Baseball League, and for the state of Alaska. There are people who still think it's the top of the world, all covered with ice."

And then they hear about this peculiar baseball game.

The uniquness of the event attracted a horde of fifty-seven people from the 7,000-person town of Marshall, Michigan, led by trip organizer Dale Rosene. The 1998 game marked the fifth time the group of junior high students and teachers made the trek to the Midnight Sun game as part of a three-week science education Alaskan journey. Rosene and his pals were loud fans in

The Midnight Sun Game always brings the fans flocking to Growden Park. LEW FREEDMAN

the third-base bleachers, readily heard in support of the Goldpanners despite being dwarfed by the crowd of 3,300.

"If they (the Goldpanners) don't win, it's not their fault," said Rosene, pointing to his kids.

The game was supposed to begin at 10:30, but was fifteen minutes late getting under way. The Michiganers were consistently the most energetic fans. When Purcell sought to get the wave going, he wisely chose the Michigan section as the starting place.

The Goldpanners' right-fielder was Tim Nettles, the son of former Goldpanner and Major League star Graig Nettles. The younger player has been aware of the Midnight Sun game much of his life.

"I've been hearing about it for years," said Tim Nettles. "It's a strange event. I talked to my dad about it. He said, 'When I played, the first pitch went right by the catcher's head.' It's just a fun experience, not something that everyone gets to do."

The Goldpanners took a 2-0 lead on a Lockhart home run. In the fourth inning, though, as a few clouds drifted over, it seemed as if Nettles had trouble handling a fly ball in right. The Kelowna shortstop, Shaun Curley, lost two grounders in the darkness.

"My night vision is pretty good," joked Nettles later. "I eat lots of carrots."

It was plenty light enough to read the word G-O-L-D-P-A-N-N-E-R-S spelled out in gold in a horseshoe arc on the artificial turf infield. But then, the letters are about the size of a human being. Overall, it would be considered plenty light out—if you were driving around in a car with headlights on rather than trying to connect with a pitched ball.

At the closest half-inning to midnight, play was halted for the traditional singing of The Alaska Flag Song. Nancy DeLeon did the honors in a strong voice.

Former Goldpanner manager Jim Dietz said singing of the state anthem was about his favorite part of the Midnight Sun game.

"I always got chills when they played the Alaska Flag Song," said Dietz.

Around 1 A.M., a dazzling pink sunset illuminated the sky. Runs continued to pile up and the game went on. The Goldpanners took a 10-9 lead, then Kelowna inched ahead, 13-11. Then, in the bottom of the ninth, Lockhart parked a home run and Fairbanks prevailed, 14-13.

"I stuck my bat out," said Lockhart, making no claim that he saw the ball as it hurtled towards the plate. "You really had to focus."

Lockhart homered, stroked a single and walked three times, though. A good night at the plate under any circumstances. In baseball lingo, you might say Lockhart had a good eye. In Midnight Sun game lingo, you might say Lockhart had X-ray vision.

By the time the players listened to a short pep talk from Cowgill and gathered their gear, it was nearly 5 A.M. 5 A.M.? No matter. The sun was high in the sky. It might just as well have been noon sun as midnight sun.

18

THE FANS

Taking players into their hearts and homes

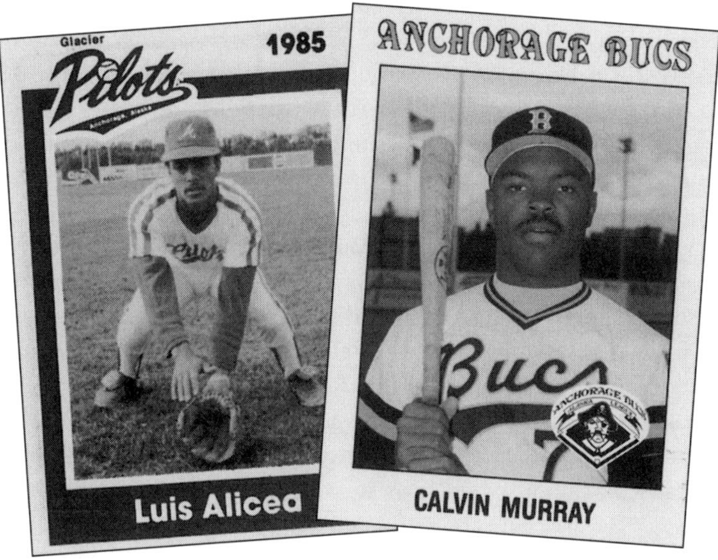

THERE ARE four beds in the basement of the two-story house on Anchorage's east side. And a pool table, too. You can sleep at least one on the pool table. Sometimes it's necessary at the Sheltons. Like when seven members of the Anchorage Glacier Pilots move in for the summer.

"I can't say no," said Mac Shelton, the team's coordinator of player housing and a woman who has been summer mom to some sixty Pilots.

Some summers, Mac and Chuck Shelton, who has been the Pilots team president for most of the 1990s, welcome so many ballplayers into their home that it might as well be a Motel 6. A very crowded Motel 6. They have a dog house, too, but you don't want to get into Mac Shelton's dog house.

Mac Shelton is a small woman with a big voice. She has very blonde hair and very specific ideas about how things should be done. She cooks for her boys. She washes clothes for her boys. She loves her boys. But she also believes in discipline. There are definitely house rules at the Sheltons. In fact, Mac, who makes a point of greeting each summer guest personally at the airport, has a list of printed rules that she hands to incoming players immediately.

Among the rules: 1) "If you open it, close it"; 2) "If you turn it on, turn it off"; 3) "If you break it, repair it"; 4) "If you make a mess, clean it up"; 5) "If it doesn't concern you, don't mess with it."

Oh yes, and Pilot players are not allowed to utter the word "Bucs" in her home. Spell it out, if you must, but don't say it. The Anchorage Bucs are the on-field bad guys, and players are prodded, cajoled, urged to beat the Bucs every time they meet.

If players follow the rules, they earn Mac's loyalty and love forever.

"Mac is just a great person," said David Wright, a 1999 Pilot from the University of San Diego. "Mac is an outstanding cook. We follow the house rules, or else there'll be trouble. She's a strong-willed person."

Tom Nicholson, a two-year second baseman, said he was handed the house rules at the airport, something he found a little intimidating as he tried to cope with jet lag.

"It's, don't do anything in her house you wouldn't do in yours," said Nicholson.

In some minds, the Alaska Baseball League's summer son program is the league's most important legacy. Long after on-field performances dim in memory, relationships forged over a two-month period hold fast.

The idea to place visiting collegians in local homes originated under Red Boucher in Fairbanks. Families volunteered to house and feed players and the plan worked so smoothly and was so popular that all other Alaska teams adopted it.

What this meant was that 19-year-olds away from home had someone to watch over them. They had the security of a roof, meals and adults to turn to for advice. Usually, summer parents take in one or two players. The Sheltons, whose record for squeezing players into their home in a single summer is nine, are unusual. Families later watch players advance through the minors and cheer for them when they reach the majors.

Dick Lobdell, the Pilots broadcaster, said the summer parent program is the single best thing to come out of the ABL.

"The great thing about it is the longstanding relationship between the players and the families," said Lobdell. "Here's these Anchorage kids who got to have a brother for the summer."

Bucs general manager Dennis Mattingly said having reliable summer parents is critical.

"That makes your program," he said.

Dave Foreman, the long-time Pilots official, and his wife Penny, served as summer parents.

"There was one kid who thought they'd be playing in snow," said Penny Foreman.

During the 1994 season, the Foremans housed Ohio State shortstop Chris

Bev Walters spends her summers making Bucs players feel at home. Major leaguer Calvin Murray calls her "Mom." LEW FREEDMAN

Williams, who saw this gigantic animal lingering outside the window.

"There's a moose out there!" yelled Williams. "What do I do?"

"Don't go outside," was Penny Foreman's sage advice.

Although summer parents have no obligation beyond providing the basics, most who handle the role want players to appreciate Alaska. Hosts take players sightseeing to nearby Portage Glacier, or to Denali National Park, or on fishing trips to the Kenai River or Kachemak Bay.

Sharon Woods, a retired elementary school teacher, became a Pilots host mom in 1972. A huge baseball fan who grew up in San Francisco, favoring the Giants of the Willie Mays–Willie McCovey era, it took a gift of season tickets in 1971 to attract her to the ABL.

"I fell totally in love with everything," she said.

The first player she hosted was Glen Johnson, from Stanford University, by way of Juneau. Woods said her mother gave up her room for him and allowed him use of her car and her credit card.

"He never overstepped his bounds," she said.

In 1984, one player who stayed with Woods was future Major Leaguer Kip Gross. Gross played for the Boston Red Sox in 1999, but earlier played in Japan. He occasionally telephoned Woods from there.

"He's called me from Japan, Puerto Rico, and Mexico," said Woods. "He calls me out of nowhere. He just loved Japan. He had his own translator and a $10,000-a-month apartment."

The famous "Bucsmobile." Nolan Ryan's son Reese and three teammates bought the 1983 Crown Victoria in 1997 for $400. LEW FREEDMAN

Tim Peters, a University of Arkansas player, was her other player that season. He signed with the Montreal Expos' organization and after a few years in the minors settled in Texas. Although fifteen years have passed, Woods hears from Peters at Christmas.

"I love hanging around the guys," said Woods. "They talk baseball. They're fun and I love showing off Alaska. I feed them a lot, root for them, show them Alaska and show them a feminist can be a warm, caring person. They're such chauvinists."

One of her favorites was pitcher Eddie Guardado, now a reliever with the Minnesota Twins, who was the neatest boarder she ever had, so meticulous he ironed his blue jeans.

"A nice lady," said Guardado. "I talk to her a lot. It was the best time I had in baseball, except for making the majors. Alaska was a great experience. Sharon is always saying I have to come up. One of these days I'm gonna get back."

Woods housed David Crowder and Gary Gros, both from Nichols State, in Louisiana, in the early 1990s.

"Those southern boys are the best," she said. "They say, 'Yes m'am,' and 'No m'am." Gros said, " 'My dad would hit me upside the head if I didn't say yes sir, or yes m'am.' "

The following spring she took a road trip with the team.

"Me and thirty-five guys on a bus to West Texas," said Woods. "We won nine out of ten. The coach wanted me to stay."

Blake Stein, the lanky Major League pitcher, was also one of Woods' house guests.

"Blake Stein calls," said Woods. "He'll say, 'I was sitting on the couch telling my girlfriend about Alaska.' "

Stein, traded from the Oakland A's to the Kansas City Royals during the 1999 season, had a blast in Alaska. He fished on the Russian River and wherever else he could wet a line. His father caught a king salmon on a visit. In fact, his dad, Bruce, dropped his suitcase off and drove right to Ship Creek to fish.

"I saw a moose real close," said Stein. "It was standing right next to me. I got to meet a lot of guys I'm playing against now. I think that league up there had a lot to do with me being drafted. I hadn't really been seen before the NBC. It helped me out tremendously. I wouldn't have missed it for anything."

Woods said she always considered it a responsibility to show players as much of Alaska as possible, so she made certain they saw Portage Glacier, took the tram up Alyeska Mountain ski resort, and saw other tourist sights like Hatcher Pass and Independence Mine that are within driving distance of Anchorage. And she set up fishing trips with her friends.

One time, to repay her, Crowder and Gros cooked red beans and rice. Guardardo cooked a Mexican meal for her—and even cleaned the stove.

Anyone who has hosted players long enough has some special memory and any player who came to Alaska and worked at it enjoyed it.

Rico Rossy, a second baseman with the Kansas City Royals and Seattle Mariners, who for years exchanged Christmas cards with Pilots general manager Ron Okerlund, said being in Anchorage was one of the best summers of his life.

"Such beautiful country," said Rossy, an avid fisherman who caught silver and red salmon and a king salmon which has been growing in size throughout the 1990s. These days Rossy calls the fish a seventy-five pounder.

"It used to be smaller," he said, laughing. But that fish still fed plenty of people. "I had it cut into steaks and sent the steaks to Puerto Rico. It traveled 5,000 miles to get eaten."

Rossy said when he retires from baseball he wants to bring his wife and children to Alaska.

"We'll go camping and sightseeing," said Rossy.

Oakland A's outfielder Ryan Christenson lived with Lisa and Steve Horn for two summers while he was with the Peninsula Oilers, and still talks to them. He fished for king salmon in the Kenai River, took a float trip, and caught halibut. He took a flightseeing trip to Denali National Park.

"A bear chased the plane," said Christiansen. "It was pretty big."

Tom Goodwin, the ex-Goldpanner, lived with former University of Alaska

Fairbanks athletic director Ed Lawrence, who later became director of umpires for the minor-league system.

"It was always light out," said Goodwin, who said he has one special Alaska souvenir. "I took a license plate home. They're probably still looking for it."

Former Pilot Luis Alicea, a second baseman with the Texas Rangers, lived with ex-Pilot general manager Lou Sinnett, who called him "a wonderful kid." A Californian, Alicea said he chose to play in the ABL instead of in the Cape Cod League because of the scenery.

"I loved it up there," said Alicea. "I really did. I loved the wilderness and the outdoors life. I remember catching my first salmon on the Talkeetna River. I had never fished much, but every time there was something to do I did it because it was a new experience. A moose, that was a sight to see at the beginning. Then it was a regular thing."

Alicea and other players fished a spot in Talkeetna right near the Alaska Railroad tracks. Some people leaned out of a train and yelled that they were in bear territory, though they didn't see any bears. Then fishing on the Kenai River, they saw bears right across the water two nights running.

Alicea, who has a thin, dark mustache and an easy smile, said when he left Alaska he left salmon in Sinnett's freezer. He was hoping it would be canned and shipped to him, but he never received it.

"They had food for the winter," said Alicea.

One thing players hope for when they settle in with a family is access to wheels. Some regular summer parents insure beaters for two months a year and park them the other ten.

For years, Diane Owens housed Anchorage Bucs players and loaned them a bright blue Mustang. When born in 1985, the Mustang's original color was Navy blue, but it was involved in an accident and when touched up, it became, well, brighter. In the late 1990s the car had either 163,000 miles on it, or 263,000. Owens lost track of how many times the odometer went around. Each group of Bucs added to the car's lore.

In 1997, the passenger-side door wouldn't open from the inside, the windows were hard to crank and there were no rear shocks, so passengers bounced.

"We call it 'The Beast,' " said Buc Geoff Geary.

Geary and his roommate Adam Huxhold installed a baseball on top of the stick shift.

Another famous Anchorage summer baseball vehicle is the 1976 blue Chevy Blazer driven by Pilots players who stayed with Tony Webb. Interestingly, a couple of generations of the same family, former Kansas City Royal Jaime Bluma and his younger brother Marc, now in the Toronto Blue Jays' organization, drove the truck, Jaime in 1993, Marc in 1997.

The carriage of the Blazer began deteriorating long ago. In 1994, former

Things are close and cozy between fans and players at Mulcahy. LEW FREEDMAN

Pilot pitcher Mike Drumright, later a number one draft pick of the Detroit Tigers, stepped right through the floor to pavement and the metal closed in on his leg like quicksand.

"Two of us had to hold him while the metal was peeled back," said Webb.

Marc Bluma was quite impressed when he saw daylight through holes in the floorboards.

"When you drive over a puddle, you get wet," he said.

The Blazer left the Pilots family soon after Bluma. Webb actually found a buyer.

None of these vehicles matched the Bucsmobile, though. It is the Anchorage Bucs' version of the Batmobile. The man behind the Bucsmobile is Reese Ryan, a Texas Christian pitcher who was the second son of Hall of Famer Nolan Ryan to pitch for the Bucs. His older brother Reid pitched earlier. Nolan Ryan generously donated autographed baseballs to the Bucs that were given away at ballgames.

The Bucsmobile is a 1983 Crown Victoria painted in black and gold and plastered with slogans like "Go Bucs," "Honk 4 Bucs," and "Luv a Buc."

Reese Ryan and three teammates went to a used car lot during the summer of 1997 in search of a proper ride. The salesman, no doubt bearing in mind the "sucker-is-born-every-minute" saying, asked for $3,000.

"We acted like we were leaving," said Ryan.

Mac Shelton has no trouble putting up as many as seven Pilots players for the summer—as long as they put up with her house rules. LEW FREEDMAN

The price quickly dropped to $1,200. Ryan made a counter offer.

"It doesn't even run, I bet," he said. "We'll give you $300 for it."

The salesman asked for $900.

"Look, I've got $400," said Ryan.

The deal was consummated. Ryan and friends then had fun with spray paint. They were a rolling team billboard the rest of the summer.

"People honk at us and wave and stare," said Ryan. "Nobody knows what to think."

At the end of the season, the Bucs bought the car from Ryan and put it in storage at Diane Owens' South Anchorage home. And there it stayed.

Dead battery? No insurance?

Nope. Nobody could find a key to the ignition.

Some summer parents practically adopt the ballplayers. John and Bev Walters definitely make the Anchorage Bucs who've stayed at their home since 1984 feel like members of the family.

Bev is the loudest rooter at Bucs games, cheering for her guys from a regular seat on the left side of home plate. John, who goes by "Bud," works the beer stand at Mulcahy and hardly ever sees home action.

Over the years the Walters have hosted such Buc luminaries as Calvin Murray and Brooks Kieschnick.

"We get letters and cards," said John Walters. "They know the rules. They have to get in touch and let us know what they're doing each Christmas. Brooks, Calvin, we know their kids. We know their families. We know where they're at. They're family."

A year ago, Rick, the Walters' youngest son, took a trip to the Lower Forty-eight to see former Bucs Pepper Arredondo and Bobby Walters at their colleges, and some ex-Bucs in the pros.

"I grew up watching everybody," said Rick, now in his thirties. "I was kind of a younger groupie. I wasn't old enough to go out with them."

Probably no one has been tighter with the Walters than Murray, who played two years in Alaska, and moved into the majors with San Francisco in 1999.

"Calvin got so close to us," said John. "No matter what time of night he came in he'd wake me up and say I'd have to go look at his fish."

Once, that was at 4 A.M.

The Walters have a special wall in the family home in the Chugach foothills on the east side of Anchorage. It highlights photographs of former Bucs with their families.

"I call it my wall of fame," said Bev. "I love the boys. I love the sport. I'm not a Pilots fan. I'm a baseball fan."

Much like Mac Shelton, Walters reacts strongly if a Pilots player friendly with one of her boys, comes to visit.

"I made them close the curtains," she said, "so no one knew they were in my house. I said, 'Quick, take your uniform off.' "

Murray and Bev were so close that he called her "mom" when they hugged goodbye at the airport. That got some attention from passersby who overheard, Bev Walters said with a laugh, because Murray is black and she is not.

When Murray was called up for his Major League debut, Bev Walters frantically tried to call and congratulate him. She was so happy for him.

"He's my baby," she said. "I'm so excited."

On a mid-summer night, son Rick took the Walters' 1999 players, Bobby Womack and Brandon Rogers, on a fishing trip thirty-five miles from Anchorage. Although she had already cooked them a lasagna dinner, Bev made a box lunch of turkey sandwiches, chips and soda.

"They're always hungry at midnight," she said.

Womack, an outfielder from San Diego State, later said, "I didn't catch a bite, I caught a cold."

But his stomach was full.

"She's a very good cook," said Womack. "She does so much for us. You've got this lady with open arms right from the start."

Although Mac Shelton doesn't know Bev Walters, there are similarities between them. They both love their players and love baseball. The Sheltons have a special wall, too. They framed and mounted uncut sheets of Pilot baseball cards from 1989, 1990, 1991 and 1994, cards printed before the NCAA prohibited the practice.

Mac grew up in Michigan. Gordie Howe, the Hall of Fame hockey player, used to visit her home when she was young. Her dad, the late Jim Cody, was an umpire who moved to Alaska in 1960. He had his collarbone broken by a Tom Seaver pitch, said Mac, who referred to the Goldpanners as "The Bedpanners." Cody umpired Pilots games in their early days, and that made her an ABL fan.

Mac and Chuck Shelton, who have been married since 1965, began as house parents and gradually got more involved with the team. The living room fireplace mantle features autographed baseball cards and balls from many of the guys who lived with them. The queen of Pilot summer parents also has an assortment of baseball earrings. One earring is in the shape of a baseball. Another is an earring that says, "Longhorn baseball." It's in honor of pitcher Scott Dunn, who played at Texas and lived in Alaska with her.

"They're all favorites," said Mac, who has attended three former Pilots' weddings.

Mac does up to nine loads of laundry a day in the summer and she leaves players pizza hot pockets, sandwiches and soup for lunches. At night, she cooks a hot meal, usually tacos, roasts, scalloped potatoes, or spaghetti.

"They eat once a day, all day," said Chuck, who is balding with a blond mustache, and is renowned for cooking Sunday breakfasts requiring three pounds of bacon and three dozen eggs.

Mac's rules rule. If it's time to get up, the players better get up, or they get splashed by cold water. The players are expected to carry the groceries for her and mow the lawn.

Many players' friends show up to play pool, darts, or cards, including members of the B-U-C-S. They are welcomed and sometimes stay overnight. Chuck Shelton said he is a realist, that he realizes players will drink.

"I do say, 'If you're going to have a beer, stay here,' " said Chuck. "One time I counted five guys in the house in the morning. I couldn't even get in the living room. You know what was funny? I didn't even know which ones were Pilots."

From a volunteer, send-over-a-kid parent, Chuck Shelton has eased into the presidency of the team. That means he manages a $200,000-a-year budget, works year-round gathering sponsors, coordinating schedules, and planning player, coach, and team travel.

But player relationships matter most to him.

"We make them part of the family," said Shelton.

At Chez Shelton, it's more homey than a hotel.

19
GAMES

Ninth-inning homer breaks up no-hitter in best game ever

THE SCENE crackled with the tension. 0-0. Ninth inning. Anchorage Buc Don August throwing a no-hitter. Anchorage Glacier Pilot John Hoover throwing a two-hitter and striking out everyone carrying a club.

There was one down in the bottom of the ninth when Mark McGwire strode to the plate for the Pilots. The setting was the stuff of movie fiction.

Dennis Mattingly paced in the Bucs dugout. "Don't give him anything to hit," Mattingly said out loud. "Do not throw him a fastball," Mattingly thought to himself.

August was pitching a masterpiece on this night of July 7 in 1982. So was Hoover. He had sixteen strikeouts. And it was Bucs against Pilots, teams which shared the same ballpark and competed for Anchorage fans. Young Mark McGwire, who brought no hitting reputation to Alaska, spent the previous month impressing people with his size, power and ability to place hits in gaps and over fences.

Most of McGwire's dynamic feats lay in the future, but for the 2,200 fans who saw the way he ended the greatest game ever played in the Alaska, his legend began that evening at Mulcahy Stadium.

The pitch flew out of August's hand—and came in fast. It left the park even faster. McGwire swung and connected. The towering smash sailed over the left-center field wall, just about the deepest part of the park, clearing a light tower and seemingly headed for the Bahamas. It was clearly ready for take-off.

"He hit that ball so far," said Mattingly. "It was a little dot leaving in the dark. That ball had stewardesses, movies, the whole thing on it. McGwire was the last threat they had as far as we were concerned. It was just smoked. That baby was just rocketed. I wanted to see where it came down. If you were there and saw it, it was something you wouldn't forget."

August, who later pitched in the majors with the Milwaukee Brewers and was still throwing for a living in the late 1990s in the Taiwan Major League, turned his back at the crack of the bat. Then he walked into the dugout, put his glove down and said, "Shoot."

August was understandably subdued, and McGwire understandably jubilant.

"I was looking for the fast ball all the way," said McGwire. "He got it up right where I like it."

McGwire admitted he was going for the big blow, seeking to end it with a single swing.

"Why not?" said McGwire. "One run wins it and I'm a power hitter. I was definitely thinking home run."

This Bucs-Pilots game is the greatest in the more than one hundred that the teams have played against each other. Much argument is offered suggesting it is the best ever seen in Alaska.

Double shutout. Two magnificent pitchers in control of their stuff. A man headed for greatness breaking up a no-hitter in the bottom of the ninth to claim the game 1-0 for the Pilots.

"The shot heard around Anchorage," said Dick Lobdell. "That was quite a ballgame. Up comes McGwire. Man, oh man, did he hit that ball."

"The 1-0 Game." That's what people call it and everyone knows what they're talking about. Or sometimes it's called "The McGwire-August Game."

There have been many, many great and memorable games involving Alaska baseball teams. Many took place in Wichita, where the setting was dramatic and the results meaningful. But many, like the 1-0 Game, struck like lightning, in Alaska. On what seemed likely to be an average night at the ballpark, some kind of history was made.

Dennis Cook, now with the New York Mets, pitched a no-hitter for the Peninsula Oilers against the Glacier Pilots in 1993. In consecutive weeks in 1985, Mat-Su Miners pitchers Gil Heredia, now with the Oakland A's, and Jim Long, pitched no-hitters against the Oilers.

As nondescript as any circumstance, though, was the setting for the third no-hitter in Miners history in July, 1994. Scott DeWitt, out of Lassen Junior College in Susanville, California, was pitching the second game of a Sunday afternoon doubleheader against the Pilots at Mulcahy.

In the bottom of the seventh inning, DeWitt cradled the ball in his glove as he listened to "Take Me Out to the Ballgame" being played over the loudspeaker. It was only then that it dawned on him that it wasn't a nine-inning game and he needed just three outs to end it.

DeWitt got his outs, his no-hitter, and a 1-0 victory. Travis Wyckoff, the Pilots' losing pitcher, threw a one-hitter. The only hit in the game was a solo home run by Miners' designated hitter Phil Olsen in the fourth inning.

That's it. One hit in the game. The pitchers were so dominating the game took just one hour and fifteen minutes to play. Waiting to buy a hot dog could have cost you an entire inning.

"That's by far the best I've ever pitched and lost," said Wyckoff.

It was an astonishing game, both for brevity and numbers. How is it that two pitchers are nearly flawless on the same day? Almost never happens.

To make things even more surreal, in his previous start, DeWitt gave up nine earned runs in one-and-a-third innings. To the Pilots. The Pilots came into the no-hitter batting .323 as a team. All DeWitt wanted to do was get beyond the first inning.

"You get lit up one time and you shut 'em down the next," said DeWitt, a 6-foot-4, 200-pound redhead who is now pitching in the minor leagues.

Wyckoff, a former Wichita State pitcher from Kansas, telephoned his father, Steve, with a game report. "Dad," said Travis, "I pitched and I only gave up one hit." Pause. "But I lost."

"You what?" replied Steve.

Usually, a one-hitter will get you the W. Somewhat astonishingly, though, in the thirty-year history of the team, six Glacier Pilots have thrown no-hitters and three of them lost.

DeWitt struck out eight, walked two batters, hit one, and had a man reach on an error. But the biggest threat to the no-hitter was a shot off the bat of Pilot first baseman Steve Carver. Carver drove a pitch to deep centerfield long enough for a home run if aimed elsewhere. But Miner Mike Flood ran it down.

DeWitt may not have been aware of the game's scheduled length, but he was aware that there were a whole bunch of zeroes on the scoreboard. His teammates, true to baseball superstition, did not discuss his performance while in progress. DeWitt heard murmuring among the 600 fans, though, and the Pilots made comments, trying to psych him out. Didn't work.

When he threw the last pitch, forcing Pilot Troy Kent to ground into a double play, DeWitt simply thought, "Wow."

Teammates rushed over and hugged him.

"It's probably my biggest highlight ever," said DeWitt. "It's one of those things you might only do once."

When DeWitt returned to his host family's house he was rewarded with a steak dinner.

Sometimes an entire tournament can be magical. In the 1994 Bucs Invitational, Bucs pitcher Mark Redman, who made the Minnesota Twins in 1999, tossed a no-hitter. Bucs teammate Andrew McNally settled for a one-hitter.

In the 1999 Bucs Invitational, pitchers flirted with no-hitters every day. The Oilers' Chris Clark lost a no-hitter and the game to the Bucs in the last inning. John Eric Hernandez of the Miners, the league's player-of-the-year, chased a perfect game before losing his no-hitter.

The Bucs' least likely no-hitter came in 1986 from Jeff Bloom from little Tufts University near Boston, who had a knack for producing mystical results despite being far from a flamethrower.

"I could have caught him with work gloves," said Mattingly.

Nonetheless, he could have been called "No-hit" Jeff. Between April 6 and April 19 of that year, Bloom pitched three straight no-hitters, an unbelieveable accomplishment, even if Tufts played a mostly NCAA Division III schedule. Talk about being in a zone. The performance earned Bloom nationwide attention and Mattingly recruited him based on the publicity.

"You don't throw three no-nos without having something," said Mattingly. "I don't care if it's Little League."

Bloom provided the best thank-you possible. He added to his no-hit resume in June. Bloom no-hit the Island Movers in Hawaii over nine innings, retiring the last twenty batters in the 3-0 triumph.

"I didn't think I had it tonight," he said after the game. "I didn't think I warmed up enough."

Bloom was pitching in the Hawaii heat rather than the Alaska chill, so maybe that's why it didn't make any difference.

If Bloom rose to the occasion against better competition, then Flint Wallace's June, 1995 Bucs no-hitter was more predictable. Too bad only 340 fans predicted it with their presence at the mid-week game against the Mat-Su Miners.

Wallace's very excellent first name added spark to the proceedings. A 6-foot-1, 180-pounder from Texas Christian, Flint sounded very Texan. One could imagine referring to him as Steely-eyed Flint. Raw-boned Texan Flint. Or Scratch-a-match-on-your-grizzled-face Flint.

Or on this night, Firing Flint. Wallace disposed of the Miners in under two hours, striking out nine batters with a zipping fastball, darting curveball, and slow-motion changeup.

It took Wallace until the sixth inning to realize the Miners had no hits. And he had to survive a nerve-wracking finish in the 2-0 win. Buc left-fielder Bobby Brown made a diving catch to end the game. Brown had to belly-flop on the grass to spear the ball as the fly angled away from him.

"It was lots of fun," said Wallace. "It's definitely something I'll remember."

One game that will be long remembered is the Pilots-Kamloops Sandpipers twenty-one inning-contest of June 1992, the longest game in ABL annals.

Twenty-one innings. Lasting six hours, thirty-minutes. Six hours, thirty-nine minutes? It lasted as close to forever as can be imagined. The game began a little past 7 P.M. and ended a little before 2 A.M.

Shortly after 1 A.M., the police arrived in the Mulcahy press box. Residents at a nearby apartment complex begged for the public address announcer to cease so they could get some sleep. Cut it off, said the police. The sound was spiked, the game continued.

On and on it went. Paul Sousa, the starter for the British Columbia team, lasted twelve innings and threw 169 pitches, pretty much two full games' work. All pitchers combined for 628 pitches.

Pilot left-fielder Sean Hugo, who brought a twelve-game hitting streak into the matchup, extended it when he stroked a single after going oh-for-eight. Another Pilot, Carl Hall, went oh-for-nine and saw his average fall from .441 to .349 in one game.

The longer the game lasted, the more intensely the players coveted victory. After run-saving, game-saving plays, they celebrated.

"At 2 A.M., I think most of the players are used to being at a party," explained Pilot third baseman Nate Olmstead. "So I guess they were just partying at the game."

In the end, Olmstead gave the Pilots the best reason to party. He slashed an RBI single to right in the bottom of the twenty-first to give Anchorage the 5-4 win.

There was a discrepancy over just how many fans stuck it out. One reading had it at barely a dozen, another count at fifty. One fan shouted, "Could this be the first game called because of daylight?"

He probably never saw the Midnight Sun game.

It was a game that was three times as long in innings as the DeWitt-Wyckoff struggle and more than five hours longer on the clock.

Still, for sheer drama and pure baseball, no game ever bested the McGwire-August confrontation.

That was the summer McGwire became a first baseman and occasionally he made mistakes. Pilot pitcher John Hoover, who briefly played in the majors with the Texas Rangers, was actually calling the novice at that position "Mr. E" for his errors. Hoover, out of Fresno State and later a member of the 1984 U.S. Olympic team, ceased using that phrase after McGwire's monstrous blow preserved his masterful shutout.

"The home run was over those light towers, four hundred or five hundred feet," said Pilots coach Jack O'Toole. "It was one of the greatest games I've ever been involved in."

For McGwire, too, at the time.

"I'm dreaming," said McGwire of the game-winning bomb. "To break up a no-hitter, too. How often do you see that?"

Maybe never again.

20

MARK McGWIRE

He pitched before he hit

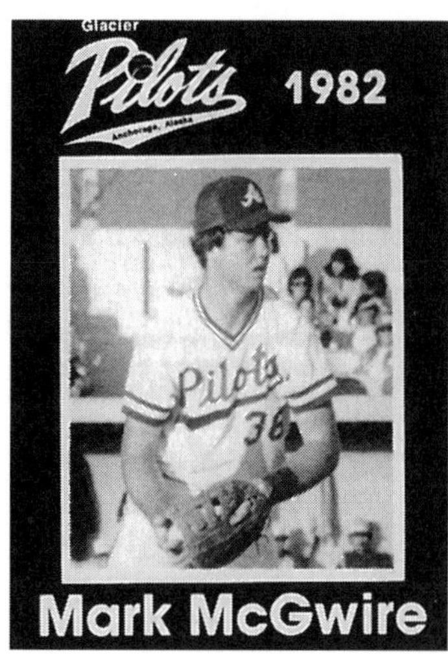

MARK McGWIRE'S season with the Anchorage Glacier Pilots occurred long before he became universally recognized as the Babe Ruth of his generation.

But there were hints.

Like the time he hit the towering home run off Don August to break up that no-hitter. Like the time he crunched Dennis Mattingly's windshield.

Anchorage teams in the Alaska Baseball League provide instructional clinics to local kids. During the summer of 1982, Mattingly brought his sons to one clinic at Kosinski Fields, ballfields located adjacent to Mulcahy Stadium.

Mattingly selected the wrong parking space. McGwire stepped up to the plate, and ripped a pitch deep. It crash-landed on Mattingly's vehicle. Say goodbye to the ball. Say goodbye to the windshield.

"That baby was splattered," said Mattingly.

That's one way to get noticed in the Bucs-Pilots rivalry.

At age nineteen, McGwire was already 6-foot-5, but he was slender, not nearly as thickly muscled as he was as a 250-pounder with the St. Louis Cardinals in 1998 when he surpassed Ruth and Roger Maris to claim baseball's single-season home-run record. He was still a raw hitter, but when he connected, he powdered the ball.

McGwire played in Alaska after his freshman year at the University of Southern California. Although a .415 hitter in American Legion ball, he was then primarily a pitcher. McGwire was 4-4 with a 3.04 earned run average his first college season, not shabby at all. He also batted .200, with three homers and 11 RBIs, in 75 at-bats.

Don Dennis of the Goldpanners scouted McGwire as a pitcher and passed up the chance to add him to his roster.

"If it wasn't so embarrassing, I'd go back and pick an all-reject team," said Dennis, meaning McGwire isn't the only young player he misjudged.

When McGwire joined the Glacier Pilots he was not a heralded player. He was supposed to work on his pitching form. But the Pilots were short of first basemen. A combination of injuries and defections added up to a need for an opening-day first baseman.

McGwire started out hot and stayed hot. McGwire batted .404 with 10 home runs and 44 RBIs in Alaska games, then added three home runs and seven RBIs in Wichita.

In his single pitching outing, McGwire surrendered two hits, two walks, four earned runs and received the loss. He got nobody out, which means he officially went into the books as pitching zero innings.

"He has the highest earned run average in the history of the Pilots," said statistician Dave Foreman. "Infinity."

Not that McGwire is remembered for that. McGwire ended up at first base partially because the Pilots thought they were so well-stocked they ignored the chance to sign future major leaguer Tim Wallach. When the Pilots realized they were short-handed, assistant coach Ron Vaughn, also an assistant at USC, stepped forward and said, "There's a guy who can play first base."

Vaughn, now a major league scout, played a critical role in McGwire's development. He saw the hitting potential and encouraged McGwire. However, Okerlund remembers the Pilots being required to call Southern Cal coach Rod Dedeaux for permission to use McGwire at first.

"He hesitated because he wanted him to be a pitcher," said Okerlund.

McGwire distinguished himself in the Pilots' daily lineup quickly. He started off going eight-for-twelve and hit the ball with authority. Even his foul balls made an impression on coach Jack O'Toole. O'Toole said his wife Katie was struck by a line-drive foul off McGwire's bat.

"McGwire hit my wife," said O'Toole. "It made her cry. When he hit a foul pop-up, it went up the elevator shaft."

Meaning it traveled sky-high. These days McGwire attracts mobs to batting practice because he routinely sends the ball into outer space.

Until McGwire's season-long pursuit of Maris' record and his arrival at 70 homers, few baseball fans realized he played in Alaska. But the story was more widely disseminated as McGwire and the Chicago Cubs' Sammy Sosa Cubs excited the populace with their quest.

Tom Seaver is generally acknowledged as the greatest player to pass through the Alaska league, and Dave Winfield put up Hall of Fame numbers, but it may well be that by the time he retires McGwire will surpass them both in fame and recognition. A year after setting the single-season record, he passed the career 500-homer mark.

Dick Lobdell said McGwire was fun to have around.

"He was one of my favorite players," said the broadcaster. "I just liked his personality. He was interested in the radio aspects. It was interesting that for as little experience as he had at first base, he picked it up so fast."

There was little doubt, though, that McGwire was a different person then. O'Toole said he was young and immature, "just a baby."

McGwire grew up in California and attended college in California, so coming to Alaska represented the first time he was away from home for an extended period of time. He also had a girlfriend he missed. McGwire lived with Okerlund, and Okerlund said the young man was constantly on the phone.

"I couldn't use the telephone," said Okerlund. "He was on it all the time. I had to call him on that a couple of times."

McGwire's girlfriend, later his wife, visited, and he borrowed Okerlund's car for a trip to the Kenai Peninsula. The muffler gave out on the Seward Highway, nearly fifty miles from Anchorage, and McGwire was scared to call Okerlund because he was afraid he'd be so mad.

"It just rusted off," said Okerlund.

McGwire pleaded homesickness and wanted to leave early. But Jim Dietz, the Pilots manager between his stints with the Goldpanners, wouldn't let him. He said McGwire was so homesick he actually broke down crying, and was headed for a telephone to request plane fare from his father, John, to get him out of Alaska.

"He was sitting down by the fence crying, saying, 'I want to go home,' " said Dietz.

Dietz believed the talented McGwire would greatly benefit from finishing the summer season. So he intercepted McGwire's dad and told him that. The older McGwire refused to send the money, McGwire completed the season and had a tremendous year. Later, said Dietz, McGwire admitted it was the best thing for him.

In the book, *Mark McGwire, Home Run Hero* by Rob Rains, McGwire recounted the incident.

"He (Dietz) sat me down and we had a long talk," said McGwire. "He told me I was going to have to deal with being away from home a lot if I wanted to play pro ball. What he said made sense."

In 1998, when McGwire was revving up his record pursuit of Maris, he suffered a minor injury and sat out a few games. Dietz visited him in St. Louis then and gave McGwire souvenirs of the 1982 Alaska season, a Pilots yearbook and a tournament program from that season. McGwire gave him a hug.

"Sometimes the Alaska league means a lot more to those guys when they're in their thirties than it does at the time," said Dietz. "They get older in life and they appreciate it more. Mark was so excited to get that program and yearbook."

It was both a commentary on McGwire's widespread popularity and a fascinating glimpse into the hobby of baseball card collecting that as he zeroed in on Maris, the rare 1982 McGwire Pilots baseball card skyrocketed in value.

The card sold for hundreds of dollars in Internet on-line auctions, as collectors previously unaware of its existence sought the item. McGwire, freckle-faced, with thick hair sticking out from his baseball cap, looks terribly young in the blue-bordered Pilots card.

The demand for the card remained high following his record-breaking season. Anchorage sports card dealer Warren Schuessler, who for years has sold cards at Mulcahy Stadium during Bucs games, said he hears from collectors all over the country.

Schuessler started the 1999 Bucs Invitational with seventy-two different kinds of McGwire cards, including the coveted Glacier Pilots card. He sold two during the tournament, one to a visiting scout, and the other by mail to a man in California, each for $225. Schuessler said he heard of the McGwire card selling for as much as $800 during the frenzy of 1998.

Fresh out of Glacier Pilot McGwires, Schuessler's remaining prize McGwire card displayed the slugger with Team USA in the early 1980s. The price tag was $200.

While McGwire thrilled the country during the 1998 season, Red Boucher lamented that Joe Armstrong didn't live long enough to see the chase. Armstrong and McGwire formed a close bond.

"He treated the boy like a son," said Boucher. "I think Joe and Alaska had a significant impact on him. Every time I look at Mark McGwire I think of him in a Pilots uniform."

By 1982, Boucher lived in Anchorage and when he attended Glacier Pilots games he sat with Armstrong.

"I remember Joe nudging me in the ribs and saying, 'He's pretty good, isn't he?' " said Boucher.

O'Toole thought so. McGwire now puts on such a show in batting practice that people come extra early to his games. His power mesmerized the country during the home-run hitting contest at the 1999 All-Star game in Boston. The venerable Pilots coach said McGwire did the same kind of thing in Anchorage long ago.

"Not ball after ball," said O'Toole. "But you could depend on it. If he took fifteen cuts, it would go out."

Jim Carnell, now a dentist in Spokane, Washington, played for Gonzaga and was a McGwire teammate with the Pilots and his memory gives more credit to the big guy's wallops. Along with those of Cory Snyder, another future major leaguer and later a McGwire Olympic teammate.

"I remember in batting practice, he and Cory Snyder, they'd just sit there and bomb balls out," said Carnell, himself a New York Yankee draft pick. "He and Snyder would be there launching. I'd sit there and go, 'Oh, my God.' It was unbelievable."

The shots landed on the track inside Anchorage Football Stadium, beyond the Mulcahy left-field wall.

McGwire, said Carnell, "kept to himself in the dugout. He was always one hundred percent focused on the game."

The next school year, Gonzaga played Southern Cal and Carnell, a third baseman, faced McGwire, who still made mound cameos.

"He pitched and struck me out," said Carnell.

After a different at-bat, Carnell wound up on first when McGwire was playing the field.

"I'm finally being able to play and hit," Carnell said McGwire told him.

Years later, when McGwire played for the Oakland A's and was just establishing a reputation as a feared slugger, Carnell met up with him and McGwire gave him game tickets.

As McGwire closed in on the single-season record, Carnell said he got goose bumps.

"It's almost like Babe Ruth," said Carnell.

O'Toole, who turned seventy-eight in the summer of 1999, saw Babe Ruth play when he was a kid. In fact, O'Toole must be one of the few baseball people in the world to have his picture taken with both Ruth and McGwire, whom he shared a spot with in the Pilots team shot.

O'Toole, who grew up in Detroit, went to a Tigers-Yankees game with his mother when he was six or seven, in the late 1920s, wearing his best sailor suit. In those days, when overflow crowds turned out, team officials simply roped off outfield territory and permitted spectators to stand there. The O'Tooles were in the outfield, behind the ropes, and Ruth was warming up, shagging flies. O'Toole's mom yelled to Ruth.

"Have a picture taken with the kid," she shouted. Ruth ambled over and "he put his hand on my shoulder," O'Toole said.

Ruth's single-season record of sixty homers was broken by Maris. His career record was broken by Hank Aaron, who finished with 755. McGwire has the goods to set a new record, said O'Toole.

"If nothing happens to him, he might break Aaron's record," said O'Toole.

In September, 1998, when McGwire was closing in on Maris, Boucher had a dream. In the dream, Boucher was back in his Goldpanners' uniform, arguing with Jim Dietz and an umpire at home plate in Mulcahy Stadium when McGwire stepped into the batters' box and blasted a home run.

"He was wearing a Cardinals uniform," said Boucher. "I start shouting, 'What is this? He's out of uniform!' It was his sixty-sixth home run. Dreams don't make sense."

A few nights after the dream, Boucher predicted McGwire would break Maris' record in a specific game, in a specific at-bat, in a specific inning. He got the game and at-bat right and was off by only one inning.

McGwire has long admitted that Alaska played an important role in his development as a player. In an interview several years after his Pilot season, McGwire said, "Going to Alaska changed my life. It was the most pivotal time in my career."

Having a player of such stature make that kind of statement is the best free advertising a program could have.

21
RANDY JOHNSON

One of the wild and crazy guys to make the Majors

COURTESY OF SANDRA TENUTO

IF HE WAS going to be featured on a baseball card for the first time, what would he want it to say on the back? Young Randy Johnson thought the question over for about two seconds. "A wild and crazy guy," he said.

Oh, wild and crazy like the silly Czechoslovakian brothers on the "Saturday Night Live" show?

"No," said Johnson. "Psycho. Kind of like Norman Bates crazy."

OK.

Johnson, then a gangly, hard-throwing pitcher from the University of Southern California, uttered those magical words in the summer of 1984, his one season with the Anchorage Glacier Pilots.

Back then, there weren't twenty different types of baseball cards printed each year. Minor league teams did not routinely issue sets. Some Alaska league teams printed card sets some of the time, but for most players the idea of appearing on a baseball card was still part of the childhood dream signifying they made the big-time.

Johnson, the 6-foot-10 southpaw who might have been the most feared pitcher of the 1990s with the Seattle Mariners, Houston Astros and Arizona

Diamondbacks, was very much an unfinished product when he played for the Pilots. His pitches were startlingly fast, but his throws were not always in the same zip code as home plate. Like many of the young men who come north to compete in Alaska, he had the right stuff, but it was too soon to tell if he could develop into a poised, polished star.

Like Seaver, Winfield, and McGwire before him, though, Johnson did, and he deserves to be mentioned as one of the greatest players ever to wear an ABL uniform.

But back in 1984, that was not a sure thing. Johnson had some work to do.

"He could throw the ball 218 mph, but he had no idea where it was going," said Pilots coach Jack O'Toole.

O'Toole occasionally used innovative methods to psych up Johnson. Once, Johnson, the scheduled starter, complained that he couldn't get loose and shouldn't pitch. Standing nearby was Pilot Mark Gardner, another future major leaguer. O'Toole called to Gardner and pointed at a player on the other team.

"Mark," said O'Toole, "do you know that number thirty-two over there?"

"I go to school with him," said Gardner.

O'Toole looked back to Johnson and said, "He called you a pussy." Johnson got angry and said, "Give me the ball."

Johnson fanned the first two batters and when number thirty-two stepped in he fired a fastball.

"He drilled him right in the ribs," said O'Toole smiling at the memory. "He was just young and raw. His problem was he was wild. If I were the opposing manager, I'd tell my players not to swing."

Johnson's speed and control often make him impossible to hit in the majors. In the ABL, his lack of control sometimes left batters shaking in their spikes.

"He was wilder than a March hare," said Miners' general manager Stan Zaborac.

Pilots coach Lefty Van Brunt was catching Johnson in the bullpen one day, waiting for the regular catcher to put on the gear. Van Brunt was in a half crouch and when Johnson's fastball tailed off, wham!

"I couldn't get over and down," said Van Brunt. "Ask me about my big toe. It did a number on the nail."

Although Johnson is remembered as being wild, perhaps because the occasional warmup pitch rocketed to the screen, his record belies some of the reputation.

Johnson went 4-2 with a 3.18 earned run average for the Pilots. He struck out thirty-six men in thirty-four-plus innings and gave up only twenty-five hits and twenty-one walks. Those numbers definitely show promise.

Steve McFarland, the Pilots manager that year, said Johnson was a fun guy. McFarland said Johnson was a photography fanatic who usually had his camera around his neck. Indeed, years later Johnson's photos were featured in a national magazine spread.

Once, after a Pilots loss, McFarland couldn't understand why several players were in stitches. As is the custom on poor-weather nights at Mulcahy, the home team had to cover the field with tarp.

"They were laughing and screaming," said McFarland, who now lives in Scottsdale, Arizona, near Johnson. "I couldn't figure it out. Randy came in with his hands all beat up, Pilots jacket torn. He said, 'Hey, coach, I need a new jacket.' He'd been in the middle of the tubing of the tarp when they rolled it out."

McFarland said Johnson, who is not a very good hitter, and later made fun of his own ability in commercials, bugged him all summer to let him bat.

"He said, 'Let me hit. Let me hit,' " said McFarland. "He said, 'McGwire came up here and did it.' He wanted to follow in his footsteps. He wanted to hit the roof of the curling club in Fairbanks because he heard Winfield had. I wouldn't give him the opportunity in a game."

Interviewed at the Major League All-Star game in Boston in 1999, Johnson remembered hitting a lot.

"I did get to take a lot of batting practice," said Johnson. "It was fun while I was there."

Johnson left indelible memories with Alaskans just by being a typical, silly, nineteen-year-old.

On a trip to Fairbanks, Johnson rode with Van Brunt in his Lincoln Continental instead of the team bus because he was the scheduled starter.

"He rode with his feet out the window the whole way," said Van Brunt. "He didn't have a pair of socks. He was barefoot. I told him they'd get windburned. I had to give him a pair of mine. They barely covered his heel."

Lou Sinnett, then the Pilots assistant general manager, recalled waiting in the airport for a flight to Kenai for a series with the Oilers when Johnson broke out a boom box. Johnson is tall and skinny and he looks as if he's all arms and legs.

"He starts doing a break dance," said Sinnett. "If he didn't look like Big Bird. That was a sight to behold."

Although Johnson was productive, his season was cut short. He started a July game and pitched to just one batter, who walked. Then he complained of arm problems and was removed. In an oddity, the runner scored, the Pilots never led and Johnson was tagged with the loss.

"I remember it was really cold and I came down with inflammation of my shoulder," said Johnson, "and I left about halfway through the season. It was a great opportunity to play there."

Soon after the short appearance, Johnson left Alaska.

"His arm was stiff," said McFarland. "It was mutally agreed."

Johnson is one of the best players to hone his abilities in Alaska, but some three hundred players were good enough to advance to the majors. Alaska was a stepping-stone for many.

"It has to be the growing season for future professional players," said Dan Cowgill, the 1999 Goldpanners' manager who also played in Alaska. "It's a forty-five-day growing season, instead of a ninety-day growing season."

Ninety days is pretty much the length of Alaska's intense vegetable growing season where the world's largest cabbages are raised for competition at the State Fair.

"The players blossom just like that," said Cowgill.

When it comes to listing the best Peninsula Oiler players of all-time, team executive Mike Baxter starts with Frank Viola, who won a Cy Young Award for the Minnesota Twins. He remembers Bill Spiers batting .418 in 1986 before going on to the majors, and Casey Bookout crushing the ball at .382 in 1997. Pitcher Dave Stieb, a seven-time All-Star, was another Oiler. Stieb was a late Oilers addition in 1977 when they won the NBC.

"We needed an outfielder and his older brother Steve was a catcher for us," said Baxter. "Dave had just finished high school and was signed to go to Arizona State. We can't find an outfielder to come in and Steve told Mark Newman, the manager, 'My brother's an outfielder.' Everybody's got a brother or a cousin who's outfielder, but we brought him up."

Stieb was installed in centerfield.

"He made an incredible throw and threw a guy out at the plate," said Baxter.

The Oiler legend is that Newman met Stieb at the third-base line running off the field and said, "You're pitching tomorrow."

Stieb never stopped pitching.

There are times when Alaska league officials see a player and label him a "can't-miss" prospect. There are times when they can say, "I told-you-so."

"It's interesting to follow them and see if your intuitions were correct or not," said the Pilots' Dave Foreman. "You have a feeling about some players who can't miss. Eddie Guardado was not one of them."

But Eddie Guardado is now a middle reliever for the Minnesota Twins.

"Alaska was a great experience for me," said Guardado, who pitched for the Glacier Pilots.

Kevin Smallcomb, a coach, then manager of the Pilots, said Guardado's achievement caught him off-guard.

"He didn't seem like the best pitcher on the roster and there's Guardado in the big leagues," said Smallcomb, who also coaches at Mendocino Community College. "They all have career goals. I follow Alaska league players in the majors. Every one of them, not just the Pilots."

Players like the Mat-Su Miners' Steve Trachsel, a 1990 Alaska star, who served up the pitch McGwire hit to break Roger Maris' record.

"He dominated us," said Smallcomb. "He used to stuff it up our butts. Any time I'm reading box scores, I'm thinking about Alaska. I think, 'How did we get that guy out?' "

In many cases, they didn't. Or the guy got all the Pilots out.

Anchorage Buc Anthony Telford made a lasting impression, dominating with a 5-0 record and 1.58 earned run average in 1986 before leaving the team to attend summer school at San Jose State.

"His athletic director made him go back to summer school because he flunked bowling," said Bucs GM Dennis Mattingly. "Maybe he was being sarcastic with me. I said, 'How do you flunk bowling?' "

Telford said the secret of his success was simple.

"I want to win worse than anybody," said Telford. "I can't stand to lose."

Telford threw a 90 mph fastball and an exquisite curve, and returned to the Bucs the next year while negotiating with the Baltimore Orioles, his future employer.

Jed Hansen, a former Buc from Stanford who played for the Kansas City Royals in 1999, loved the outdoors almost as much as the baseball. He visited his host family's remote cabin.

"There's nothing like pulling a trout right out of the water and frying the fish for dinner the same night," said Hansen.

A popular former Pilot with a long Major League career is infielder Luis Alicea. Alicea played on the 1985 club.

"Very effortless, real fluid," is Steve McFarland's description of Alicea's fielding skills.

Alicea, still taking ground balls for the Texas Rangers, enjoyed himself tremendously in Alaska, and said the talent level was so high in the ABL.

"There's good competition there," said Alicea. "Most everybody gets drafted. I'm still playing. You've got to be lucky. Even if you work hard you've got to be lucky and have no bad injuries."

Casey Candaele was a Pilots second-baseman in 1982 who few thought would go beyond being an NBC all-star. Candaele is still hanging in at AAA, trying to get a last callup.

"He did it with hustle. He was an average runner, an average thrower, but he had a big heart," said Jim Dietz. "Never in my wildest dreams did I think he would make it. I thought he might be a good minor leaguer."

Candaele played hard and he had a sense of humor. Ron Okerlund said Candaele lived down the street and once walked home drunk, fell in a ditch and spent the night sleeping it off there.

"He used to love to slide on the tarp," said Okerlund. "He did belly flops."

Once, Candaele pulled the trick later seen in the movie *Bull Durham* when players didn't want to play a game and turned on sprinklers to soak the field at night. The Pilots had to postpone a game. Years later, in Anchorage to speak at an athletic banquet, Candaele confessed to the stunt.

"He admitted it," said Okerlund. "He was the instigator. He said, "In case you want to know who did it, Ron.' "

Rico Rossy, another former Pilot who is from Puerto Rico, made the majors at second base. Rossy nearly matched Johnson with distinctive comment when asked what he'd like a baseball card to say about him. "Baseball has been bery, bery good to me," said Rossy, an imitation of "The Saturday Night Live" character.

"I tell everybody if they get the chance, to go," said Rossy of Alaska. "The baseball part, I think, helped me more than college. The talent, the instruction."

Tom Goodwin, a former Goldpanner with the Colorado Rockies, said he went to Fairbanks at just the right time in his college career.

"It helped me grow from my freshman to sophomore year," said Goodwin. "When you face new guys, that kind of stuff, from colleges we never played, it helps. I had to get over being a little homesick. That just kind of helped me grow up."

Jon Zuber of the Philadelphia Phillies played for the Mat-Su Miners and was a Wichita pickup for the Oilers. He said playing every day gave him a whole new outlook when he returned to the University of California.

"It gave me so much confidence," said Zuber. "It made me feel like I could play and that I belonged. I played every single day. I just got myself feeling more comfortable and confident."

Zuber made the most of that growing season Cowgill described.

Terry Francona, now the Phillies manager, played for the Goldpanners. His father, Tito, was a major leaguer, and Francona wanted to follow him. He ultimately did so, but the younger Francona was inexperienced when he went north.

"The baseball was a little ahead of me," said Francona. "I had to scrap to keep up."

Francona's showed his stuff off-the-field in Fairbanks in an unusual way.

"I caught a salmon with a hockey net," he said.

Mark Gardner, the Pilot used as a foil to provoke Johnson, had a great time away from Mulcahy. He saw moose, bears, rivers, glaciers, and fished.

"Every day was a new adventure," said Gardner. "I played golf at 10:30 at night. There were moose roaming around. We were advised to skip that hole."

J.T. Snow, the San Francisco Giants first baseman who was a 1986 Oiler, can top that story.

The first time Snow fished with his host family he wore hip waders and stepped into the Kenai River to cast. The water seemed awfully cold. Nah, the boot is waterproof, he was told. Snow decided to check the boot, anyway. He waded ashore and took it off. There was a hole.

"There was water up to my knee," said Snow. "My foot was blue."

Snow said playing in Alaska was just like playing in the minors.

"I think it prepares you pretty good for professional life," said Snow, who said someday after his baby son grows up he would like to take him to Alaska to fish and watch ABL games.

One player with the potential to become an Alaska great was the Giants' Barry Bonds. However, despite being recruited by Fairbanks several times, Bonds, who seems destined for the Hall of Fame, always went to summer school.

"I wanted to finish school early," said Bonds years later.

One year, Bonds made it to Fairbanks—in time to watch the last game.

"I just watched the sun, sun, sun," he said.

Then he accompanied the team to Wichita and represented the Goldpanners in the NBC.

"My experience was basically the tournament," said Bonds.

Mike Benjamin, a Pittsburgh Pirate second baseman, played for the Goldpanners in 1985 and benefited greatly from the competition. But Benjamin was also on a sightseeing rafting trip that nearly turned tragic. On a bus ride to Anchorage, the Goldpanners took a Nenana River raft ride.

"We had a team vote on taking the raft trip and it was like twenty-four to two," said Don Dennis. "The two who voted against it were both in the boat that went over."

One Goldpanner raft overturned, tipping players into the churning river.

"The water was about thirty-five degrees," said Benjamin, who was in a trailing boat. "They told us, 'You've only got about ten minutes if you fall in.'"

Benjamin threw a rope back to struggling teammates.

"I could only throw it about five feet," said Benjamin.

It was a close call and players were shaken up, but no one was seriously harmed.

Tim Layana, later a Major League pitcher, was the last one fished out, according to Dennis.

"He was one of the ones in the most danger," said Dennis. "His Goldpanner hat went floating down the river."

Layana, who had short stays with the Cincinnati Reds and the Giants, was unfortunately killed in an automobile accident in 1999.

In the 1980s, the Alaska league included a team called the Palouse Empire Cougars. They were an off-season version of Washington State University before the NCAA changed its rules to limit the number of players from one college who could play for the same summer club.

Boston Red Sox catcher Scott Hatteberg was a Palouse Empire player added to the Pilots for Wichita.

"It was a great time up there," said Hatteberg of his Alaska visits. "A lot of fishing. I couldn't help but catch them. I'd love to get back there. There were a lot of good teams. A lot of guys I'm still playing with."

The undisputed top Palouse player was John Olerud, a former batting champion who is now with the Seattle Mariners. Olerud also played for the Oilers in the 1980s. People tend to forget Olerud was a star pitcher as well as pure swinger. One season Olerud was 15-0 for Washington State while hitting .464.

They also forget that the easy-going, gracious Olerud had life-threatening brain surgery for an aneurysm during college.

Olerud's head was cut open by doctors in early 1989, less than a year after he was named the college player-of-the-year. Suffering from severe headaches, Olerud collapsed during a December drill. A six-hour operation was followed by rehabilitation and the requirement to wear a helmet on the field at all times. It made Olerud hot and sweaty and certainly wasn't as comfortable as wearing a baseball cap, but Olerud adjusted. He played for Washington State a few months after the operation and hit .350 during the first stage of his remarkable comeback.

Then five months after surgery, he appeared in the ABL and was again a full-fledged star. Olerud didn't pretend to be at full strength by summer, but he looked it when he played.

"Every step of the way I feel I was real fortunate," said Olerud. "I feel real lucky to be here. I'm just glad it's behind me."

Ahead of Olerud was a brilliant baseball career.

Olerud went directly to the majors with the Toronto Blue Jays, without stopping in the minors, and in 1993 won the American League batting championship.

Olerud is still a .300 hitter, and he too may end up among the Alaska Baseball League's greatest alumni.

22

THE NINETIES

Alaska keeps cranking out stars

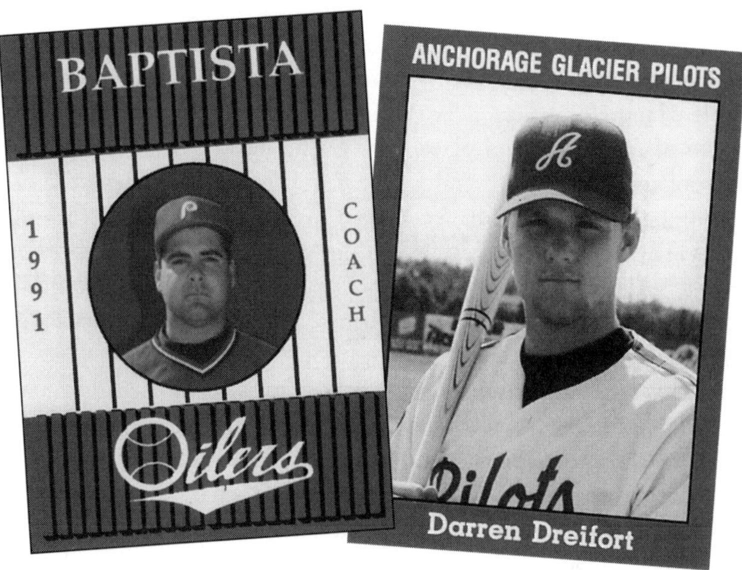

J.D. DREW stood on third base, waiting for the perfect moment. Anchorage Bucs pitcher Bobby Robinson went into his windup and then, out of the corner of his eye, Robinson saw a blur.

Drew darted down the third-base line. Head lowered, arms churning, he sprinted for home. Robinson threw home. Drew ran home. Catcher Barry Patton tried to block home. Drew slid. The ball thudded into Patton's glove. The dust flew.

Safe.

Drew, a daring outfielder for the Peninsula Oilers, stole home. Stealing home is almost a lost baseball art. Stealing home may be the game's most exciting play, but it is rarely attempted anymore. Only the very confident try the maneuver since by all logic the thrown ball should be able to beat the running runner to the plate.

The secret is to study the pitcher's delivery. Does he have a big kick, a big windup? Does he take a long time to throw? If the pitcher takes longer than 3-to-3.5 seconds serving the ball up to the plate, then he is vulnerable to a savvy runner.

The Oilers watched and talked, watched and informed Drew that all systems were go.

"We had a stop watch in the dugout," said Drew, who played for the Oilers in 1995. "We talked about it earlier."

The gamble paid off. Swipes of home tend to demoralize the other team. Bucs manager John Baptista called Drew's move "a surprise attack. You know you're sleeping."

At college and Alaska, Drew fooled a lot of people a lot of the time. He left Florida State in 1997 as the number one draft pick of the Philadelphia Phillies. He held out for a $10 million signing bonus, though, earning the enmity of many fans and players. When he didn't get it Drew played in an independent league for several hundred dollars a month. A year later he was the number one pick of the St. Louis Cardinals and did sign for millions of dollars. The controversy over his holdout was slow to die, but Drew is a soft-spoken, religious man and a top-notch player who hit more than .400 in a September, 1998 St. Louis call-up, then became a starter for the Cardinals the next season.

Disliked in Philadelphia, Drew's popularity was unmatched in Alaska.

Oilers executive Mike Baxter said he thinks Drew "might end up being" the team's all-time best player. To prove their faith in Drew's future, the Oilers used his picture on the cover of their 1999 yearbook.

Decades have passed since the Goldpanners started it all and great players filled Alaska lineups in the 1960s, 1970s and 1980s. Drew could become the Alaska Major League star of the 1990s, but it is too early to tell. There is also competition.

The 1996 U.S. Olympic team alone featured four former ABL players. Travis Lee and Jacque Jones of the Goldpanners, Chad Green of the Oilers, and Brian Loyd of the Glacier Pilots, were members of the American squad that won the bronze medal.

The raves which followed Lee's career matched or eclipsed the scouts' gushing about Drew.

Lee, who signed to play for Jim Dietz at San Diego State before he ever set foot in Alaska, was a high school phenom. Dietz figured it would be good experience for Lee to hit against ABL pitching. What could he lose? So in 1993 Lee joined the Goldpanners—and he hit .386.

"It was interesting to see a guy come out of high school with as much maturity as he had," said Dan Boone, then a Goldpanner coach. "He was the best player on our team coming out of high school. And he hasn't slowed down one bit."

That's the truth. Lee played for Fairbanks again in 1994, became a member of Team USA, where he batted .405, and represented his country in the

1996 Olympics in Atlanta. In three college seasons, the sweet-swinging lefty batted .339, .350, and .355.

"I told his dad Gary halfway through his freshman year to get a financial planner because his son was going to be a millionaire," said Dietz.

That was also the truth. Lee agreed to a multi-million-dollar deal with the Arizona Diamondbacks and by 1998 was the team's starting first baseman.

Lee said Dietz never intended to make him a regular with the Goldpanners.

"He wanted to bring me up to take batting practice for two weeks," said Lee. "I had nothing else to do."

He showed how special a player he already was. But Lee was young, barely a month past his eighteenth birthday, and later said that made him uncomfortable.

"I was just nervous the whole summer," said Lee. "I'm coming in a high school guy and all those other guys are college dudes."

Like some major leaguers who refuse to watch movies because they think it will strain their eyes, Lee thought rest was the prescription to keep his hitting sharp in Fairbanks. While others fished, he slept.

Jacque Jones, the other Goldpanner 1996 Olympian, was another can't-miss guy. Jones, out of Southern Cal, has speed and swings a deadly stick. That's why he is the leadoff hitter for the Minnesota Twins. His 1999 rookie season saw him hit close to .300 all year.

Jones played for Fairbanks in 1994 and it was swiftly recognized this was a player who would ascend the charts.

"One of the things I like best about Jacque Jones is that he hits the ball to all fields," said Mark O'Brien, who was a coach when Jones competed in Alaska. "He can hit with pop to all fields."

Jones developed a special bond with his Fairbanks family, Terry and Barbara Aldridge and their three children. During his college years, they spoke on the phone monthly. The family kept pictures of Jones on a wall and on the refrigerator and the kids wrote him letters.

"I'd like to go back on vacation and spend time with my host family," said Jones.

After USC seasons hitting .335, .353, and .375, playing in the Olympics, and working his way through the minors, Jones has the makings of a player who can be a cornerstone of the Twins franchise.

Loyd, a Fullerton State All-American who caught for the Pilots in 1994, is in the Toronto Blue Jays chain, but as a smooth-fielding catcher who has a good bat, he seems destined to break in with the parent club soon.

Loyd might well be the Glacier Pilots' most active fisherman of all time. He caught red salmon, king salmon, halibut and even sea bass on Resurrection

Bay near Seward during his summer in Alaska. Scheduled to alternate at the position, he played his game, and then secure in the knowledge he would sit out the next day, Loyd stayed up all night fishing.

Regarded as a strong, all-around catcher, Loyd works well with pitchers, has a good arm and anticipates action on the field.

"He's a real intelligent receiver," said five-year Pilots manager Kevin Smallcomb, who did not coach Loyd in Alaska, but saw him play in California. "Just a smart kid. He knows how to read swings."

Loyd did not hit well for the Pilots—maybe because fishing was a higher priority—but hit over .300 three times in college and approached that figure in AA Knoxville. Loyd always thinks about the glorious fishing in Alaska.

"I'm planning to come back," he said.

The fourth Olympian, Green, humorously compared the Oilers' Bingo Hilton to the Athletes Village.

"I've seen Monica Seles and Vlade Divac walking around," said Green of the famous tennis player and the well-known NBA player.

Not at the bingo hall.

A star at the University of Kentucky, Green has lightning speed.

"That guy's going to steal you blind," said O'Brien. "He's very dangerous when he gets on base."

Green, a number one draft pick of the Milwaukee Brewers, said it was a thrill being part of the American team at the opening ceremonies.

"It was a great feeling to walk in," he said.

A better feeling than fishing the Kenai River, which he did often with the Oilers. The salmon he caught were nothing to brag about, said Green, not very big. Which left Green with another goal to fulfill after he makes the majors: return to Alaska and catch a larger king salmon.

Sometimes the ABL becomes a temporary haven for a drafted player who can't agree on a contract. Rather than sit home watching TV, the player heads to Alaska to play ball.

Pitcher Darren Dreifort played for the Glacier Pilots in 1991. After playing on the 1992 Olympic team, Dreifort was drafted in the first round out of Wichita State by the Los Angeles Dodgers in 1993. While talks between his dad and the team stagnated, Dreifort served as the Pilots' designated hitter, risking his future.

"I just want to play baseball," said Dreifort when he got to Alaska. "You can get hurt walking down the stairs. If you get hurt on the baseball field, it happens."

The contract was signed, Dreifort joined the Dodgers and these days is a member of the club's starting rotation.

The greatest reliever in Pilots history is a different hurler from Wichita

State. Marc Bluma, a member of the 1997 and 1998 teams, finished his Pilot career with twenty-one saves, including eleven in 1998 when he ended his season abruptly by smacking a wall in frustration, breaking his hand.

A thrower with a chunky build and a heater that zips, Bluma, now in the Blue Jays' system, is the perfect closer. He strides in from the bullpen with the air of cockiness so necessary to the mentality of a finisher. In Anchorage, he was so good that any time Kevin Smallcomb called, he expected the game to end in about five minutes.

"It's security knowing he's out there," said Smallcomb. "He can also get hot in less than two hitters. He can get ready to throw in eight or ten pitches. He prides himself on that."

The day Bluma recorded the tenth save of his record-setting season, he mowed down three visiting Athletes in Action batters in the ninth inning on strikes.

"When I get in my rhythm," said Bluma, "that's how it is. I don't step off the mound. I like to work fast. They're going to have to beat me on what I feel is my best pitch."

That rarely happened.

One of the Anchorage Bucs' best all-time players, Andrew Beinbrink, was also just starting out in professional ball in 1999. Beinbrink, a three-year Buc, played third base for Arizona State and batted .402 his senior year.

Beinbrink distinguished himself off the field, too. He designs flowered shorts, sewing his own, though it made more sense for him to work on that hobby in Arizona than Alaska.

"It's too cold," said Beinbrink, citing one factor that inhibited his stitching in the northland. And? He had no sewing machine with him in Anchorage.

Beinbrink, the league's 1996 player-of-the-year, ended up spending so much time in the state he wondered if he might qualify for the annual Permanent Fund Dividend check given to locals from oil money.

"I'll get a residency check," said Beinbrink. "I need it."

Another Pilot who is a budding star is slugger Ryan Ludwick. Ludwick, younger brother of Major Leaguer Eric Ludwick, also an ex-Pilot, played the 1997 season in Anchorage during one summer off from University of Nevada Las Vegas. Mashing home runs faster than a totalizer board could compute them, Ludwick equaled the 1971 team record of 19 set by Ron Pruitt.

You could tell Ludwick would be an honest-to-goodness power hitter by what type of pitches he hits. Ludwick swats balls long-distance that he has no business touching.

"I love those balls down," he said of throws that might be termed bad tosses. "I like coming up on the ball."

Closer to the majors than Bluma, Beinbrink or Ludwick are such former

ABL stars as Buc Dusty Allen, who played three seasons in Anchorage, and in 1999 played at AAA Las Vegas for the San Diego Padres. And Pilot Steve Carver, the 1994 league player-of-the-year, who in 1999 played at AAA Scranton for the Phillies.

Adam Kennedy, an ex-Goldpanner, made his Major League debut with the St. Louis Cardinals late in the 1999 season. Kennedy, who played collegiately at Northridge State, owns the all-time best single-season Goldpanner average. His .432 in 1995 broke the twenty-one-year-old record of .425 set by Steve Kemp.

For every star who goes on and enhances the reputation of the Alaska Baseball League, new ones appear to replace them. In 1998 and 1999, the Mat-Su Miners introduced unheralded pitchers who baffled the opposition.

In 1998, Jeremy Cunningham fooled batters with a slider more overpowering than his fastball. Cunningham finished 5-1 with a 1.47 earned run average.

"Guys who throw ninety-five mph have the luxury of throwing and missing by a few inches," said Cunningham, a Cal Poly San Luis Obispo player. "I've got to hit my spots."

A year later the Miners uncovered another little-known gem. John Eric Hernandez led Chico State to the NCAA Division II championship. He had no idea if he could out-smart more experienced hitters from big schools.

But Hernandez dominated in Alaska, going 8-1 with an 0.85 earned run average. A player from a tiny high school on Catalina Island, Hernandez threw three straight no-hitters there and in Alaska nearly ended the season with one as well. His finale shutout of the Peninsula Oilers was a one-hitter.

"I'm pretty much in shock," said Hernandez, a polite, soft-spoken player. "It just worked out for me.

Just worked out. As if Hernandez's right arm had nothing to do with the result. The Detroit Tigers, who drafted him, are wondering if Hernandez can tie a whole new group of hitters in knots.

A few years from now John Eric Hernandez may well be an Alaska Baseball League graduate who is a hot topic in the big leagues.

23

HOME COOKING

Alaska high schools produce their share of pros

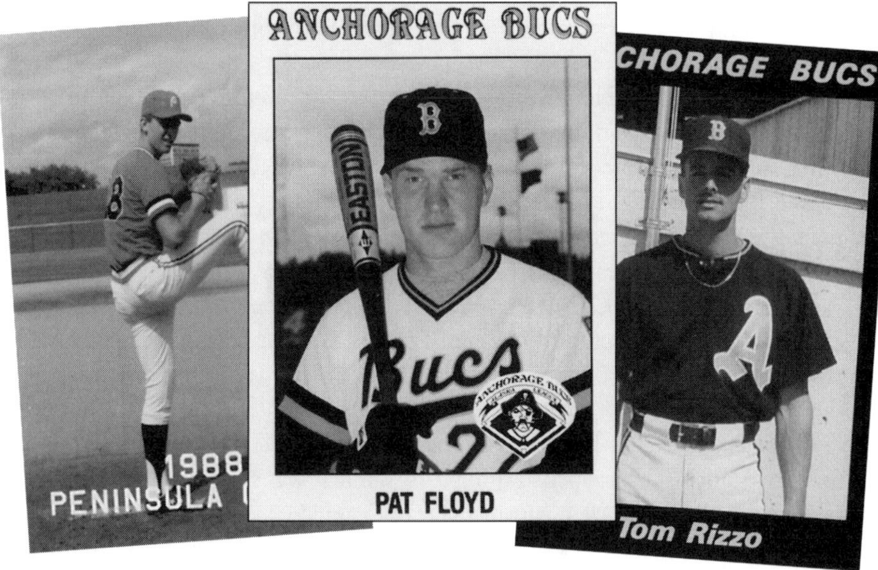

PAT FLOYD was the last one. The last of three Floyd brothers to play for the Anchorage Bucs. Max started the connection in the early 1980s. Scott followed. Then Pat, as the 1980s turned to the 1990s.

They came out of Kodiak, the large island in the Gulf of Alaska known for its king crab and monstrous brown bears. They came from the remotest possible place in the United States for a baseball player. But they were Floyds. They came out of Joe Floyd, the offspring of a man who virtually invented kids' sports opportunities in Kodiak.

Joe Floyd was his own kind of brown bear, tenacious and tough enough to jump-start ideas and see them through to fruition. He is Mr. Sports in Kodiak. He began the American Legion baseball program in Kodiak. He was athletic director at Kodiak High. The high school Christmas basketball tournament is named for him. And the local track is dedicated in his name.

Baseball in Kodiak. There wasn't much competition and the conditions were rugged. Rugged? Well, when it wasn't cold and windy, it was cold, windy and wet. Pat Floyd once said that his Legion team played only about fifteen games a season "and half of them were rained out."

Still, Max, Scott and Pat were good enough to play with and against anybody, and they made the link with the Bucs and Dennis Mattingly early.

Mattingly once said of Joe Floyd's brood, "I wish he had about five more of them."

Max Floyd played third base, outfield and catcher for the Bucs in the mid-1980s. Scott was a pitcher a couple of years later. And Pat was a great-hitting DH and outfielder who was fortunate to play on the dominating Bucs teams of 1990 and 1991, after spending 1987 and 1988 with the Palouse Empire Cougars.

What made the Floyds unusual was that they were Alaskans. From the time the Fairbanks Goldpanners began recruiting top-flight collegians from other states, it became difficult for the Alaska-bred ballplayer to shine in the Alaska Baseball League. They were at a disadvantage. Until a few years ago, there was no spring high school ball in Alaska, only summer American Legion. Seasons were short, weather conditions frequently awful.

For a while, Alaska players were overlooked. When the Bucs formed in 1980, they made it part of their mission statement to provide expanded chances for Alaskans. But the Bucs found that if they were going to compete, they also had to rely on collegians.

The league responded by passing a rule allowing teams roster exemptions to carry Alaskans. That opened things up. While it was still rare for Alaskans to become regulars, they were part of the team, gained experience, got the chance to be seen and develop, and periodically made breakthroughs to become key contributors.

Pat Floyd did that. In 1991, Floyd, who played at the University of the Pacific, batted .366 for the Bucs team that as he put it "won everything." Everything they entered. The league. Tournaments. And Floyd's average was the highest on a remarkable club.

"Just everything fell for me," said Floyd, now a guidance counselor at Colony High in Palmer, Alaska. "It was just a fun year of playing baseball. It was one of the best years I ever had.

"When you're trying to make it on the club and they find out you're from Alaska, you had to work to earn their respect. That's why it was so much better when I proved myself."

The performance was more satisfying because Floyd's role wasn't as significant with the Cougars. In one game, Floyd was due to bat in a crucial bases-loaded situation. But Palouse manager Bobo Brayton called him back for a pinch hitter.

"Floyd, you're sawed," said Brayton, figuratively and literally taking the bat out of Floyd's hands.

The pinch hitter? A freshman named John Olerud. Olerud tripled, clearing

Chugiak High graduate Joey Clark goes into his windup on the Mulcahy Stadium mound. Clark, drafted by the Montreal Expos, played for the Glacier Pilots. Lew Freedman

the bases while Floyd stewed in the dugout, thinking, "I could have done that."

He might have. Even if Olerud did turn out to be such a great player that Floyd now collects Olerud baseball cards.

Another "Alaskan" who made an impact with the Bucs was Tom Rizzo. A former minor leaguer, Rizzo was in the Air Force at Elmendorf Air Force Base, helping a Bucs official coach a legion team when he was asked to fill in. That was in 1992.

"They needed an arm one night," said Rizzo.

Two years later, still playing, the then-twenty-eight-year-old Rizzo distinguished himself as a valuable utility player, making the league all-star team. That season a guy who thought he was finished with top-quality baseball, played second base, third, left field, and was a designated hitter and relief pitcher. Rizzo batted .309 and scored twenty-five runs. He became such a fan favorite that at his last game before being discharged and moving back to Massachusetts, the Bucs presented him with a plaque that praised his "leadership, dedication, and most of all, the hustle you have given us for the last three years." Mayor Rick Mystrom proclaimed it "Tom Rizzo Day" in the city, calling Rizzo "an outstanding role model and inspiration for Anchorage's youth."

Against the odds, some Alaskans have played professionally. Bill Noverr of Anchorage was drafted by the San Diego Padres in the mid-1980s. Tim Stanley of Anchorage played in the Montreal Expos system in the late-1980s, signing after playing for the Pilots at Wichita in 1987. In the 1990s, Cliff Anderson of Kodiak was in the Los Angeles Dodgers chain.

Trajan Langdon, the Duke All-American basketball player who joined the Cleveland Cavaliers of the NBA in 1999, signed a $250,000 contract with the San Diego Padres in 1994 when he finished high school in Anchorage. Langdon played parts of two summers in the minors, but chose to concentrate on basketball. Although Langdon did not shine in the minors, Jim Dietz, the old Fairbanks manager, still thinks Langdon's best sport might have been baseball.

The biggest Alaska baseball success story is Marshall Boze, a pitcher from Soldotna. Boze, who once struck out twenty-two men in a Kenai American Legion game, received a $25,000 signing bonus from the Milwaukee Brewers in 1990. He understandably took the money and turned down the invitation to play with the Peninsula Oilers that summer.

In 1996, Boze became the first Alaskan to reach the major leagues.

"I had no idea I was getting called up," said Boze. "It really didn't hit me until I was on the airplane getting ready to land."

Although his fastball was clocked at 93 mph, he stayed with the Brewers only briefly, compiling an 0-2 record with a 7.79 earned run average and one save.

Pilots coach Jack O'Toole helped local pitcher Joey Clark come to the attention of the Expos while he was with the Glacier Pilots. LEW FREEDMAN

"Getting there was the greatest feeling I'd ever had," said Boze. "There was no better place to be than in the major leagues."

Boze would have been quite the gate attraction with the Oilers, who between 1994 and 1997 featured local hero Dennis Machado. Machado set a then-state record by rushing for 1,509 yards for the Kenai's high school football team, and pitched for the Oilers. Machado was drafted by the Montreal Expos and earned a college scholarship from the exposure.

"It was nice to be drafted," said Machado. "Later on in life I can always say I was drafted by a major-league team."

The Oilers enjoy having local players on the roster. Besides Machado, Josh Coleman and Jackson Coleman of Soldotna played for the Oilers in recent years. But it's hard for many to find a place.

"It's real, real tough on the kids," said the Oilers' Mike Baxter. "The talent base we're picking from is humongous. They haven't had the year-round ball the kids from Arizona and Florida have. Getting playing time for local kids is tough. I really like to have local guys involved."

When it works out, it's good for everyone.

"It's so good if the kid gets it right," said Baxter. "They're celebrities with the Little Leaguers."

The patron saint of local ballplayers is Pilots coach Lefty Van Brunt.

While Van Brunt's Pilots visibility is etched in fans' minds, what he does in the off-season, out-of-sight, may well be his biggest contribution to Alaska baseball.

Lefty's Warehouse. That's what people call it. It's not fancy. It's not plush. It's a place for work. Van Brunt's winter hangout is a workout center converted from an old South Anchorage warehouse. Local ballplayers, regardless of affiliation, are welcome, free of charge. The center has batting cages, pitching mounds, and its greatest asset—Lefty.

Van Brunt videotapes hitters and pitchers and tutors willing pupils. Some of Van Brunt's customers are high school players who just want to have a good season. Some have higher aspirations. Some seek junior college or college scholarships, or a chance to play for the Pilots. Van Brunt makes time for all of them.

Sharon Woods, the summer parent who sometimes works in the Pilot offices, said Van Brunt's largess is well known.

"I get calls to the office," she said. "He'll help any kid who wants it."

One of those kids was Ricky Bostick, a lanky Anchorage pitcher who sought assistance on his mechanics and then went on to Orange Coast College in California. In a 1999 tournament, Bostick pitched a superb, though losing, three-hitter against the Pilots. Van Brunt was an interested spectator and afterwards said he was proud of Bostick.

"When I got there," said Bostick of Lefty's Warehouse, "I listened. He showed me how to throw, how to follow through and how to throw a cut fastball better."

Van Brunt knows that with proper instruction, some Alaskans can equalize a Californian's weather advantage. Impressing Van Brunt can get a local player onto the Pilots roster. He runs pre-season tryout camps and tells general manager Ron Okerlund who is worth taking.

In 1994, catcher Scott Silvulich of Wasilla stuck with the team. He didn't play much, though. Neither did Mischa Sorbo, a former West High infielder. But Sorbo was a Van Brunt disciple who worked on his game religiously, and displayed an enthusiastic attitude. For a while had a 1.000 average for the Pilots, even if it was only 1-for-1.

Few Alaska players see much game action. A good time to make an impression on the manager, though, is in early-season games when the roster is in flux.

In 1998, Joey Clark, a fastballer from Chugiak High, who was drafted by the Montreal Expos, was looked on as a hurler with potential. Big at 6-foot-4 and 220 pounds, he lacked experience.

"It's very seldom you see this raw talent in Alaska," said Pilot coach Jack O'Toole, who recommended Clark to the Expos. "He needs a lot of coaching. He's a rough diamond."

Clark was happy to be noticed by any Major League team.

"I don't think any of this would have happened without Jack," said Clark.

In seven Pilot appearances that season, Clark was 2-1 with a 7.27 earned run average. He pitched in junior college and returned to the Pilots for part of the 1999 season.

The Pilots made room for four other Alaskans in 1999. Pitcher Darrel Bradley of Anchorage was back for a fourth season with the club. Josh Ellis of Anchorage made the roster. And Rob Conway and Chad Bentz of Juneau came aboard. Conway, a third baseman, had the best contact possible: he played for Pilots manager Kevin Smallcomb in California.

The most intriguing addition was Bentz. Fresh out of Juneau-Douglas High, Bentz had made a name for himself not only in American Legion ball, but by spending recent summers pitching in Michigan for a Connie Mack-level team. Bentz, like Jim Abbott, was also born without a right hand, so he released his 90 mph fastball, then rapidly shifted his glove to his left hand.

Just nineteen, Bentz, a thirty-fourth-round draft pick of the New York Yankees, has 6-foot-2, 210-pound size, an asset as a high school fullback. Given several opportunities to start for the Pilots, Bentz could not carry a game smoothly for more than three innings.

He felt intimidated by players from big-time colleges and saw his fastball flatten out, then get roped to all fields. Bentz pitched 18 innings and finished 1-3 with a 9.50 earned run average. It was a bruising welcome to the Alaska league. Although his ego was wounded, Bentz said the experience was valuable.

"I've learned every single time I've been out there," said Bentz.

And he learned he has a lot to learn. The shelling left him determined to come back and show the ABL better stuff a year later.

Alaska teams will continue to make room for Alaska players. And they will be thrilled if any of those players become contributors like Pat Floyd. The Floyds, all now in their thirties, were ahead of their time.

At the start of the new century, Max Floyd was director of club and intramural sports at Wake Forest University in North Carolina. Scott Floyd was a major in the Air Force, and also stationed in North Carolina. Pat Floyd coached baseball for a while, but now he just follows it.

Pat never tried to play at a higher level. Batting .366 in the ABL in 1991 was his special season.

"Growing up, that was the top thing in my priorities," he said. "For me, it was the major leagues. My goal was already achieved."

24
THE SCOUTS

Mining for nuggets of talent

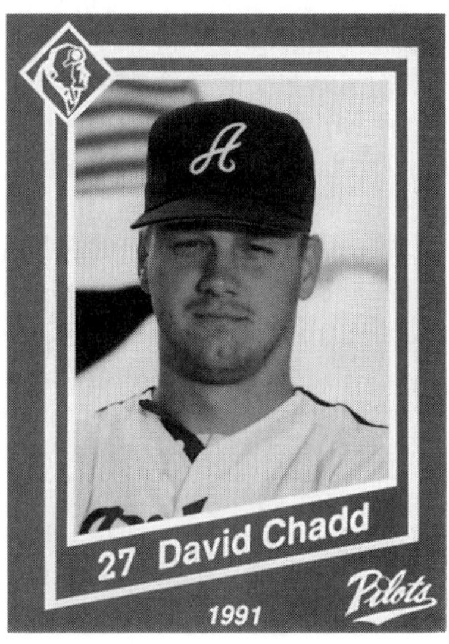

BOB OLDIS is an old wise man of baseball. Craggy-faced, with gray hair, Oldis knows his territory. When he attends Alaska Baseball League games on summer nights, he wears a heavy coat. You can't fool him. Alaska in summer is like April in the Midwest.

His is the deep voice of experience. He knows the wind can blow in fiercely from left field at Mulcahy Stadium. He is a superior weatherman, as well as a superior talent scout for the Montreal Expos.

Scouts follow players. If good ball is played in Alaska, the scouts come to Alaska. Oldis has been coming for a quarter century. He is the man who signed Warren Cromartie so long ago on Jack O'Toole's advice, and he is the man whom Jack O'Toole tips about hot prospects.

On one recent Alaska visit, Oldis stood by the Glacier Pilots dugout before a game, shooting the breeze with O'Toole. Dick Lobdell walked up and did a double take.

"If it isn't Jack O'Toole's son," he joked.

The two men have a close relationship, but father-son it isn't. Both are in their seventies.

Oldis caught for three Major League teams between 1953 and 1963, and has scouted for the Expos since 1970. O'Toole notes that Oldis is the only original Expo left.

For three decades, Oldis has been a man on the move, scouring the land for players, covering what must be more than a million miles. He said he travels 38,000 miles annually and the road always takes him to Alaska.

What is he searching for? More than impressive numbers, he is searching for impressive skills.

"If someone can run, he's gonna get our attention," said Oldis. "An aggressive swinger will open your eyes."

Now that the Bucs Invitational is established as a gathering place for all Alaska teams at the end of the season, Anchorage is at the end of the northern road for all Major League scouts. They can spend a week in Anchorage and scrutinize all the talent the ABL has to offer.

For that reason, in the summer of 1999, thirty-three Major League scouts appeared for the tournament. Pretty impressive since there are only thirty Major League teams. Some teams were seeing double.

"It saves a lot of moving around," said Rich Bordi, a San Diego Padres scout. "The consistent search for talent." Then he cracked, "I came up to see Jack."

The scouts all know O'Toole. He's got longevity, a good track record, and he's one of them, on the payroll of a big-league team. Besides, Jack and wife Katie always threw them a barbecue bash.

Thirty-three scouts in one building is a lot, very real testimony to the belief that the ABL is a hotbed of talent, filled with guys worth watching.

Not bothering to scout Alaska might mean missing out on a gem, or getting fooled by a prospect who is not one. Many times scouts know the players before they get to Alaska. Many times they know them by reputation.

"Some of them are just names to me," said Bordi, who briefly played in the majors.

David Chadd is affiliated with the Florida Marlins. He is also the rare scout with a past Alaska league connection. In 1991, one of the Pilots' NBC championship years, he was a coach. At that time his main job was working as an assistant coach for Wichita State. Chadd grew up a few blocks from Lawrence-Dumont Stadium in Wichita and said his first job as an eight-year-old was chasing balls for NBC executive Larry Davis.

Chadd has scouted Alaska six times.

"It's my favorite duty of the summer," he said. "If I was a kid playing baseball, I would want to come up here."

The scouts are not hard to spot in the stands. Most sit behind home plate. The tools of the trade are radar guns used to measure pitchers' speed, stopwatches used to time runners getting from the batter's box to first base, and notebooks used to scribble thoughts.

These are the numbers and words that determine young men's futures, decide whether their dreams are realistic or fanciful. Although some talent is easy to see, like the guy who throws 95 mph or hits 500-foot homers, several scouts may see a player and form different impressions. Some may decide he is worth a try, worth a draft pick, and some may decide he's not.

The issue is simultaneously simple and complex. Is the skinny nineteen-year-old going to bulk up and become a hard-hitting twenty-two-year-old? Will he improve? Does he have the intangibles, heart and hustle? Is he our kind of guy?

That's all hard to predict with a player who might need four years of minor-league seasoning. What will that finished product be like? It's called educated guesswork.

Scouts see thousands of players play hundreds of games every year and they must make snap judgments as well as informed judgments. They have to project, predict the murky future from an empirical present. Worse, if you think you found someone special that no one else thinks terribly highly of, unless you can convince the front office, he might not be drafted.

"You spin the wheel," said John "Spider" Jorgensen, a Chicago Cubs scout who once played for the Dodgers.

It used to be that scouts were men who led solitary lives touring the backwoods of the nation, seeking the hidden jewel in the tiny town. They wooed mom and dad, as well as junior, and they sweet-talked them into signing with the big club before a scout from another big club pounced.

No more.

In theory it's still every team for itself, but the establishment of a communal draft in the mid-1960s, rewarding teams who did the poorest on the field with the highest picks, wiped out that way of life, that way of finding the Hall of Famer who could make you famous. With the draft, it is harder to prove you are smarter than anyone else, that you out-hustled them.

Now, with expanded communications, there are no backwoods, anyway. Even those in the country find their way into the public eye. There is no less of a need for talent to replenish the big-league roster, but it's awfully hard for a scout to distinguish himself the way his predecessors did.

It's a long-gone method of working, faded out more than thirty years ago. Oldis has been around long enough to remember the old ways because as a player he was signed before the system changed, and scouts who lived by their wits and gut instinct were still working when he started in the profession. They didn't congregate in the stands as often back then.

"You'd hear stories about scouts who ran into each other and say, 'Where

Bob Oldis, left, a scout with the Montreal Expos since 1970, has been searching Alaska ballparks for potential major league talent for a quarter of a century. Pilots coach Jack O'Toole, right, also scouts for the Expos. The two men have a close working relationship. In 1973, O'Toole helped Oldis land Warren Cromartie, who went on to a stellar nine-year career with the Expos. LEW FREEDMAN

are you going tomorrow?" said Oldis. "One would say, 'I'm going to Topeka.' The other would say, 'I'm going to Oklahoma City.' The next day they'd both show up in Kansas City. Now you have a one-in-thirty chance of getting the player."

Of course, those scouts were looking for unpublicized special players, seeking the star from Nowheresville. Stars are known now, even as high schoolers.

"There are no secrets," said Oldis.

Good judgment, though, remains the number one attribute of a scout. A scout still has to make the call on whether a young player can make it at the highest level. A player might have a big reputation, but is he the real deal? He might be batting .600, but he may not be able to hit the curveball. He may strike out twenty-seven in a game, but was the opposition weak?

Salaries of Major League stars grew by the millions over the years, but team managements were reluctant to reward high draft picks with really big bucks until recently. Over the last few years, number-one draftees started getting big checks to sign their John Hancock on the dotted line. Hence, teams engage in all kinds of research. It's not enough to be able to figure out if Billy can hit, field and throw, they want to know more about his personality.

"Now you've got to find out what kind of family he's from," said Oldis. "Is he on that funny stuff?"

Meaning marijuana. But also, no doubt, any other drug, or booze.

Among the players Spider Jorgensen signed are ex-major leaguer Bob Walk, for the Phillies, and Mark Grace, for the Cubs. Jorgensen said it helps to compare prospects to known players.

"You might write, 'Reminds me of Mickey Mantle,' " said Jorgensen.

And how many times has he written that?

Jorgensen smiled. "Zero," he said.

Jorgensen joked about the difficulty of signing an unknown star, especially in his specialty territory.

"You're not going to do it in Southern California unless the guy's been in jail for five years," he said.

Players know when the scouts are in the house at the Bucs Invitational and they know the scouts go to the National Baseball Congress. That's a selling point of Alaska summer ball: You will be seen.

In the 1994 Bucs Invitational, Mark Redman threw a no-hitter for the Bucs. He was hardly an unknown, though, since he came to Alaska directly from the College World Series. Still, he wanted to enhance his chances of being well-received in the pros.

"I knew there were scouts there and I had to give them my best," said Redman.

Redman was drafted and made his Major League debut with the Minnesota Twins in 1999.

Mike Drumright, a Glacier Pilots pitcher, who has good genes, being the nephew of former Major Leaguer Keith Drumright, was also very conscious of the scouts' presence when he hummed his fastball. He wanted them to write compliments in their notebooks, so they would be happy to draft him.

"That's what I'm out here for," said Drumright.

Drumright was a number-one draft pick of the Detroit Tigers, but a few years later was still trying to rise above AAA.

One humorous situation arose. Richard Graves, a scout for the Kansas City Royals, attended the Invitational while his son Ryan was serving with the Bucs. Even if Richard unbiasedly loved Ryan's pitching talent, he couldn't sign his son without drafting him. Actually, Ryan had few illusions about his baseball future.

"I'm not a prospect," he said.

There are always plenty of prospects in Alaska, though. Steve McFarland, who managed the Pilots from 1984 through 1987 and again in 1993 and 1994, said at the start of each season he told players the odds favored them.

"We used to tell these guys, 'Six or seven of you are going to make the majors,' " said McFarland. "You didn't know which six or seven. You could tell certain guys would be big-league ballplayers, or would get the chance. But they were so young. It's a proving ground. If you can do well in the Alaska league, you are going to be a player. All of the scouts knew that."

Oldis, who has threatened retirement, said it's hard to picture skipping his annual Alaska visits.

"I can't stay away," he said.

Maybe he just wants to find one more special player. One of his favorite signings for the Expos was Shane Rawley. When Oldis saw the future Major Leaguer for the first time, he was pitching for Indian Hills Junior College in Iowa and he weighed about one-hundred-and-thirty-five pounds. Yet Oldis spotted potential.

"You get a lot of satisfaction out of something like that," said Oldis.

Oldis' intuition paid off that time, and who's to say it won't again with some unheralded player running around the outfield in Anchorage?

25

THE UMPS

Sometimes they find the fans tougher than the weather

UMPIRING AT first base, Scott Taylor was an easy target for the spectators in Home Brew Alley, the first-base side stands at Mulcahy Stadium where the most committed Anchorage Glacier Pilots fans sit.

Out of nowhere a carrot landed at Taylor's feet. No subtle hint there, huh? A fan found a creative way to hint at Taylor's need for better vision. What did Taylor do? He picked up the carrot, took a bite out of it, and threw it back. The fans laughed.

Another time, on a close play at first base involving a Pilot runner, Taylor turned to Bill Ferguson, one of the most devoted Pilots' fans, and yelled, "Fergie, what have you got?"

Ferguson, so close to the Pilots for so long that he was chosen to throw out the first pitch for a home game during the 1999 season, called "Safe!"

"Wrong," Taylor yelled back. "He's out."

Taylor, who attended umpire school in California and Florida, umpired minor league baseball in the Texas League between 1982 and 1986, and handled college baseball in the Plains states. He ran across Dave Strike, an Alaska League umpiring veteran, who urged him to come north.

Seeing Alaska sounded like a fun thing to do. So Taylor became an ABL ump in 1996. Then he gave up umpiring and stayed in Alaska awhile. Taylor got a job in marketing for the Pilots, changing his uniform from umpire blue to Pilots blue.

Much like the players, most umpires are from out of state and come to Alaska only for the short season. They are generally experienced college umpires. Taylor, who is from Oklahoma, called games in the Big Eight, Southeastern Conference, the old Southwest Conference, and the Missouri Valley Conference.

Some umps return for years. Others try it once. However, because they umpire every day, the fans get to know them quickly, and they aren't cut any slack.

Mark Hoops, an umpire originally from Indiana and now living near Chicago, was working on Cape Cod in 1991 when he wrote to the ABL asking to join up.

"I wanted to get a sampling of other leagues," said Hoops.

The late Coral Seymour, then the Oilers' general manager, called to welcome him aboard. Hoops was assigned to ump home games of the Glacier Pilots, Miners and Oilers. His first indication that Alaska would be different was his flight.

Hoops drove from Cape Cod to Providence, then flew from Rhode Island to New York, to Atlanta, to Salt Lake City, to Anchorage, to Kenai. It took twenty-three hours. The league put him up in a hotel in Kenai and he contacted his father long distance.

"I called my dad the next day and said, 'There's a moose walking outside my window,' " said Hoops.

Hoops had a wonderful summer. He fished for halibut and caught one that weighed one-hundred-and-twenty-five pounds. He fished for king salmon on the Kenai after night games. He umpired a game between the Pilots and the Korean National Team and got a souvenir ball with Korean writing on it.

A Mat-Su fan took Hoops and another umpire on a tour of local gold mines. Some were shut down, some still producing. Although he got a souvenir nugget or two, he was most impressed by a sign propped up on a card table on a side road approaching one mine. It said trespassers would be shot on sight.

During one game at Hermon Brothers Field, Hoops wondered if that threat might apply to all umpires. Hoops was running the game behind home plate when the Miners played the Oilers. Kenai led 8-1 when rain began falling hard. After a twenty-five-minute rain delay, Hoops asked local officials if they could treat the field to keep it playable. They said yes. It took an hour. The teams squeezed in another inning-plus and it started to pour again. By then it was 8-6 Kenai.

"Mat-Su really wanted to get the game in," said Hoops.

Officials attacked the field again. Meanwhile, Hoops and his partner retreated to their dressing area, a tool shed located above the concession stand behind home plate. They were befuddled when they heard thumping on the walls.

"Fans were throwing rocks at us," said Hoops. "It was like fifty-cent draft night."

Nonetheless, they bravely emerged and finished the game. Which lasted until about 1:15 A.M. About twenty-five fans remained. Drunk or sober, no one took a head count.

A former Alaska umpiring regular is Bob Homolka. In a one-year period beginning in late 1994, Homolka, who in real life is a professor at Kansas State University, umpired in the NBC championships, Big Eight Conference tournament games, an NCAA regional in Tennessee, the College World Series in Omaha, Nebraska, National League replacement games during the players strike, and several real National League games when players returned.

Hoops said he once listened to a Homolka argument with an irate manager at the NBC. A shortstop made an unreal stop of a batted ball. The throw was obviously late. However, Homolka called the runner out.

"The runner is three steps beyond first base," said Hoops.

The opposing manager ran onto the field yelling. And he kept protesting. Hoops stepped between the manager and Homolka. Finally, Homolka shouted, "He was out because he was coming from the other way."

The baffling statement pretty much ended the dispute.

Homolka, in his late fifties, has thick gray hair and a solid build. He has umpired for a quarter of a century, mostly at the collegiate level. So when he got to do Major League games he was excited.

"What a thrill," said Homolka. "Oh, heavens."

Homolka turned to umpiring when he realized he was not going to make the majors as a player. He played collegiately at Iowa Northern and got a once-over from the Pittsburgh Pirates, but realized he was too slow to go far.

Homolka next tried coaching high school ball in Arizona, but the funny thing was he was too obnoxious to umpires and kept getting tossed out of games.

"I figured I'm umpiring so much from the bench, that's maybe what I should be doing," he said.

Umpires are supposed to blend with the action. They are supposed to have the wisdom, knowledge and temperament of judges. Homolka realized he had to change his demeanor. He gradually calmed down, though he admits that when he first began umpiring college games behind the plate, he was not ready.

"Oh, I was bad," said Homolka, conceding that his strike zone was all over the place.

Umpires must have thick skins. If they flip out every time a player or manager challenges them, there would be no one left on the field to play the games. If they let themselves be baited by fans, they wouldn't be able to concentrate on balls and strikes. Some umpires say they never hear derogatory shouts criticizing everything from their eyesight to their ancestry. Homolka doesn't pretend to be deaf.

"You can't block it all out," he said. "I love the fans. The hecklers, I don't care. That's part of the game."

There are certain general guidelines dictating whether a player or manager will survive an argument with the ump to play or watch another inning. It's accepted that players cannot contest balls and strikes. Each one is a judgment call and with a couple hundred a game the ump can't debate every one. It's accepted that if managers scream too long, they will be ejected. Likewise, if they utter curse words, they will almost surely be heaved.

There are times when managers just want to make a point. There are times when managers merely want to show their players they are behind them. And there are times when managers hope to inspire the troops. There are times when managers cross the white line knowing they are about to be sent into exile. Other times their actions aren't premeditated and their ejection comes as a surprise to them.

Bucs manager Mike Oakland recorded some kind of achievement during the 1999 season when he was thrown out of the team's first game of the season and last game of the season.

"It has to be the culmination of a lot of things, the whole game going to a boil," said Oakland. "Sometimes, if I'm so mad, I know I'm not coming back."

He used to think that a timely ejection would fire up players.

"It worked for about an inning," he said. "Then I figured it's better to be in the dugout."

During one recent season, Homolka ejected Bucs manager Mark O'Brien and Pilots manager Kevin Smallcomb in the same week. The Smallcomb confrontation was as theatrical as any Broadway play.

Homolka ruled that a Pilot runner was hit by a ground ball and therefore out. Smallcomb said the ball never touched his man. Face-to-face, chest-to-chest they argued. The two were so close that the brims of their caps were knocked askew. They kicked up a dust storm.

Smallcomb was gone. Later, though, he wasn't angry.

"At the time I'm irritated," he said. "I want to win my argument. I'm like a lawyer in court."

If so, Homolka was the judge who held him in contempt of court.

Not every umpire comes to Alaska from college games. In the 1970s, after his fame was established as the first black umpire in the majors, Emmitt Ashford came north. By then he was retired from pro ball and it was understood that his eyesight was not as sharp as it once was.

Once, Goldpanner manager Jim Dietz thought he was robbed of a game in Anchorage and Ashford's vision figured into it. A certain play left Dietz suspicious that Ashford favored the Glacier Pilots. Of course, the thought occurred because of Ashford's housing arrangement. When in Alaska, Ashford lived with the Pilots' Jack O'Toole. To this day, O'Toole has a framed photograph of Ashford on his wall from the ump's 1971 or 1972 Alaska days.

"He was a funny man," said O'Toole, who shared a sip or two of whiskey with Ashford.

If you asked O'Toole, Ashford was the fairest umpire who ever lived. Here he was staying with O'Toole and what does he do? Throw him out of a game.

Ashford called them like he saw them. Dietz just didn't think Ashford saw them well enough. During this crucial Goldpanner-Pilot game (they all seemed crucial back then) a ball was hit deep to the left side.

"This was a foul ball over the third-base dugout," said Dietz. "The leftfielder didn't even go into foul territory. It was so far foul there was no sense going over to it. You're talking about a ball that's two hundred feet foul. All of a sudden, Emmitt calls " 'Home run.' "

Home run? Dietz stormed out of the dugout.

"I say, 'Emmitt, is this game fixed?' " recalled Dietz. "He goes, 'Coach, I really didn't see it. But I'm gonna stay with my call.' "

Again after the game, Dietz brought up the play and Ashford admitted he didn't see the ball.

"That's obvious," said Dietz. "That's the most phantom home run I've ever seen in my life."

Although Dietz is the typical manager, fighting for every edge, in this instance he believed Ashford's vision really was an issue.

"He had really bad cataracts," said Dietz. "It was a wonder he could find his way to Jack's house."

It was a wonder O'Toole let Ashford in after he exiled him from a game. But O'Toole is no shrinking violet. No season is complete unless he gets thrown out of a game.

It took until the last week of the season, O'Toole's thirtieth in uniform with the Glacier Pilots, in the Bucs Invitational, for a forced hike to be imposed on him in 1999.

Each year, at the start of the season, O'Toole speaks to the newly-arrived players and tells them that there are two things they can't control—the weather and the umpires.

"God takes care of the weather and Kevin Smallcomb and I take care of the umpires," is the message O'Toole delivers.

That basically means they'll do the arguing.

O'Toole harangued home-plate ump Pat Griffen from the dugout during a 9-0 Pilots loss, and when he was informed he was history, he charged to the plate as fast as his septuagenarian legs could carry him.

The coach ripped into the ump, accusing him of having a strike zone resembling "what you seldom see in a garage anymore." That being a horse's waste product, O'Toole later translated.

O'Toole completed his command performance by shoveling dirt on the plate—with great difficulty. Much rain had fallen and the field was layered with a solidifying agent to prevent the dirt from turning to mud.

"That dirt was hard to move," said O'Toole.

One of the most surreal incidents in the history of umpiring occurred during a 1989 Glacier Pilots-Miners game at Mulcahy Stadium. A base umpire pulled a calf muscle and the Pilots searched the stands for a fill-in.

Talk about turning the tables. Fans always think they know better than the umps. Bill Lehmkuhl, a local radio sales executive, got the chance to prove it.

"I was looking in the stands for anyone," said Pilots coach Lefty Van Brunt. "We wanted to keep playing. I knew he knows baseball, so I called him down."

Lehmkuhl, who had some experience umpiring Little League and softball, was in mid-beer. Stunned, he trotted out to the base paths wearing blue shorts and a T-shirt from a hockey tournament. Lehmkuhl was involved in one close play at first base and made a decisive, arm-waving safe call, one that not everyone agreed with. It took one inning for officials to round up a substitute ump with more experience. Lehmkuhl went back to his seat. At least he handled his assignment with style.

So did Scott Taylor. During a 1996 Pilots game, Taylor was on the bases. In the sixth inning, he disappeared from the field. Unbeknownst to fans, he headed to the Pilots' clubhouse, accompanied by a pitcher with barbering skill. When Taylor reappeared in the eighth inning, fans, who thought he was injured, yelled: "Where did you go?"

Taylor tipped his cap and revealed that his long locks had been transformed into a brush cut. Fans roared with laughter.

It was the last game of the regular season and the trick marked Taylor's exit from Alaska Baseball League umpiring.

26

ONLY-IN-ALASKA

Only-in-baseball, and only-in-Alaska-baseball

MIKE OAKLAND remembers the first road trip he took during his first year as a coach with the Anchorage Bucs. Oakland, who became the Bucs' manager in 1998, was riding in a car along the Seward Highway with then-manager Mark O'Brien.

O'Brien gave him a heads-up on viewing wildlife on the road to the Kenai. The key was watching for cars pulled over. It meant tourists were stopping for animals.

They were cruising along and saw a Dall sheep and a moose, and O'Brien remarked how it was a shame they didn't have a camera. Then they saw a bunch of cars stopped. "Pull over, pull over," said O'Brien. There was a huge grizzly bear munching on a moose carcass.

"It was an awesome thing to watch him rip that thing apart," said Oakland.

The bear was only about two hundred yards away and could have pounced on any spectator in seconds. Oakland and O'Brien hung close to the vehicle.

"He was too far away from us," said Oakland.

Which could have been famous last words. It's been four years but the sight of that bear chowing down is very clear in Oakland's mind. It was a welcome-to-Alaska experience.

Pilots manager Kevin Smallcomb experienced a grizzly bear moment on the same highway, parallel to the Alaska Railroad tracks.

"Coming along the tracks is a grizzly bear," said Smallcomb. "And there's a train coming. The bear stops in the tracks, turns around and runs."

Even a bear can recognize when it is out-sized.

"But he stayed in the tracks," said Smallcomb. "For maybe three miles, he'd stop, turn, snort, get mad, and run again."

Finally, the bear dashed away from the tracks, presumably to view nearby Portage Glacier.

Baseball is the storytelling game, a sport that moves to its own rhythms. Baseball is a sport that cannot be rushed. Players lean against the batting cage and talk. Players sit in the dugout and talk. Baseball stories time-travel well.

Alaska Baseball League players and coaches have it better than anyone. Not only do they experience the same offbeat, quirky baseball incidents that occur nationwide, they get a bonus experiencing offbeat, quirky Alaska incidents, too. Their story repertoire should outdo any other players'.

There are only-in-baseball tales, only-in-Alaska tales, and best of all, only-in-Alaska-baseball tales.

Some stories get better with age. When Red Boucher managed the Goldpanners in the 1960s, he coached third base. And he had flair.

"One time he came running down the line right behind the guy," said Don Dennis. "The runner slid and Red slid, too. The umpire said, 'You're out' to the runner. 'And you're out of the game' to Red."

Before becoming manager, Smallcomb was a coach for the 1991 NBC champion Pilots. On that team, half the infield spent more than half its time fishing. That is, second baseman Steve Sisco and third baseman Clay King.

"I told them they had to stop fishing so much," said Smallcomb.

Didn't work. King ranked fishing first. He was going to take advantage of Alaska.

"Coach," he said, "you're just going to have to sit me down. I'm just going to fish."

Although it cannot be termed managerial retribution, partway through the season King sported two black eyes. A bad-hop grounder off the infield dirt gave King a shiner in his right eye. Soon after, he was leaning against the cage in batting practice and someone hit a foul ball. The ball flew back into the mesh and whacked him in the left eye. Another black eye.

"But he did not stop fishing," said Smallcomb.

Some stories are never forgotten.

In the 1970s, the Glacier Pilots recruited a player named Dennis Sherow. He was a very good player, an unsigned draft pick of the Montreal Expos.

"When he got to the airport, there wasn't anybody from the Pilots," said Mike Baxter, the Oilers executive, recalling the swift thinking of former Peninsula general manager Max Swearingen. "Max identified himself as being 'From the ballclub.' He knew who Sherow was."

Swearingen took Sherow to Kenai. The Pilots couldn't find Sherow.

"Then they come down to play us a few days later and there he was," said Baxter. "To this day, there's not a league meeting I go to where it doesn't come up."

There was a quasi-replay in 1999. Will Waldrup, a pitcher from Arizona State, showed up on the roster of the Bucs and Goldpanners. One day, Dennis Mattingly was talking to Don Dennis. Dennis mentioned he had Waldrup coming in soon. Mattingly said, "Don, he's been here since June 5."

Silence on the other end of the phone. Then, "The coaches don't know that. They think he's coming July 5," said Don Dennis.

When Palouse Empire was in the league, manager Bobo Brayton made it clear he would just as soon fish as play ball. He was just as happy on the Kenai River as at Oiler Park.

"He'd go fishing and we were lucky he came to the game," said Baxter.

Although prices of resident and out-of-state fishing licenses change, there has always been a great disparity in the cost. Summer baseball players don't count as official residents. One year, a coach, a player and team trainer with the Oilers bought the cheaper resident licenses. And they got caught by state Fish and Game enforcement officers.

"They were fined $200," said Baxter.

One other local tradition involves the "Kenai mud" used to build the mound. Former Kenai Mayor Vince O'Reilly, who also served as an Oilers' official, trooped players to a secret location to find the proper dirt.

"He'd make them wade through the water," said Baxter. "It was just dirt. They'd come back and say, 'That crazy old man.'"

Lefty Van Brunt was long retired from playing, but on July 14, 1994, his birthday, Van Brunt was activated for fun. The Glacier Pilots were playing the local American Legion All-Stars. Van Brunt pinch-hit in the eighth inning and tapped a grounder to the mound. Then he took the mound in the ninth. One batter hit safely, but a grounder into a double play followed. Out of the inning.

"Not too bad for a sixty-two-year-old," said Van Brunt.

It was the first time Van Brunt pitched since 1968. Two-thirds of an inning, 0.00 earned run average.

"I like those numbers," said Van Brunt. "And at least I didn't strike out."

Pilots coach Jack O'Toole donned a Detroit Tigers minor league uniform in 1939 and, with few interruptions, has been in the sport ever since. At 78 in 1999, he may be the oldest man in uniform in baseball in North America. Lew Freedman

Anything goes in Alaska. Maybe short of human sacrifices.

During the 1999 season, with the Mat-Su Miners in a major slump, the players felt something drastic was called for, so they made a sacrifice. Not a sacrifice fly, or a sacrifice bunt. They burned a bat in the dugout.

"We needed to break out of our funk," said outfielder Brian Oxley.

The appeasement of the baseball gods paid off. The Miners beat the Anchorage Bucs, 6-3.

Few players know what Alaska weather will be like. If they are from hot-weather communities, where the temperature regularly reaches the nineties, they are caught off-guard by mid-summer nights in the fifties.

Anthony Pennix, an outfielder on the 1999 Pilots team from tiny hot-weather Brookneal, Virginia, said he sought wardrobe advice from the club.

"They told me to make sure I didn't bring all just summer clothes," said Pennix. "They told me I didn't have to bring anything too heavy, though, like a trench coat."

A trench coat?

Former Pilots manager Steve McFarland (center) and coaches Brent Kemnitz (left) and Jack O'Toole have experienced the tense rivalry between the Panners and the Pilots, but only Kemnitz was in on the plot to stage a mock battle in a runner-up game between the rivals during the NBC tournament.
LEW FREEDMAN

Oiler Andy McCullough made his Alaska debut in 1998. Manager Scott Marr and teammates were surprised when on a chilly first day of workouts McCullough trotted out in shorts and short sleeves. It was, Andy, where are your clothes at?

"I pack no shorts," added Marr.

At least McCullough stuck around. Mike Baxter met Kevin Burford, an outfielder from California, at the airport and drove him to a hotel. After Baxter dropped him off, Burford verbally agreed to a contract with the San Diego Padres.

"He never made it to the office or the field," said Baxter. "He said, 'I need a plane ticket.' San Diego did reimburse us for the plane ticket."

Stories abound of the fierce Pilots-Goldpanners rivalry. But former Pilot manager Steve McFarland, now in player development for the Chicago Cubs, has a take on that subject that comes with a twist.

In 1984, the Pilots and Goldpanners advanced to Wichita, and met in the comparatively meaningless runnerup game. It was the thirteenth time the teams played that season and they were staying at the same hotel. Talk about familiarity.

Neither McFarland nor Fairbanks manager Dave Snow knew the players colluded on something weird, though Pilots coach Brent Kremnitz was in on the scheme. About the fifth inning, the Pilot pitcher reared back and fired a fastball that sailed over the batter's head. The second pitch made the batter duck, too.

"I'm thinking, 'What the hell is going on?' " said McFarland.

The third pitch zoomed to the backstop and players charged the mound from the Goldpanner dugout. Pilots ran out to support their pitcher. They briefly squared off and wrestled, and then the players squirmed into a lineup, arms around each other and broke into a can-can.

The whole thing was a hoax, a fake brawl.

"When the fight broke out, I'm panicked," said McFarland. "Then they go into a can-can. I couldn't believe it. It was nuts. I think everybody was stunned. It was comical, but it kind of showed what Alaska baseball is all about, the camaraderie that builds."

Most baseball played by Alaska teams is played under the watchful eye of team management, but sometimes, to save money, top officials skipped in-season Hawaii road trips. The Pilots were in Hawaii and two of their top pitchers were future major leaguers Ben McDonald and Russ Springer, teammates from Louisiana State. They rented mopeds and went body surfing.

Innocent enough, right? Well, Springer hurt his shoulder. McFarland decided to keep the news quiet. Springer missed his turn against the Island Movers and the broadcasters were suitably vague.

Back in Anchorage, Joe Armstrong wasn't fooled. He dialed McFarland in a New York minute and asked, "What the heck is going on?"

"Joe was just livid," said McFarland. "He was all over me. They're kids. They're in Hawaii. What are you going to expect?"

When it comes to baseball chit-chat, it's hard to top Jack O'Toole. O'Toole knows a million stories. It is Pilots tradition for the team to gather on the field just before the game and listen to a Jack joke. The only problem is that all of O'Toole's stories are off-color in content or language.

O'Toole grew up in Detroit and in 1939 signed a Tigers contract to play in the minors in Waycross, Georgia. Then he was an infielder for Class C Newport News in the Piedmont League and Class AA at Chattanooga. By then it was 1941 and World War II changed everything. The Army brought O'Toole to Alaska and he stayed when discharged in April, 1946. Then he coached for years in Anchorage and moved right into the Pilots' organization.

With little interruption, O'Toole has been wearing a baseball uniform for sixty years. So it was not so surprising to see O'Toole in his Pilots whites during the summer of 1996. Except for the fact that he was standing by the side of the highway. On the way to Mulcahy Stadium, where the Pilots were meeting for a bus ride to Palmer to play the Miners, O'Toole's car broke down.

So there he was, hitch-hiking, a then-seventy-five-year-old man in a rumpled Pilots uniform in a desperate hurry.

According to O'Toole, "The guy who picked me up said, 'Where's your club?' " Good question. "I said, 'I'm trying to get to them!' "

O'Toole made the bus on time.

27

BUSINESS AS USUAL

Infighting and money woes

STRONG-WILLED MEN with firm opinions and the vocal chords to back them up.

That pretty much characterizes the men who built and run the Alaska Baseball League. They know what they don't want, know what they want, and more often than not over the years were suspicious of the motives of anyone who disagreed with them.

If there has been an ABL weakness, the five-ton elephant weighing down the league, it has been factionalization: off-field battles that at times sadly eclipsed on-field heroics. From a distance it often seemed as if each team staked out a me-me-me position instead of a we-we-we stand.

The first major schism between teams dates back about twenty years. There was a dispute over some of the old Valley Green Giants finances, a complaint that the Oilers weren't paying their dues, and a clash between Don Dennis of the Goldpanners and Jack Brushert, then general manager of the Pilots. The creation of the Bucs infuriated the Pilots and helped drive a wedge between existing teams, too.

Bickering split the league. In a startling move, the Oilers, Pilots and the

Miners, then succeeding the Valley Green Giants, broke off to found the Alaska Independent Baseball League in 1980. The Goldpanners and North Pole Nicks welcomed the Bucs into the original Alaska Baseball League. The timing was great for the Bucs as they upgraded from Adult League to ABL.

"I could make it three and three," said Bucs general manager Dennis Mattingly. "It was the golden door for us. We'd give everybody some games."

Joe Armstrong had already made his feelings known about the Bucs. He didn't want them, didn't think the league needed them. So the Pilots did not exactly welcome the new kid to school.

The division lasted two years and the ABL returned to normalcy in 1982, though it was a peace that more resembled North Korea-South Korea cohabitation than full-fledged calm. Relations were testy between the clubs. Jim Dietz said he attended league meetings where the snapping and snarling was frighteningly nasty.

"There were some real strong-willed men in those rooms," said Dietz. "Individually, I was friends with all of them."

Dietz believes Don Dennis saved Alaska baseball because of his aid for the Valley Green Giants and North Pole. Others would disagree, and said his idea to place the ABL in the forefront of Pacific Rim expansion nearly killed them.

Exacerbating difficulties were financial woes. The Pilots were hurting for money following the Agbaba regime. While Dennis thought the league's scope should expand to embrace teams from Hawaii, Japan, Korea and Taiwan, others felt such ventures were too costly. They wanted a schedule grounded in Alaska.

The Miners won the 1987 NBC crown, but the price was dear. Soon after the championship—and a first prize of $12,000—was claimed, it became apparent the Miners had serious problems. The Miners announced they were $80,000 in debt, and then a figure of $120,000 was mentioned.

"These are debts that have accumulated over the years," said general manager Stan Zaborac, who said the team took out a loan just to make the trip to Wichita.

And then the Bucs said they faced $50,000 worth of debt. The team agonized over whether or not to declare bankruptcy, or to take a leave of absence from the league.

Miners club officials decided the team couldn't play in 1988. The Bucs chose to sit out. So did the Pilots. And then the North Pole Nicks pulled out.

John Lohrke, at the time the Nicks' general manager, and more recently president of the Oilers, said the Oilers have it made compared to other teams.

"Thank God for bingo," he said.

Alaska baseball was teetering. The Oilers were sound. So were the Goldpanners. The Palouse Empire Cougars of Washington were in and so were the Hawaii Island Movers. But the quartet represented merely a remnant

As the signs on the outside of Mulcahy Stadium indicate, the Anchorage Glacier Pilots and Bucs have gotten past the days when they told each other to take the ball and go home. Rivals for ever, they still co-exist in the shared stadium. LEW FREEDMAN

of the Alaska Baseball League. That season Mulcahy Stadium was dark. No baseball in Alaska's largest city. It was the grimmest of summers for Anchorage baseball fans.

Many wondered if the Bucs, Miners, Pilots or Nicks would ever play again.

The money shortage was the immediate problem, but trouble had been brewing in several ways for several years. It was all the team leaders could do to sit at the same table without resorting to insults or, nearly, to fisticuffs.

League meetings used to be held in Commissioner Emmitt Wilson's office at Teamsters headquarters. Don Dennis said one time someone from outside the room called security. Either the yelling was overheard in the building, or someone outside looking through a large picture window worried that a riot was breaking out.

Wilson, the old Goldpanner shortstop, was caught in the middle. He tried to run the commissioner's office with authority, but no matter what ruling he made he was accused of favoritism or prejudice.

Wilson became commissioner in 1975 and by 1985 incoming missiles landed from all directions. Some teams ripped Wilson for an unbalanced schedule. Some teams blamed him for hiring poor umpires. League bylaws prohibited teams from publicly criticizing the commissioner, but the rule was violated.

Pilots manager Steve McFarland blasted the quality of umpiring and accused Wilson of favoring the Goldpanners. Wilson suspended McFarland for five games.

The Oilers' Coral Seymour attacked the umpiring, too, and said if the current administration wouldn't fix it, then the league should change administrations. During a radio interview, an irritated Wilson said the quality of umpiring was no worse than the quality of players on the field. He subsequently apologized for the remark.

Wilson nailed Seymour with a fine of $300 for his comments. And Pilot general manager Ron Okerlund was hit with a $300 penalty, too, as the debate grew more intense. The entire ugly episode played out in the media.

Years later, Wilson, who stayed as commissioner until 1990, reflected on his role at a time when the Bucs and Pilots hated each other and conflict engulfed the league.

"It became more difficult," said Wilson. "The Pilots didn't want them around. Understandably, they didn't want to give up their monopoly. Whatever decision you made, you were wrong. When I ruled against Fairbanks, they complained. When I ruled against the Pilots, or Kenai, they held it against me personally. I thought I ruled against Fairbanks more harshly. I thought it was very petty."

Not only did the disputes take the fun out of the job, Wilson called the increasingly bitter atmosphere "the beginning of the downfall."

Meaning teams seceding from the league.

To the surprise of many, three of the absent 1988 clubs came back, restructured, on surer financial footing. Only the Nicks died. But the ABL was no longer unified. For most of the next decade, the league was rent. Palouse dissolved after the NCAA limited the number of players allowed on the same team from the same school. Hawaii hung in, though.

What emerged for the second time were two, three-team leagues. The Goldpanners, Bucs and Island Movers kept the original Alaska Baseball League name. The teams did not seek the NBC title, but turned their attentions to other post-season tournaments. The new Alaska Central Baseball League consisted of the Pilots, Miners and Oilers, who maintained the tradition of August visits to Wichita. The executive director of the ACBL, Jack Slama, another Teamsters official, later would prove extremely influential as a conciliator.

There were plenty of tough times in the 1990s. A Mendocino, California, team was invited into the league in 1992, but folded after playing ten games. The Blue Jays quit by fax and Joe Triano, the team's top executive, concluded a farewell message on the answering machine with, "I'm outta here."

In 1993, a Japanese team scheduled to play in the Bucs Invitational withdrew a week before the tournament. Also in 1993, a Kamloops, British Columbia team folded after a road trip to Alaska. Kamloops played some games that counted in league standings, but did not fulfill its entire obligation. This was all quite embarrassing.

Most Alaska teams operated on a monetary tightrope. The reputation of

Pilots general manager Ron Okerlund led the team's charge back from the financial perils of the 1980s.
LEW FREEDMAN

the league was jeopardized by the split and by money ills. The Cape Cod League in Massachusetts was on the rise. While most other leagues used aluminum bats, the Cape Cod League struck a deal with Major League baseball to pay for wood bats. Wood bats are used throughout the minors and give a truer reading of an athlete's capabilities, essential information to a pro team.

In the mid-1990s, in large part due to the efforts of Slama, the leagues inched closer to rapprochement. The teams created an umbrella organization called the Alaska Baseball Federation. The Federation was a way to provide another set of standings for an increasing number of crossover games between leagues.

The Federation was a small step for mankind, but it left players and fans completely confused. Nobody knew which game counted in which set of standings. Although there were only six teams, newspapers needed three sets of standings to account for Alaska baseball action.

Alvie Shepard, an ace Bucs reliever in 1994, tried to fathom the situation.

"The Pilots aren't in our league," said Shepard, a number-one draft pick of the Baltimore Orioles a year later. "That's weird. We've got Hawaii, which is a thousand miles away, and the Pilots in the same town and they're in a different league."

Then in 1997, a wonderful thing happened. The Mat-Su Miners, the poorest team in the league, and a team taking its life in its hands financially by accepting a bid to Wichita, won the NBC title. It was a serendipitous, feel good victory.

"It's the underdog syndrome," said Dan Cowgill, a coach for that team. "Stan Zaborac and his wife Nell are two great people. We had uniforms without numbers. Uniforms without letters. There was nothing to drag the field. And that's the kind of team we brought up. Unheralded guys. We decided we would get better and enjoy the experience and see what happened. They had something to prove. I think we brought up players with the right character."

Somehow the Miners pulled it off and pulled through. It was an emotional point of agreement, anyway. Everybody in both leagues was happy for the Miners.

Meanwhile, the Pilots, knocked off-balance by Agbaba's debt and the rise of the Bucs, finally overcame the setbacks. Lou Sinnett said he felt the burden of fundraising every minute of his tenure as general manager between 1989 and 1997.

"That was kind of a heavy weight on me," said Sinnett, who established a Pilots pull-tab store at the Dimond Center, Alaska's largest shopping mall.

Okerlund, an accountant by trade, took over for a second stint as general manager, and hired Scott Taylor, the former umpire, to work in sales and marketing. Chuck Shelton, the president, hustled all over the community. The combination paid off.

After years of lobbying, in 1998 Slama brought the feuding parties together. Slama deserved a Nobel Prize nomination. President Clinton should have sent him around the world to settle wars.

"Jack never let the lines of communication fall apart," said Don Dennis. "All the credit belongs on his shoulders."

The ABL was back together again. It was agreed the top two teams would annually represent Alaska in Wichita. And it was agreed that the league would replace the alumnium bats with a wood composite bat, a recent invention that resembles regular wood, but has the staying power of aluminum and is roughly equal in cost. Slama even arranged for an $8,200 donation to cover the costs of the bats for a season. Unification, at last.

"Nine years in the making," said Slama. "It's been a long process. We had a sense maybe some of the other leagues were creeping up on us. This will be positive publicity in the eyes of the baseball community."

He was right.

"I've longed for it forever," said Sinnett. "When we split I wondered if any of us would survive."

Teams took the field in 1998 with a new spirit of cooperation. After a season under one flag, things looked even better.

"Everybody got over the hard feelings," said Okerlund.

It was an important fresh start for the old league.

28

THE OILERS

The team of the Nineties

OPENING DAY. Always a joyous occasion in the baseball world. The sounds of the ball connecting with the bat, the ball thumping into the leather glove, are sweeter. The hot dogs never smell better.

But the Peninsula Oilers' season opener in June of 1998 was tinged with melancholy. Over the winter, general manager Coral Seymour, the club's most enthusiastic backer, died at age sixty-seven after suffering a heart attack. This was the first time the Oilers began a season without him.

It wasn't too busy yet at the Oiler Park ticket booth, where Lona Payment, wearing a red Oilers jacket with black lettering across the front, reminisced about the man who seemed irascible to some, kind-hearted to others, and passionate about the Oilers to all.

"Coral would tease me mercilessly," said Payment with a smile at memory of their banter. "But then I was always doing things to deserve it."

In a league where team leaders could rule with the firmness of dictators in foreign lands, no one was more identified with his club than Seymour. And in a league where team leaders were renowned for stubbornness, no one could be more bull-headed.

Peninsula Oilers team president John Lohrke, formerly general manager of the North Pole Nicks, welcomes fans to the opener of the 1998 season at recently renamed Coral Seymour Memorial Park. Oiler Park was renamed that year to commemorate Seymour, the team's longtime president, general manager and occasional groundskeeper, who had died that January at the age of 67. LEW FREEDMAN

No one could deny, though, that the bald and bespectacled Seymour was tenacious battling for Oiler interests. Everyone respected Seymour's commitment. They just didn't always have a ton of fun negotiating with him.

"The guy loved the game of baseball," said Bucs general manager Dennis Mattingly. "Coral was a hard man to deal with, but he was fair. He had a lot of Missouri mule in him. Not to say I didn't like him."

Seymour also made the Oilers into winners. Just like the Pilots and the Goldpanners, the Oilers quickly established a reputation and a tradition.

Formed in 1973, the Oilers won their first National Baseball Congress title in 1977. It took eleven innings to do it, but the Oilers beat the Goldpanners, 6-3, for the championship. Kenai's Howard Shapiro walked with the bases loaded for the go-ahead run. Shapiro hit a home run and had four RBI's in the championship game, too, but outfielder Bob Skube was the Most Valuable Player. The team was managed by Mark Newman, later a minor league executive for the New York Yankees, and Dave Stieb, headed for Major League stardom, was a top starter.

It took until 1993, under current Oral Roberts coach Sunny Golloway, for the Oilers to win a second national title. Kenai bested the Beatrice Bruins of Nebraska, 9-1.

"You don't have a great season in Alaska unless you come here and win this tournament," said Peninsula catcher Jeff Poor. "That's the truth."

Poor was the truth during the tournament. He was MVP. The Oilers celebrated by dousing Golloway with a cooler of water, much like the sideline trick then starting to sweep through the National Football League.

The Golloway regime was fruitful. Kenai won the NBC again in 1994, topping the Wichita Broncos, 8-1. This time Golloway nearly drowned in an outpouring of Gatorade. His team just couldn't help showing its appreciation. Braden Looper and Olympian Chad Green became Major League first-round draft picks.

"I have said that this team has the best collection of talent I've ever been associated with," said Golloway.

Golloway was an assistant coach at the University of Oklahoma when he joined the Oilers in 1993 and his back-to-back NBC titles were wrapped around a Sooners' College World Series triumph. The Oilers were so loaded—Ryan Christenson of the Oakland A's and Doug Mientkiewicz of the Minnesota Twins were also there—that Golloway still marvels at those teams' quality.

Kenai Borough Mayor Mike Navarre throws out the first pitch of '98 at Coral Seymour Memorial Park.

Lew Freedman

Against a backdrop of leafy trees and old fashioned advertising billboards, Oilers players loosen up in the outfield at Coral Seymour Memorial Park. Lew Freedman

"You don't have the scholarship money at a school to put that together," said Golloway. "It's very hard to assemble that talent on an amateur level anywhere."

The 1994 team was so good, said Golloway, for a while he felt the club was not living up to its potential.

"We were going through the league handily," said Golloway, who more recently has guided Oral Roberts to the NCAA regionals. "I thought we were underachieving. I was looking for a little bit more because I thought there would be more pressure in Wichita."

Golloway came back to start 1995, but had to make the tough choice to quit and accept the Oral Roberts head coaching opportunity early in the summer.

"I really wanted to go after that three-peat," said Golloway.

But the job offer was too good to pass up.

"What a tremendous run and what a tremendous time in my life," he said.

Golloway left Alaska with several notches on his fishing pole, too, from catching silver salmon. He never nabbed a king, but you can't say the big one got away from him. Not with two NBC titles on his resume.

The 1990s were very good to the Oilers. National titles are an impressive measuring stick, but in other years the Oilers were contenders. They were as consistent as any Alaska team locally and outdid the others nationally. Part of that was savvy recruiting by Golloway, but Seymour played a role in acquiring players, too.

"He was very well known to coaches throughout the country," said Mike Baxter, now the team's baseball operations chief. "We have connections with many, many schools. Florida State. West Virginia. Coral made them. There's no question the team wouldn't be where it is without Coral."

Golloway called Seymour "a great general manager. Whatever I needed done as a head coach he'd see to it. I just had a great respect for his love of the game."

Instead of solely relying on players from big-name schools, Golloway shifted gears. He put more than the usual number of junior college players into the mix and Seymour let him.

"I felt they would be a lot more hungry if they had something to prove," said Golloway. "I wanted players who wanted a championship, not somebody looking for a vacation. As old-school as people thought Coral was, he was innovative."

Seymour was out-spoken and his delivery lacked tact, but Baxter said if people penetrated the outer shell, they met a different man.

"Once you got past that you saw what a great guy he was," said Baxter. "He was the guy out there painting the fence and fertilizing the field."

Oilers Manager Scott Marr signs autographs and talks with the young fans on the field after a game.

Lew Freedman

Oilers outfielder Phil Downing meets the local press. LEW FREEDMAN

Mat-Su general manager Stan Zaborac put aside league meeting rhetoric. The two men talked a lot.

"Wherever we happened to be," said Zaborac. "Every time the Oilers came to Hermon Brothers. For a lot of years, I drove our bus. Coral and I sat together and harassed one another. He would call umpires names and then go out to dinner with them after the game."

Seymour died unexpectedly in January of 1998. He seemed as vigorous—and loud—as ever. It can't be said that he died on his own terms, but it was impossible to imagine Seymour departing this earth in the middle of the baseball season.

When Seymour died, the local newspaper, *The Peninsula Clarion,* wrote an editorial. It read in part, "When it came to the Peninsula Oilers, Coral Seymour batted 1.000. He easily could be called the Peninsula Oilers' most valuable player. Or the team's biggest booster. Or the baseball organization's hardest worker."

Dick Lobdell, the Pilots' official, echoed the editorial.

"He was the Oilers," said Lobdell. "Who do you see selling raffle tickets in the stands?"

Or, as Baxter put it, pushing the broom.

Not every recruit Seymour signed up worked out, of course. One year, the Oilers were gathering at Sea-Tac International Airport in Seattle in anticipation of some early-season games against the Kelowna Grizzlies in British Columbia. Seymour was present to greet the players.

As one player approached after disembarking from his flight, the general manager stuck out his hand to shake and said, "Hi, I'm Coral Seymour." Only the player brushed right past him, saying, "Just a minute."

And right there at the airport the guy signed a professional contract with a Major League club. The player turned back to Seymour and said, "Goodbye."

The real test for the Oilers in 1998 was to see how they would handle a season without Seymour, without his bellowing voice rolling over the field from behind home plate encouraging them.

The 1998 opener featured Miss Alaska, Joslyn Tinker, from nearby Soldotna, singing the national anthem. Mike Navarre, the Borough Mayor, threw out the first pitch.

And then they were playing baseball. Baxter wandered through the stands, selling programs for two dollars. Players showed off new Oiler caps. The team

Mike Baxter heads the Oilers baseball operations—and sometimes operates the bus as well.

LEW FREEDMAN

Lona Payment, staffing the ticket booth, says she misses Coral Seymour teasing her at the park.

LEW FREEDMAN

hats are red, with a white "P," and except for black brims, resemble those of the Philadelphia Phillies. But there was an addition. Since it was the twenty-fifth anniversary year for Kenai, the hats also included a diamond-shaped insignia to commemorate the season.

Centerfielder Phil Downing, from Southern Utah University, was making his Alaska debut.

"It's a great place," he said. "You hear a lot about it. People say, 'That's the place to be.' "

Manager Scott Marr, in his third season, had been around long enough to notice the difference in atmosphere. He didn't hear Seymour.

"I miss him," said Marr. "You always hear his loud voice, getting fired up."

Late in the season, the Oilers held a special night to honor Seymour. His wife Marjorie and other family members attended. There was a nice crowd at the ballpark which former mayor Vince O'Reilly said was really designed by

Seymour himself, more from ideas off the top of his head than from written plans.

In the ceremony, the Oilers offered Seymour the greatest tribute they could imagine. They changed the name of their home field to Coral Seymour Memorial Park.

The ultimate honor, of course, would be winning another national title. The Oilers did qualify for Wichita and played well, finishing tied for fourth. A year later, they came close to ending the century with a third title. The Oilers were runners-up to the Dallas Phillies.

It was an Oiler team that thrived on magnificent pitching depth, exactly what's necessary in a long tournament. The staff ace was Jeff Nichols of Rice, who came to Kenai late, straight from the College World Series, but mowed down batters with ease the rest of the summer. The poised Nichols, who showed exquisite control, might well be the next Oiler headed for the majors.

Before the games began, Golloway sent a message to current coach, Gary Adcock, of Purdue, a half-teasing, half-wishful directive: Win the tournament so the Oilers can call themselves the Alaska team of the nineties.

In the championship game, the Oilers led early, but lost, 5-4.

"We thought we might have it in us," said Baxter. "We just about got it done."

A hat trick of titles in the 1990s would have been special, but the Oilers were still the biggest Alaska National Baseball Congress winners of the decade.

Warm-up time at Coral Seymour Memorial Park looks like a tryout camp with all of its activity.

Lew Freedman

29

THE ABL IN THE NEW MILLENNIUM

Still king of the mountain

NEARLY FORTY years after he founded the Alaska Goldpanners, and thirty-seven years after his first trip to the National Baseball Congress tournament, Red Boucher was surprised and touched by the telephone call he received from Larry Davis in Wichita.

At the age of seventy-eight, Boucher was headed into the NBC Hall of Fame.

"They must be running out of people," joked Boucher, who was inducted into the hall in August 1999, in a class that included Mark McGwire.

When informed of his election, Boucher asked NBC officials if he should bring along a polar bear this time.

Lance Deckinger, the NBC associate vice president, said he wouldn't put it past him.

"Knowing him, he'd just leave it with us," said Deckinger.

Don Dennis, the man Boucher brought to Fairbanks to succeed him, said Boucher's election was long overdue.

"It should have happened a long time ago," said Dennis. "He brought more color to that tournament than anyone except for Hap Dumont, the guy who founded it. Certainly for Red not to get in before now is some kind of oversight."

The same night Boucher learned of his selection, he made a rare pilgrimage to Mulcahy Stadium. The Pilots and Goldpanners were playing. Boucher made no secret of his allegiance. A bright, red Goldpanner baseball cap covered most of his gray hair, and in-between chain-smoking cigarettes, he shouted cheers for the Fairbanks club.

When the game ended, Boucher made his way to the field, and soon made his way into the Goldpanners' post-game huddle. He posed for pictures with the players and gave them a husky-voiced pep talk. Boucher said he expected them to go undefeated the rest of the season and reach the NBC tournament.

They could not follow up on his wishes, on either count.

Boucher made it to Wichita, even if the Goldpanners didn't. NBC officials presented Boucher with a plaque that now perches on a shelf in the office of his Anchorage townhouse and they even turned the never-shy, never-taciturn Boucher loose with a microphone.

"I got to speak to the fans of Wichita," is the way he put it.

Boucher reminisced about McGwire's days in Anchorage, the way Joe Armstrong believed in him, and he told the fans about a lesser-known player, a catcher named Floyd Watson from the Goldpanners' first NBC team in 1962.

Watson, a University of Arizona player, caught the last three games of the season in terrible pain from a slipped disk. He needed surgery right after the tournament.

"Mister Guts," said Boucher.

Boucher signed many autographs. Then he got to make his second pep talk of the season, visiting the Peninsula Oilers' dugout before their first game. He talked about Alaska's glorious history at the NBC and how many fine ballplayers preceded them.

"I expect you to live up to that," said Boucher.

The Oilers did, nearly walking off with the crown.

No longer holding a monopoly on collegians the way it once did, the ABL must compete for talent with numerous leagues across the land and with Team USA, which tries to scoop up the very best players. Once upon a time, the Goldpanners had the pick of the crop, then shared the pick of the crop with the Pilots, but no more.

"In the early days, there was no Cape Cod League, no Team USA," said Glacier Pilots coach Jack O'Toole. "Alaska was a novelty. Both teams could get some awful studs. You could get some hellacious players."

Yet the Oilers placed second in 1999—ahead of Team USA. And the Anchorage Bucs tied for fourth. The ABL remains a powerful force.

Glacier Pilots Manager Kevin Smallcomb sees young Alaskans getting serious about their baseball futures at local clinics. LEW FREEDMAN

And Alaska offers what no one else can: the spectacular beauty of the Last Frontier. Players can play every day, but also see bears, moose, and Mount McKinley, raft rivers, fish for salmon and suit up where the sun seems like it never sets.

Goldpanner manager Dan Cowgill has been to Alaska as player, coach or manager regularly since the 1970s. Each fall he returns to his regular job as a California college professor toting two types of carry-on baggage.

"I bring back stories and I bring back fish," said Cowgill. "To me, that's what it's all about, the experience."

There have been growing pains and changes, unfortunate personality conflicts and territorial fights, but as the Alaska Baseball League moves into the twenty-first century, it is once again unified and facing the world with a single voice and strategy.

Two years into the Slama-inspired treaty, peace is holding.

The team leaders have cooperated so well, Stan Zaborac said he wouldn't mind scheduling his Miners against only Alaska teams in the future.

"That's what people want to see," said Zaborac. "I think the fans would rather see the Alaska teams play twelve times."

Alaska against Alaska always sold best.

Alaska in the year 2000 is a very different place from Alaska in 1960. It's a wired world and not only does Alaska receive same-day television and first-run movies, phenomenal developments in communication put the rest of the world only typing fingertips away on the Internet.

Some things change little, though. Baseball is essentially the same sport. The nineteen-year-olds fresh off freshman year, are, well, still nineteen-year-olds. Many players who come north still sign professional contracts, and many reach the majors.

The little boys who watch them play and dash down to the field after games seeking autographs are still little boys with awe in their eyes and dreams in their hearts.

With one difference. One day soon, one of those homegrown little boys will grow up to dominate the ABL and become a Major League star. ABL teams have conducted clinics for years, but in the 1990s it has become obvious the Alaska player is dramatically improving.

Kevin Smallcomb remembers the one-day sessions from his first Alaska year, and how they differ from present-day clinics.

"In 1991, it was 'Baby-sit our hellions for four hours,' " said Smallcomb. "Before parents sent kids without a glove. Now these kids come with a baseball, pants, hats, belts. They're ready to play."

Spring and fall weather won't get any better, so the growing season Cowgill spoke of will never expand, but the Alaska ballplayer is better equipped than ever to take on the sport in the big-time. That is one legacy of the ABL.

As they were a quarter of a century ago, Glacier Pilot homers are stil cause for home plate celebrations at Mulcahy Stadium. LEW FREEDMAN

Today's players can get words of wisdom from legendary Jack O'Toole. LEW FREEDMAN

Boucher long ago left his mark on Alaska baseball, and he long ago left Alaska baseball in any kind of official capacity. He was a state legislator and became lieutenant governor. Never looking back, always looking forward, Boucher became intensely involved pioneering Internet work with Compaq computers, seeking to bring sophisticated, wireless digital communication to the remote villages of the Alaska Bush.

But as Boucher approached his eightieth birthday and Alaska baseball approached its fortieth, for the first time in years he began bringing forth fresh ideas to promote the ABL.

"I would like to see Alaska baseball and the NBC recognized in the National Baseball Hall of Fame," said Boucher.

For a start. He also thinks the ABL should work with league cities' chambers of commerce to reach tourists, placing brochures hyping the league in hotel rooms; that an annual league winter banquet should be held featuring a former Alaska player turned Major League star; and a campaign should be undertaken to woo Team USA to the state for its permanent home.

And combining his favorite interests, Boucher would like to see Internet videostreaming of an Alaska Baseball League game-of-the-night.

"What a recruiting tool that would be," he said. "Tune in tonight."

Sound crazy? They said Red Boucher was crazy when he formed the Alaska Goldpanners and brought a bunch of college kids to play the nation's best in Wichita.

Maybe he was. And just maybe any Arctic visionary needs a little high-wire act in his soul.

Tune in tonight.

Randy Johnson COURTESY OF SANDRA TENUTO

FOR THE RECORD

- ❑ Teams, Stadiums and Managers
- ❑ The Midnight Sun Game
- ❑ NBC Tournament Highlights

Alaska Baseball League Teams

Fairbanks Goldpanners, 1960–
Anchorage Glacier Pilots, 1969–
Peninsula Oilers, 1973–
Valley Green Giants, 1976–79
Mat Su Miners, 1980–
Anchorage Bucs, 1980–
North Pole Nicks, 1980–87
Hawaii Island Movers, 1986–
Palouse Empire Cougars, 1986–91
Mendocino (Calif.) Blue Jays,
(10 games in 1992)

Alaska Baseball League Stadiums

Fairbanks Goldpanners—Growden Park
Anchorage Glacier Pilots—Mulcahy Stadium
Peninsula Oilers—Coral Seymour Memorial Park
Anchorage Bucs—Mulcahy Stadium
Mat-Su Miners—Herman Brothers Field
Hawaii Island Movers—Rainbow Stadium
Valley Green Giants—Hermon Brothers Field
North Pole Nicks—Newby Field
Palouse Empire Cougars—Bailey Field

ABL Managers

Fairbanks Goldpanners:
Red Boucher 1960–69
Lyle Olson 1970
Jim Dietz 1971–77
Ben Hines 1978–82
Dave Snow 1983–84
Tim Kelly 1985
Mike Weathers 1986–88
Pat Harrison 1989
Jim Dietz 1990–93
Rick Baumann 1994
Stacy Parker 1995–96
Don Leppert 1997
Dan Cowgill 1998–99

Hawaii Island Movers
Les Murakami
Carl Furutani
Dave Nakama
Tom Gushiken
Kallen Miyate
(years unavailable)

North Pole Nicks:
Jerry McClain 1980–81
Dan Cowgill 1982
Mike Gillespie 1983–85
Frank Sanchez 1986
Jim Gaddis 1987

Valley Green Giants:
Gary Adams 1976
Tom Wheeler 1977–78
Jerry McClain 1979

Anchorage Bucs:
Dennis Mattingly 1980
Jim Coveney 1981–82
Jerry McClain 1983–84
Gil Stafford 1985
John Hughes 1986–87
(No team in 1988)
Mike Garcia 1989–91
Ed Cheff 1992–93
Mike Garcia 1994
John Baptista 1995
Mark O'Brien 1996–97
Mike Oakland 1998–99

Anchorage Glacier Pilots:
Paul Deese 1969–72
Ray Young 1973
Paul Deese 1974
Augie Garrido 1975–76
Marcel Lachemann 1977–78
Gene Stephenson 1979
Chuck "Bobo" Brayton 1980–81
Jim Dietz 1982–83
Steve McFarland 1984–87
(No team in 1988)
Rick Zimmerman 1989
Pat Doyle 1990–91
Bill Mosiello 1992
Steve McFarland 1993–94
Kevin Smallcomb 1995–1999

Peninsula Oilers:
Bob Pomeroy 1974–75
Lyman Ashley 1976
Mark Newman 1977–79
Dan Radison 1980
Mark Newman 1981
Dan Radison 1982
David Hall 1983
Bob Todd 1984
Kirk Champion 1985
Pat Roessler 1986–87
Jim Bagnall 1988
Doug Smith 1989
Bo Hall 1990–91
Frank Mutz 1992
Sunny Golloway 1993–94
Sunny Golloway and Chris Pedritti 1995
Scott Marr 1996–98
Gary Adcock 1999

Mat–Su Miners:
Dan Peta 1980
Jim Frye 1981–84
Jim Fleming 1985–87
(No team in 1988)
Steve Abney 1989
Bill Mosiello 1990–91
Mark Martinez 1992–93
Steve Abney 1994
Steve Payne 1995
Ron Hauczinger 1996
Dave Ravitz 1997
Pete Wilk 1998–99

Palouse Empire Cougars:
Chuck "Bobo" Brayton 1986–91

Mendocino Blue Jays: (Calif.)
Joe Triano

Goldpanners results in the annual Midnight Sun Game

YEAR	FAIRBANKS		OPPONENT'S SCORE
1960	11	Fairbanks Pioneers	1
1961	10	North of Range Military All Stars	4
1962	8	North of Range Military All Stars	3
1963	1	Wichita (Kan.) Dreamliners	3
1964	5	Grand Junction (Co.) Eagles	10
1965	4	U. of Southern California	3
1966	8	Oregon State University	3
1967	3	Kumagai-Gumi of Japan	6
1968	7	University of Santa Clara	0
1969	2	Boulder (Co.) Collegians	5
1970	3	University of Arizona	4
1971	12	Stanford University	3
1972	4	Ponchatoula, La. Athletics	5
1973	5	Brigham Young University	8
1974	7	Washington State University	6
1975	4	Vanderbilt U. (11 inn.)	3
1976	6	Westwood, Calif. Bruins	0
1977	12	Red Deer M&K Generals (Alberta)	11
1978	1	El Dorado Coors (Kan.)	10
1979	8	University of North Carolina	2
1980	16	University of Wisconsin	5
1981	11	Intermountain (Utah) Badgers	4
1982	9	San Francisco 49ers	3
1983	9	Anchorage Bucs	6
1984	1	Republic of China (Taiwan) (Goldpanners awarded 9-0 forfeit)	2
1985	8	Moraga (Calif.) Marauders	0
1986	8	San Francisco Senators	1
1987	1	Mat-Su Miners	2
1988	8	Hawaii Island Movers	5
1989	7	San Diego Sea World Killer Whales	3
1990	8	San Bernadino (Calif.) Tribe	3
1991	9	South Lake Tahoe (Calif.) Stars	8
1992	3	Victor Valley (Calif.) Mets	1
1993	10	South Lake Tahoe (Calif.) Stars	4
1994	15	San Diego (Calif.) Stars	6
1995	10	San Francisco Seals	4
1996	5	Anchorage Bucs	3
1997	8	Kelowna Grizzlies (British Columbia)	2
1998	14	Kelowna Grizzlies (British Columbia)	13
1999	7	Oceanside (Calif.) Waves	1

Goldpanners all-time Midnight Sun record: 31-9

National Baseball Congress Championhips Won By ABL Teams

Fairbanks Goldpanners: 1972, 1973, 1974, 1976, 1980
Anchorage Glacier Pilots:1969, 1971, 1986, 1991
Peninsula Oilers: 1977, 1993, 1994
Mat-Su Miners: 1987, 1997

ABL Members of the NBC Hall of Fame

Rick Monday, Fairbanks Goldpanners
Bob Boone, Fairbanks Goldpanners
Tom Seaver, Fairbanks Goldpanners
Chris Chambliss, Anchorage Glacier Pilots
Dave Winfied, Fairbanks Goldpanners
Graig Nettles, Fairbanks Goldpanners
Red Boucher, Fairbanks Goldpanners (founder)
Mark McGwire, Anchorage Glacier Pilots

ABL Top Pitchers and MVPs at National Baseball Congress Tournament

Top Pitchers:
1997 Mario Ramos, Peninsula Oilers
1996 Andy Kimball, Peninsula Oilers
1994 Mike Drumright, Anchorage Glacier Pilots
1991 B.J. Wallace, Anchorage Glacier Pilots
1990 Jim Yanko, Anchorage Glacier Pilots
1986 Derek Stroud, Anchorage Glacier Pilots
1982 John Hoover, Anchorage Glacier Pilots
1976 Greg Harris, Fairbanks Goldpanners
1974 George Milke, Fairbanks Goldpanners
1971 Randy Jones, Anchorage Glacier Pilots
1969 Jim Crawford, Anchorage Glacier Pilots
1963 Dave Dowling, Fairbanks Goldpanners

Most Valuable Players:
1994 Jesse Zepeda, Peninsula Oilers
1993 Jeff Poor, Peninsula Oilers
1991 Chris Hmielewski, Peninsula Oilers
1987 Ken Kremer, Mat-Su Miners
1986 Steve Bales, Anchorage Glacier Pilots
1980 Kevin McReynolds, Fairbanks Goldpanners
1977 Bob Skube, Peninsula Oilers
1976 Greg Harris, Fairbanks Goldpanners
1974 Steve Kemp, Fairbanks Goldpanners
1973 Lee Iorg, Fairbanks Goldpanners
1972 Kerry Dineen, Fairbanks Goldpanners
1971 Bruce Bochte, Anchorage Glacier Pilots
1969 Chris Chambliss, Anchorage Glacier Pilots
1963 Sam Suplizio, Fairbanks Goldpanners

Notable Marks by ABL Teams and Players at the NBC Tournament in Wichita

Individual Players

most home runs one game
John Olerud, Peninsula Oilers
(tied record 1988) 3
most home runs one tournament
Chris Hmieleski, Peninsula Oilers
(second most 1991) 8
Richie Grayum, Peninsula Oilers
(third most, 1988) 7
most total bases one game
John Olerud, Peninsula Oilers,
(1988) 15
most total bases one tournament
Chris Hmielewski, Peninsula Oilers
(second most, 1991) 42
most RBIs one tournament
Chris Hmielewski, Peninsula Oilers
(tied, 1991) 25

Teams

most hits one tournament
Anchorage Glacier Pilots
(second most, 1982) 110
Fairbanks Goldpanners
(tied sixth, 1980) 101
highest team batting average:
Anchorage Glacier Pilots
(tied first, 1991) .410
pitchers in most games one tournament:
Jim Crawford, Anchorage Glacier Pilots
(tied first, 1969) 7

No-hit games:

Tom Seaver and Mike Paul (combined),
7 innings, Fairbanks Goldpanners,
6-0 over Brandon, Nebraska, 1964
Jim Yanko, 5 innings, Anchorage Glacier
Pilots, 11-0 over Clarinda, Iowa
most wins one tournament:
Greg Harris, Fairbanks Goldpanners,
(tied for second 1976) 4

ALASKA BASEBALL LEAGUE PLAYERS WHO ADVANCED TO THE MAJOR LEAGUES

ABL Players on Exclusive All-Time Major League Lists

WINS: 311 by Tom Seaver
Fairbanks Goldpanners (1964-65)
1967-86 New York Mets, Cincinnati Reds, Chicago White Sox, Boston Red Sox

HITS: 3,110 by Dave Winfield
Fairbanks Goldpanners (1971-72)
1973-1995 San Diego Padres, New York Yankees, California Angels, Toronto Blue Jays, Minnesota Twins, Cleveland Indians

HOME RUNS: 522 by Mark McGwire
Anchorage Glacier Pilots (1982)
1986- Oakland Athletics, St. Louis Cardinals

North Pole Nicks
21 Players

Kevin Blankenship
Chris Donnels (also Goldpanners)
Paul Faries (also Goldpanners)
Steve Finley
Mark Grace
Luis Gonzalez
Eric Karros
Brian Keyser
Chad Kreuter (also Goldpanners)
Pat Larkin
Scott Lewis
Tory Lovullo
Jeff Robinson
Roger Samuels (also Goldpanners)
Alex Sanchez
Mike Schooler
Doug Simons
Andy Stankiewicz
Jim Traber
Colin Ward
Jeff Wetherby (also Goldpanners)
Todd Zeile

Valley Green Giants
7 players

Floyd Chiffer
Tom Niedenfuer (also Oilers and Pilots)
Cliff Pastornicky
Ron Roenicke (also Goldpanners)
Dave Rucker
Dave Schmidt (also Miners)
Paul Zuvella

Mat-Su Miners
19 players

Rich Amaral
Jeff Brantley
Jack Daugherty (also Pilots)
Mike Devereaux
Tom Edens
Gil Heredia
Jack Howell
Jeff King
Scott Livingstone
Keith Miller
Jeff Reboulet
Stan Royer (also Goldpanners)

Dave Silvestri
Marvin Benard
Jim Bruske
Craig Counsel
Ryan McGuire (also Pilots)
Doug Mientkiewicz (also Oilers)
Jon Zuber (also Oilers)

Palouse Empire Cougars
4 players

John Olerud (also Oilers)
Aaron Sele
Scott Hatteberg (also Pilots)
Dave Wainhouse

Peninsula Oilers
80 players

Jim Adduci
Rich Aurilia
Jason Bates
Kevin Bearse
Andy Beene
Terry Bell
Terry Blocker
Mike Brown
Jim Bullinger
John Butcher (also Pilots)
John Cerutti
Jeff Cirillo
Dennis Cook (also Goldpanners)
Ron Davis
Mark Dempsey
Lance Dickson
Bill Doran
Cal Eldred
Steve Engel
John Fulgham
Jim Gaudet
Rich Hacker
Chip Hale
Atlee Hammaker
Neal Heaton
Rick Horton
Darrell Jackson
Dave Johnson
Mike Jones
Don Kainer
Jeff Keener
Rick Keeton
Jimmy Key
Jeff Kunkel
Tim Laudner
Jack Lazorko
Rick Leach
Bryan Little
Billy Long
Dwight Lowry
Gary Lucas
Rick Luecken
Steve Macko
Scotti Madison
Dave Magadan
Ron Meridith
Brad Mills
Steve Mura
Otis Nixon
Paul Noce
Chris Nyman
Randy O'Neal
John Olerud (also Palouse)
Javier Ortiz
Ken Patterson
Dave Pavlas
Ricky Peters
Marty Pevey
Allan Ramirez
Mark Redman (also Bucs)
Mark Ross
Stan Royer (also Miners)
Dan Schatzeder
Tony Scruggs
Pat Sheridan
Craig Shipley
Bob Skube
J.T. Snow (also Pilots)
Billy Spiers
Bobby Sprowl
Dave Stieb
Bob Tewksbury
Bobby Thigpen (also Pilots)
Jeff Treadway
Frank Viola
Pete Young
J.D. Drew
Ryan Christenson
Braden Looper
Doug Mientkiewicz (also Miners)

Anchorage Bucs
32 players

Michael Aldrete
Don August (also Goldpanners)
Brant Brown
Mike Campbell (also Goldpanners)
Scott Chiamparino
Keith Foulke
Ed Giavanola
Jerry Goff
Greg Gohr
Jed Hansen
Brooks Kieschnick
Chuck Jackson
Geoff Jenkins
Bobby Jones
Kevin Jordan

Wally Joyner
Jeff Kent
Mike Lansing
Tim Layana
(also Goldpanners)
Kevin Maas
Mike Macfarlane
Mike Magnante
Brad Moore
Calvin Murray
Al Osuna
(also Goldpanners)
Kevin Polcovich
Tim Pugh
Mark Redman (also Oilers)
Darryl Scott
(also Goldpanners)
Anthony Telford
Tom Urbani
Kevin Wickander

Anchorage Glacier Pilots 110 players

Rick Aguilera
Luis Alicea
Jamie Allen
Doug Ault
Dave Baker
Reggie Baldwin
Chris Bando
Marty Barrett
Jeff Barry
Joe Beckwith
Alan Benes
Jaime Bluma
Bruce Bochte
Aaron Boone
Dan Boone (also Goldpanners)
Bill Bordley
Mike Brumley
Terry Bulling
Todd Burns
Casey Candaele
Rick Cerone
Wes Chamberlain
Chris Chambliss
Steve Chitren
John Christensen
Pat Clements
Gary Cooper
Tim Corcoran
Mike Couchee
Jim Crawford
Warren Cromartie
John Cummings
Jack Daughtery
(also Miners)
Steve Davis
Darren Dreifort
Keith Drumright
Steve Dunning
(also Goldpanners)
Craig Eaton
Juan Eichelberger
Rob Ellis
Eric Fox
David Frost
Mark Gardner
Mike Gates
John Gibbons
Kip Gross
Eddie Guardado
Chris Gwynn
David Haas
Darryl Hamilton
Mickey Hatcher
Scott Hatteberg (also Palouse)
Ray Hayward
Jeff Heathcock
Don Hill
Roger Holt
John Hoover
Steve Howe
Dave Hudgens
Bobby Hughes
Randy Johnson
Randy Jones
Terry Jorgensen
Terry Kennedy
Ray Krawczyk
Roger LaFrancois
Jody Lansford
Dave Leeper
Richie Lewis
Jeff Liefer
Carlton Loewer
Eric Ludwick
Damon Mashore
Ben McDonald
Bill McGuire
Ryan McGuire (also Oilers)
Mark McGwire
Joe McIntosh
Billy Moore
(also Goldpanners)
Tom Niedenfuer
(also Miners and Giants)
Scott Nielsen
Dan O'Brien
Dave Oliver
John Orton
Bob Pate
Ken Phelps
(also Goldpanners)
Jay Powell
Ron Pruitt
Rico Rossy
John Russell
Bob Shirley
Roy Smalley

J.D. Smart
Chris Smith
J.T. Snow (also Oilers)
Cory Snyder
Russ Springer
Blake Stein
Craig Swan
Bob Thigpen (also Miners)
Dave VanGorder
Ed Vosberg
Dave Walsh
Steve Wapnik
Colby Ward
Dan Whitmer
Mike Willis
Bump Wills
Craig Wilson
Jason Wood
Curt Young

Fairbanks Goldpanners
161 players

Mike Adamson
Ed Amelung
John Andrews
Brad Arnsberg
Don August (also Bucs)
Chuck Baker
Dave Baker
Eddie Bane
Floyd Bannister
Bret Barberie
Jim Barr
Shawn Barton
Billy Bean
Mike Benjamin
Mike Boddicker
Barry Bonds
Bob Boone
Bret Boone
Dan Boone (also Pilots)
Brad Brink
Pete Broberg
Greg Brummett
John Butcher (also Pilots)
Mike Campbell (also Bucs)
Craig Caskey
Dave Cochrane
Chris Codiroli
Dennis Cook (also Oilers)
Jeff Cornell
Jose Cruz Jr.
Alvin Davis
Mark Davis
Marty Decker
Kerry Dineen
Pat Dodson
Chris Donnels (also Nicks)
Dave Dowling
Jeff Doyle
Steve Dunning (also Pilots)
Dave Edler
Paul Faries (also Nicks)
Benji Figueroa
John Fishel
Terry Francona
Dan Frisella
Mike Fuentes
Bob Gallagher
Danny Garcia
Greg Garrett
Rusty Gerhardt
Jason Giambi
Tom Goodwin
Dan Graham
Bob Hamelin
Rich Hand
Mike Harkey
Greg Harris
Chuck Hartenstein
Don Heinkel
Eric Helfand
Kevin Higgins
Dave Hostetler
Tom House
Jacque Jones
Mike Kelly
Steve Kemp
Adam Kennedy
Dave Kingman
Mike Kinnunen
Chad Kreuter (also Nicks)
Vance Law
Tim Layana (also Bucs)
Tim Leary
Bill Lee
Travis Lee
Eddie Leon
Doug Linton
Dennis Littlejohn
Keith Lockhart
Tim Lollar
Shane Mack
Alex Madrid
Joe Magrane
Darrell May
Brent Mayne
Oddibe McDowell
Kevin McReynolds
Pat Meares
Luis Medina
David Meier
Andy Messersmith
Bobby Mitchell
Rick Monday
Billy Moore (also Pilots)
Jose Mota
Curt Motton
Dan Naulty
Graig Nettles
Jim Nettles
Al Osuna (also Bucs)

Mike Paul
Ken Phelps (also Pilots)
Dan Plesac
Gary Rajsich
Pete Redfern
Mike Reinbach
Don Reynolds
Harold Reynolds
Rob Ritchie
Kevin Ritz
Dave Roberts
Mike Robertson
Bruce Robinson
Steve Rodriguez
Ron Roeinicke (also Giants)
Dan Rohemeier
Ron Romanick
Kevin Romine
Marc Ronan
Don Rose
Roger Samuels (also Nicks)
Scott Sanderson
F.P. Santangelo
Al Schmelz
Dave Schuler
Erik Schullstrom
Darryl Scott (also Bucs)
Tom Seaver
Bob Sebra
Dick Selma
Don Slaught
Dave Smith
Robert Smithberg
Dave Stapleton
Phil Stephenson
Todd Steverson
Brent Strom
Jim Sundberg
Gary Sutherland
Steve Swisher
Jeff Tabaka
Jackson Todd
Tim Tolman
Rich Troedson
Brian Turang
Jim Umbarger
Ty Van Burkleo
Ed Vandeberg
Tim Wallach
Don Wakamatsu
Jeff Wetherby (also Nicks)
Gary Wheelock
Sandy Wihtol
Eric Wilkins
Jimy Williams
Shad Williams
Gary Wilson
Steve Wilson
Dave Winfield
Craig Worthington
Ed Zosky

Hawai not available

SOURCES FOR THIS BOOK

Anchorage Daily News archives (special mention for work of Doyle Woody and Beth Bragg)
Anchorage Times archives
Anchorage sportswriter Matt Nevala tape recorded Randy Johnson interview
Personal interviews with dozens of current and former Alaska Baseball League players and officials

Books:
Balls by Graig Nettles and Peter Golenbock
Baseball's Barnum Ray "Hap" Dumont, by Bob Broeg
Slugging It Out in Japan by Warren Cromartie, with Robert Whiting
Mark McGwire, Home Run Hero, by Rob Rains
Winfield: A Player's Life, by Dave Winfield, with Tom Parker

INDEX

ABOUT THE AUTHOR

STEVEN L. NELSON/ALASKA STOCK

Lew Freedman is a popular author of books about Alaska as well as award-winning columnist and sports editor for the Anchorage Daily News.

A member of the Baseball Writers of America, Freedman has covered Major League Baseball® on both coasts and in the heartland, and is a repeat visitor to the Baseball Hall of Fame in Cooperstown, NY.

Freedman's numerous books about the northern state and its people include three books about the Iditarod Trail Sled Dog Race. His bestseller is *Iditarod Classics: Tales of the Trail from the Men and Women Who Race Across Alaska.*

A graduate of Boston University, Freedman has a master's degree from Alaska Pacific University. He and his wife Donna have a daughter, Abby.